This is the sixth volume in the popular Cummings Foundation for Behavioral Health series beginning in 1991 that addresses healthcare utilization and costs. The Nicholas & Dorothy Cummings Foundation, in association with Context Press, is pleased to continue the tradition of distributing complimentary copies to the directors of American Psychological Association approved doctoral programs, to selected leaders in psychology, and to key persons in the field of behavioral healthcare.

It is hoped you will find this series useful in your work. The Cummings Foundation for Behavioral Health requests that after you have finished reading it, you donate it to the library of the institution with which you are affiliated.

Additional copies for individuals only, may be obtained as long as supplies last by sending $5.00 to cover postage and handling to the following address. Regretfully repeat, multiple, and bulk requests cannot be accommodated.

Janet L. Cummings, Psy.D., President
The Nicholas & Dorothy Cummings Foundation, Inc.
561 Keystone Avenue, #212
Reno, NV 89503

Library and Institutional copies may be ordered from CONTEXT PRESS for a charge of $29.95 plus shipping and handling.

Behavioral Health as Primary Care: Beyond Efficacy to Effectiveness

Behavioral Health as Primary Care: Beyond Efficacy to Effectiveness

A Report of the Third Reno Conference on the Integration of Behavioral Health in Primary Care

Editors:
Nicholas A. Cummings, Ph.D., Sc.D.
William T. O'Donohue, Ph.D.
Kyle E. Ferguson, M.S.

Cummings Foundation for Behavioral Health:
Healthcare Utilization and Cost Series,
Volume 6
2003

CONTEXT PRESS
Reno, Nevada

Behavioral Health as Primary Care:
Beyond Efficacy to Effectiveness

Hardback   pp. 188

Library of Congress Cataloging-in-Publication Data

Reno Conference on the Integration of Behavioral Health in Primary Care:
Beyond Efficacy to Effectiveness (3rd : 2003 : University of Nevada)
    Behavioral health as primary care : beyond efficacy to effectiveness : a
report of the Third Reno Conference on the Integration of Behavioral Health in
Primary Care / editors, Nicholas A. Cummings, William T. O'Donohue, Kyle
E. Ferguson.
        p. cm. – (Healthcare utilization and cost series ; v. 6)
    Includes bibliographical references.
    ISBN 1-878978-45-4
  1. Mental health services–United States–Congresses. 2. Medical care–United
States–Congresses. 3. Integrated delivery of health care–United States–
Congresses. I. Cummings, Nicholas A. II. O'Donohue, William T. III. Ferguson,
Kyle E. IV. Title. V. Series.
RA790.A2 R464 2003
362.1–dc22

                                                        2003016854

© 2003 CONTEXT PRESS
933 Gear Street, Reno, NV   89503-2729

Printed in the United States of America

The Healthcare Utilization and Cost Series
of the Cummings Foundation for Behavioral Health

Volume 1 (1991):
Medical Cost Offset: A Reprinting of the Seminal Research Conducted at Kaiser Permanente, 1963-1981
Nicholas A. Cummings, Ph.D. and William T. Follette, M.D.

Volume 2 (1993):
Medicaid, Managed Behavioral Health and Implications for Public Policy: A report of the HCFA-Hawaii Medicaid Project and Other Readings.
Nicholas A. Cummings, Ph.D., Herbert Dorken, Ph.D., Michael S. Pallak, Ph.D. and Curtis Henke, Ph.D.

Volume 3 (1994):
The Financing and Organization of Universal Healthcare: A proposal to the National Academies of Practice.
Herbert Dorken, Ph.D. (Forward by Nicholas Cummings, Ph.D.).

Volume 4 (1995):
The Impact of the Biodyne Model on Medical Cost Offset: A sampling of Research Projects.
Nicholas A. Cummings, Ph.D., Sc.D., Editor.

Volume 5 (2002):
The Impact of Medical Cost Offset on Practive and Research: Makint It Work for You. A Report of the Third Reno Conference, May 2002.
Nicholas A. Cummings, Ph.D., Sc.D., William T. O'Donohue, Ph.D., and Kyle E. Ferguson, M.S., Editors.

The Reno Conferences

Co-sponsored by the University of Nevada, Reno and
The Nicholas & Dorothy Cummings Foundation

The First Reno Conference on Organized Behavioral Healthcare Delivery was convened at the University of Nevada, Reno in January 1999.

The Second Reno Conference on Medical Cost Offset was convened at the University of Nevada, Reno in January 2001.

The Third Reno Conference on Medical Cost Offset and Behavioral Health in Primary Care was convened at the University of Nevada, Reno in May 2002.

The Fourth Reno Conference on Substance Abuse in Primary Care was convened at the University of Nevada, Reno in May 2003.

Preface

This book contains papers that were first presented at the University of Nevada, Reno on May 17-18, 2002. This conference was generously supported by a grant from The Nicholas and Dorothy Cummings Foundation as well as by resources donated by the University of Nevada, Reno.

The goal of this conference was to assist practitioners, researchers, administrators, and decision makers to understand the practical issues surrounding how to integrate behavioral healthcare with medical surgical healthcare. There is a growing interest in the possibilities of this aim: healthier patients, lower costs, fewer barriers to accessing care, fewer medical errors, and other efficiencies. But the question arises: How does one move from the divided health care delivery system of today to an integrated care system in such a way that the benefits of making this change are achieved? To address this question we assembled a distinguished group of national experts to describe the process of integrating behavioral health. We covered topics such as administration buy in, readiness assessment, core competencies of the behavioral care provider, core competencies of the primary care physician, training strategies and curricula, as well as covering model integrated care demonstration projects in Hawaii and in the Air Force.

The context of this conference is the health care crisis facing the United States. Costs are escalating at multiples of the rate of general inflation. The managed care model is sick or dying. 40 million Americans are uninsured. The rate of medical errors is unacceptably high. The population is aging and the health care needs represented by the elderly have increased. Technological advances often bring higher costs. What can be done?

One of the key advantages to integrated care is that it can reduce demand for health care by providing patients with the health care they actually need. There is significant clinical research and clinical experience all pointing to one fact: many patients (perhaps even a majority) receiving traditional primary care or specialty care medicine also need behavioral care. These patients are having problems with treatment adherence; they are suffering from comorbid psychological problems such as depression or anxiety; they have undiagnosed substance abuse problems; they have subclinical problems such as stress; they have lifestyle problems with eating, exercise and stress management; and they have problems managing their chronic illness such as diabetes. However, these patients in nonintegrated settings are rarely having their behavioral health problems recognized and treated. Because these issues go untreated their health suffers and their medical utilization increases. Referral to specialty behavioral care such as psychiatry or clinical psychology is also not the answer as few of these patients actually comply with the referral and for many of the behavioral problems (e.g., treatment adherence or disease management) specialty mental health is not structured to treat.

x

This book is an attempt to illustrate the trend toward addressing these problems by integrating care. It has attempted to be very practical. The issues the chapter authors address are designed to assist those interested in moving toward integrated care to be able to begin to do this.

This book owes a special thanks to Stephanie Dmytriw and Carol Maiellero who provided excellent assistance in organizing the conference. It also owes a special debt of thanks to Janet Cummings, Psy.D., President of the Nicholas and Dorothy Cummings Foundation. Without her decision to support the conference it would not have happened. We should like also to thank our copy editor, Emily Neilan, for here dedicated skill and perseverance. Finally, we would like to thank all the conference presenters and chapter authors. They are the experts and innovators whose work holds the key to addressing the critical problems in healthcare today.

Contributing Authors

Michael A. Cucciare is pursuing his Ph.D. in psychology at the University of Nevada, Reno. He received his bachelor's degree from the San Jose State University. His research interests include: behavioral assessment, interpersonal communication factors in psychotherapy, and the development of psychosocial interventions for high utilizers of health care services.

Janet L. Cummings, Psy.D. is the President of the Nicholas & Dorothy Cummings Foundation and in independent practice in Scottsdale, Arizona. She is a former staff psychologist with American Biodyne (MedCo/Merck, then Merit, now Magellan Behavioral Care). She received her Bachelor's degree from the University of California, Davis, her Master's degree from the University of Texas, Arlington, and her Doctorate from the Wright State University School of Professional Psychology. She is the co-author or co-editor of six books.

Nicholas A. Cummings , Ph.D., Sc.D. is a former president of the American Psychological Association who has served on two Presidential mental health commissions (Kennedy and Carter) and as an advisor to the U.S., Senate Finance Committee and the Subcommittee on Health as well as to the Department of Health and Human Services. He is the founder of the California School of Professional Psychology, American Biodyne, National Council of Professional Schools of Psychology, National Acadmies of Practice, and more than a dozen other organizations. He is the author of 24 books and over 400 journal articles and book chapters. He is currently Distinguished Professor of Psychology, University of Nevada, Reno; President, Cummings Foundation for Behavioral Health; Chair, The Nicholas & Dorothy Cummings Foundation; and Chair, University Alliance for Behavioral Health.

Kyle E. Ferguson is pursuing his Ph.D. in psychology at the University of Nevada, Reno. He received a master's degree in behavior analysis from Southern Illinois University and a bachelor's degree from the University of Alberta. He co-authored the book, *The Psychology of B.F. Skinner* and is co-editor on two other books, *The Impact of Medical Cost Offset* and the *Handbook of Professional Ethics for Psychologists*. He is the author of over 20 journal articles and book chapters.

Dr. Vincent P. Fonseca is a physician epidemiologist consultant for the U.S. Air Force Medical Service's Population Health Support Division in San Antonio, Texas. His areas of expertise are clinical quality improvement, clinical informatics, epidemiology and preventive medicine. He is board certified in General Preventive Medicine and Public Health.

Susan L. Hall is a clinical psychologist currently at Haleiwa Family Health Center, providing assessment, diagnosis, and outpatient treatment services to children and adolescents. She received a doctorate in clinical psychology from the University of Colorado at Boulder. She has practiced in a variety of different clinical settings for over two decades and has served in both administrative and clinical roles.

Dr. Christopher L. Hunter is a clinical psychologist in the US Air Force, currently working as the Chief of Primary Care Psychology Training on the faculty at Wilford Hall Medical Center in San Antonio, Texas. His training program has been recognized as a model program for training students in collaborative care. Dr. Hunter received his Ph.D. in clinical psychology, with a specialty in behavioral medicine, from the University of Memphis.

Ranilo M. Laygo is a Senior Scientist with ORC Macro in Atlanta, GA. He received a doctorate in Counseling Psychology from Georgia State University and a master's degree in Guidance and Counseling from the University of Georgia. He has served as Project Manager on several large, federally funded multi-site projects, in addition to presenting research findings at national and international conferences in the area of mental health. His areas of expertise include treatment efficacy and program evaluation.

William T. O'Donohue is the Nicholas Cummings Professor of Organized Behavioral Healthcare Delivery in the Department of Psychology at the University of Nevada at Reno. He also is President and CEO of the University Alliance for Behavioral Care, Inc., a company selling integrated care services. He also holds adjunct appointments in the Departments of Philosophy, Psychiatry and at the University of Hawaii, Monoa. He received a doctorate in clinical psychology from the State University of New York at Stony Brook and a master's degree in philosophy from Indiana University. He is editor and co-editor on a number of books, including the *Management and Administration Skills for the Mental Health Professional*; *Integrated Behavioral Healthcare: Positioning Mental Health Practice with Medical/Surgical Practice*; *The Impact of Medical Cost Offset*; and *Treatments that Work in Primary Care*.

Patricia Robinson provides consultation services for the Bureau of Primary Care and other health care organizations. Additionally, she delivers primary care behavioral health services and clinical training at Yakima Valley Farm Workers Clinic in Toppenish, Washington. She received her doctorate in psychology from Texas Woman's University and a master's degree in psychology at North Texas State University. She is the author of two books (*Living Life Well: New Strategies for Change*; *Treating Depression in Primary Care: A Manual for Primary Care and Behavioral Health Providers*) and numerous articles and book chapters.

Dr. Christine N. Runyan is a clinical health psychologist working for the U.S. Air Force Medical Service's Population Health Support Division in San Antonio, Texas. Dr. Runyan received her Ph.D. in clinical psychology from Virginia Tech and completed post-doctoral training in clinical health psychology at Wilford Hall Medical Center. Her areas of interest and expertise are integrated care, clinical quality improvement, clinical informatics, and the integration of clinical psychology with public health.

Jason M. Satterfield, Ph.D. is an Assistant Professor and Director of Behavioral Medicine in the Division of General Internal Medicine at the University of California San Francisco. He is the Co-Director of the Behavioral Sciences curriculum for UCSF medical students and primary care residents including training in cultural competence, behavioral medicine, and psychiatric services in primary care settings. His current research interests include evaluation of cultural competency programs, medical provider well-being groups, and emotional intelligence in medical care.

Ian Shaffer, M.D., M.M.M. is the Chief Operating Officer of the University Alliance for Behavioral Care, Inc. Dr. Shaffer is a Board Certified Psychiatrist. Dr. Shaffer is a physician executive with more than 20 years of medical management experience. For 10 years he served as the Chief Medical Officer, Value Behavioral Health (VBH) and its successor ValueOptions. He led the clinical development and was a key member of VBH's Executive Management Team. His areas of management included participating in strategic planning, managed behavioral health practice and policy, including clinical services, utilization review, provider relations, credentialing, ambulatory review, and quality improvement. He has also worked on Joint Commission survey preparation, production development, network development and management, budgeting, contracting and provider reimbursement systems, risk management, NCQA surveying, clinical guidelines and outcomes development. He later served as the Executive Vice President of Quality and Outcome Strategies at ValueOptions where he developed outcomes programs and new provider oversight systems moving the company away from traditional utilization review. He was a member of the National Advisory Committee, Center for Mental Health Services, Substance Abuse Mental Health Services Administration, as well as the Past Chairman (1996) and past Executive Board Member of the American Managed Behavioral Healthcare Association.

Reginald D. Wood is a professor of psychology at Honolulu Community College. He received a BA in psychology from the University of Toronto and a master's degree, masters in business administration degree, and a doctorate in social/personality psychology from the University of Hawaii at Manoa. He is currently a psychology intern in the clinical respecialization program at the University of Hawaii at Manoa.

Table of Contents

Clinical Integration:
The Promise and the Path

William O'Donohue, Nicholas A. Cummings,
& Kyle E. Ferguson

The phrase "integrated care" has several meanings. Here we use "integrated care" in one specific sense: better coordinating behavioral health services with medical and surgical services. There are other meanings of this term, though different, that are generally consistent with our usage: e.g., placing other scientifically-based professionals in the medical surgical setting, e.g., nutritionists and dentists. However, there are some usages that are not consistent with our general thrust: e.g., placing non-scientifically based "alternative medicine" in primary care. Alternative medicine is a domain that has both gold and chaff, and until properly controlled studies separate the effective elements from the unhelpful or even iatrogenic elements, we do not endorse this sort of "integration".

Cummings, Cummings, and Johnson (1997) have provided a graphical representation of the range of possible coordination.

Thus integration can range from activities (in the order of less to more integration) such as a referral call for information exchange, to meetings to discuss

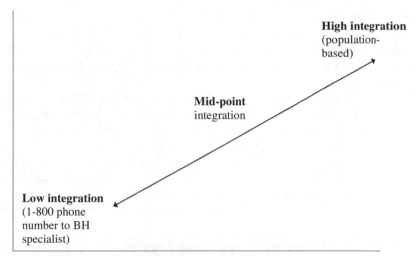

Integration can occur at any point in the continuum of intensity, depending on customer readiness and market receptivity.

Figure 1.1. Integration as a Continuum.

cases, to a collaborative meeting with a particular patient, to working conjointly in a team to deliver more comprehensive services. We have found two general domains of integrative care that are of most interest: 1) collocating a specially trained behavioral care provider in a medical setting; and 2) training behavioral care providers to outreach high medical utilizers, particularly those suffering from chronic diseases, to assess and treat unaddressed psychosocial drivers of medical utilization (see chapter by Cucciarre and O'Donohue, this volume; Cummings, in press).

Why Integrate?

There are three principle goals for integrative care:

1. Producing healthier patients
2. Producing healthier patients with less or at least more efficient resource expenditures.
3. Removing barriers to access by offering more services that are more convenient and produce less stigma

What follows are some concrete examples of these goals.

Producing Healthier Patients

Patients with chronic diseases such as diabetes, asthma, and hypertension can participate in disease management groups delivered by specially trained behavioral care providers. These services can provide treatment adherence interventions, lifestyle change programs, social support, stress management, education regarding their diseases, and treatment of comorbid psychological problems such as depression. These disease management programs are more psychologically sophisticated than many of the extant disease management programs which generally only concentrate on education and case management (see Cummings, this volume, and Cummings, in press).

Patients who do not have chronic disease but in whom the primary care physician (PCP) suspects psychosocial problems can be seen during routine primary care visits. These patients are channeled to an on-site behavioral health specialist who immediately assesses and treats their behavioral health issues.

High medical utilizers who have never been thoroughly screened for psychosocial drivers of their medical utilizers can be outreached, assessed, and treated when needed. Their unrecognized behavioral problems (clinical and subclinical) can be detected and treated and their unnecessary medical utilization can be reduced.

Creating More Efficient Resource Expenditures

By recognizing the untreated psychosocial drivers of health utilization and treating these, resources are allocated to patients' presenting problems rather than to more medical-surgical tests and procedures that will never capture patients' actual psychosocial problem, e.g., lack of social support or job stress. Because behavioral health resources, particularly in the primary care model, are generally less expensive than most medical-surgical treatments (e.g., ER visits and MRIs) this can result in more efficient resource expenditures. This can perhaps be most clearly seen in a high medical utilizer in which a program outreaches a specially chosen subset of patients (those likely by their diagnoses and usage patterns to have psychosocial issues) and thoroughly assesses these for psychosocial problems.

Eliminating inefficiencies in healthcare is of tremendous interest as health care costs are creating a crisis in the United States. In 1996, of the 943 billion dollars spent on healthcare costs in the United States, only 7% was devoted to mental healthcare, with another 1% devoted to addictive disorders and 2% to dementia/ Alzheimer's Disease. In 2002, health care expenditures rose to 1.4 trillion, which is approximately 14% of the nation's GDP. Health care costs are again rising faster than the rate of inflation. On average, premiums increased 14% in 2002 and are expected to rise at even a higher rate in 2003. It is projected that health care spending will grow at an average annual rate of 7.3% during the next decade, reaching 18% or $3.1 trillion of the GDP by 2012 (Spors, 2003).

Removing Barriers to Access

Essentially, integrated care offers all the practical advantages of "one stop shopping". It does not require the increased pragmatics involved in an external referral. Experience suggests that 20% or less of individuals who receive a referral to specialty care mental health actually comply with that referral. In an integrated care setting, patients possibly needing behavioral health services can immediately be handed off to an on-site behavioral care provider. Moreover, this provider should seamlessly fit into the primary care team and not be seen by anyone, but particularly the patient, as a "shrink in hiding". The patient should see this professional simply as one member of the team who has skills to help him or her with his or her problem. This reduces or eliminates stigma. When the problem does require specialty care the behavioral health provider can better coordinate this external referral. Finally, this can place behavioral health services in areas that are underserved such as rural and poor areas.

More Specific Aims of Integrated Care

Strosahl (1998) has suggested that integrated care can achieve these general goals by achieving the more specific aims of:

1. Improving the recognition of behavioral health needs
2. Improving collaborative care and management of patients with psychosocial issues in primary care
3. Providing an internal resource for PCP to help address a patient's psychosocial concerns or behavior health issues, without referring them to a specialty mental health clinic

4. Providing immediate access to behavioral health consultants with rapid feedback
5. Improving the fit between the care patients seek in primary care and the services delivered
6. Preventing more serious health problems through early recognition and intervention
7. Triaging into more intensive specialty health care by the behavioral health consultant

Strosahl (1988) further defines the typical services requested and provided by the behavioral health provider in primary care as:

1. *Triage/Liaison*: Initial screening visits of 30 minutes (or less) designed to determine appropriate level of mental health care intervention.
2. *Behavioral Health Consultation*: Intake visit by a patient referred for a general evaluation. The focus is on diagnostic and functional evaluation, recommendations for treatment and forming limited behavior change goals. This service involves assessing patients who are at risk due to a stressful life event. It may include identifying whether a patient could benefit from accessing existing community resources, educating patients about these resources, or referring the patient to a social service agency.
3. *Behavioral Health Follow-up*. Secondary visits by a patient to support a behavior change plan or treatment started by the PCP on the basis of earlier consultation. This service is often conducted in tandem with planned PCP visits.
4. *Compliance Enhancement*: Visit designed to help the patient comply with an intervention initiated by the PCP. The focus is on education, addressing negative beliefs, or offering strategies to help cope with side effects of medical treatment.
5. *Relapse Prevention*: Visit designed to maintain stable functioning in a patient who has responded to previous treatment; often spaced at long intervals.
6   *Behavioral Medicine*: Visit designed to assist the patient in managing a chronic medical condition or to tolerate an invasive or uncomfortable medical procedure. The focus may be on lifestyle issues or health risk factors among patients at risk (e.g., smoking cessation or stress management) or may involve managing issues related to progressive illness (such as end stage COPD).
7. *Specialty Consultation*: Designed to provide consultation services over time to patients who require ongoing monitoring and follow-up; applicable to patients with chronic stressors, marginal lifestyle adaptation, and so forth.
8. *Disability Prevention/Management*: Visit designed to assist patients who are on medical leave from job to return to work promptly. The focus of this service is on coordinating care with the PCP, job site, and patient. The emphasis is on avoiding "disability-building" treatments and patient suffering.

9. *Psychoeducation Class*: Brief group treatment that either replaces or supplements individual consultation, designed to promote education and skill building. Often a psychoeducation group can and should serve as the primary psychological intervention as many behavioral health needs are best addressed in a group format.
10. *Conjoint Consultation*: Visits with the PCP and patient designed to address an issue of concern to both; this often involves addressing any conflict between them.
11. *Telephone Consultation*: Scheduled intervention contacts or follow-up visits with patients that are conducted by the behavioral health clinician via telephone, rather than in person. This consultation may also take place via e-mail in some cases.
12. *On-Demand Behavioral Health Consultation*: Usually unscheduled PCP initiated contact with a patient, either via telephone or in person. This service is generally utilized during emergency situations requiring an immediate response.
13. *On-Demand Medication Consultation*: Usually unscheduled PCP initiated contact with a patient regarding medication issues such as compliance or possible behavioral side effects of treatment.
14. *Care Management*: Designed to contain extensive and coordinated delivery of medical and/or mental health services, usually to patients with chronic psychological and medical problems.
15. *Team Building*: Conferencing with one or more members of the health care team to address peer relationships, job stress issues, or process of care concerns.
16. *PCP Consultation*: Face to face visits with the PCP to discuss patient care issues; often involves "curbside" consultation.

In summary, in integrated care models, one or more behavioral care providers (BCP) either outreach the high medical utilizers such as patients with chronic diseases and/or are co-located with the physician in a primary care setting. Patients who see the primary care physician are then referred, as needed, to the BCP for disease management interventions and other behavioral services. The primary care setting has been viewed as the preferred setting for the delivery of behavioral healthcare services because 1) this setting does not carry the stigma that a mental healthcare setting often does; 2) the patient does not have to experience the inconvenience of making another appointment, resulting in more completed referrals (i.e., when a physician refers a patient to a BCP in another setting, patients follow through approximately 20% of the time, whereas when referrals are made to a BCP in the same setting, they are followed through approximately 90% of the time); 3) the BCP is more skilled at handling disease management issues that stem from treatment adherence/education problems than the primary care physician; 4) the physician's time is considered more costly than that of the BCP, and referrals to a BCP result in more patients seen by the physician as his or her time is freed from dealing with behavioral problems; 5) patients initially receive more services; and 6) behavioral health care services have been shown to result in medical cost offset, or savings in medical dollars as a result of implementation of behavioral services – making the integrated care model at least potentially cost effective. Thus, there is currently much interest in integrated care as it is hypothesized that this type of service delivery will improve patient access, increase the rate of evidence-based practice, improve patient health and satisfaction as well as reduce long-term costs.

The integrated care model we seek to further understand and implement has been developed by Cummings and Strosahl and implemented successfully in the Northern California Kaiser Health system, Group Health Cooperative of Puget Sound, and the United States Air Force (see Russ, et al., this volume) and in Hawaii (Laygo, et al., this volume).

Dr. Aaron Kaplan, Ph.D (Kaplan, 2002) serves as a specially trained collocated behavioral care provider in the Hawaii II Integrative Care Project (see chapter by Laygo, et al., this volume). In what follows he describes what his typical day may be like. This gives a flavor of what integrated care is actually like:

Typical Day in the Life of a Behavioral Care Provider

8:00   Arrive at work, check messages, and make phone calls.
   a.   Mr. Perez, who started taking Paxil for panic attacks, now feeling dizzy, wants to know if it could be a side effect. Call him back and discuss potential side-effects of Paxil to determine if it may be related. Also, remind him of the CBT techniques he learned for reducing anxiety (e.g., self-talk using cognitive reframing)
   b.   Dr. Tanaka leaves message asking me to contact Mr. Johnson to make an appt. with him for anger management. Call Mr. Johnson, describe behavioral health services and Dr. Tanaka's request, and make an appt.
   c.   Ms. Miller leaves message stating she has decided she wants to try an AA meeting (as I had previously suggested), and wants to know how to find out about meetings.

8:30   Get paged by Dr. Song, who has an 18-year-old female patient in tears because she recently broke up with her boyfriend. I meet pt. in exam room, and determined she needs a while to talk, so I take her into my office. Discuss with her some cognitive reframing strategies, and behavioral strategies to cope with her distress, and allow her to vent. Agree to see her in two weeks to see how she is doing.

8:45   While meeting with previous pt, Dr. Tanaka pages and asks me to see another pt. I call back and, determining it's not a crisis, have the next patient wait in the waiting room for me.

9:10   Finish with 18 yo, Check in with Dr. Tanaka, who states the pt. waiting for me in the waiting room is acting strangely and he is wondering if there is severe mental illness. I meet patient and determine he has some psychosis but not currently being treated by a psychiatrist or on meds. Help make a referral to a psychiatrist who takes Medicaid and explain to pt. that medications may help him to cope with what he is going through.

9:45   Down time – paperwork. I chart on patients so far.

10:15   Call to Ms. Ziegler, and elderly women with multiple medical problems, to check-up on her. I helped develop a system for organizing her many medications and want to see how it is going for her and discuss any problems she may be having.

10:30   Check in with practitioners. Remind Dr. Tanaka that Mr. Gusto is coming in today for a checkup, and that I listed in the progress notes some simple strategies to help him deal with Panic Disorder. Tanaka can remind the pt. of these during the visit. Mr. Tanaka then lets me know he has a pt. named Mr. Abe with depression coming in at 11:00 that he wants me to speak with afterward.

10:45   Clinic receives a crisis call from a pt. who says he's suicidal. I take the call and speak with pt. for about 20 mins, determining his suicidality, and then refer him to an appropriate community resource.

11:15   Meet Mr. Abc. Spend about one hour with him, determining that he is severely depressed, and has multiple stressors in his life he's dealing with. He also has very low self-esteem and negative thoughts. Give him some immediate cognitive and behavioral suggestions, and plan on seeing him weekly for now as there seem to be some significant therapeutic issues to work on. Also, suggest an antidepressent, and discuss it with Dr. Tanaka afterward, who agrees to start a trial of medication.

12:30   Drug reps arrive with food and presentation about a medication for hypertension. I'm invited, as part of the primary care team.

1:00   I have a weekly therapy appt. scheduled with an ongoing pt. I have been seeing for about 6 weeks with agoraphobia. Let staff know to take messages for me while I'm in session.

1:50   Session ends. I contact Dr. Song, who paged me, and had a pt. named Mr. Hanson with diabetes and hypertension, and wanted some behavioral health interventions. pt. already left, so I agree to contact him.

2:00   Another 50 minute session scheduled with a pt. with anxiety and depression who I have been seeing every other week for about 8 weeks. Plan on seeing her for at least 4 more weeks, as she has improved significantly.

2:50   Contact Mr. Hanson (the diabetic/hypertensive) by phone, and talk with
         him about diabetes and hypertension. Since he has time, we spend about
         ½ hour on the phone discussing the diseases, and making a behavioral plan
         for him to exercise more, make small changes in his diet. Also schedule a
         follow-up appt. to discuss relaxation exercises and talk about ways of
         handling stress better.

3:30   Paged by Dr. Tanaka, who is in an exam room with a pt. pt. walked in with
         an acute panic attack, and would like me to intervene to calm her down so
         he can have blood pressure checked and do physical. I spend about 15
         minutes with pt, doing relaxation exercise. Pt. calms, and I get staff to finish
         physical. We decide that pt. could benefit from some therapy for anxiety,
         and also behavioral change because she is obese and suffering from
         diabetes. I schedule an appt. to see pt. the following week for this.

4:00-4:45   Weekly smoking cessation group

5:00   Finish charting, check urgent messages – go to gym to decrease stress, then
         attempt to eat balanced meal including fish and vegetables.

A Caveat: Integrative Care is not Specialty Mental Health Care

A simple and we shall argue simplistic model of integrated care is simply to
place specialty mental health care closer or even inside a medical/surgical delivery
system. However, from the description of the day of a BCP one can see this is not
what has been done and there are good reasons for this. Placing specialty mental
health care inside medical surgical care can seemingly overcome some problems of
fragmented care (e.g., the inconvenience/barriers of an appointment, at some other
time) and can seemly gain some of the advantages of integrated care (e.g., behavioral
health skills as part of the medical care team). However, this appearance is
misleading. The limitations and problems of simply placing specialty mental
healthcare inside or beside medical surgical care include:

1. The ecologies of the two systems clash. Medical health care delivery
    particularly primary care is fast, action oriented, intermittent, and more oriented
    toward population management. Diagnosis and treatment are often
    accomplished more quickly and in a stepped care model. In contrast, specialty
    mental health care is slower (dozens or several dozens of 50 minute sessions),
    continuous (treatment is typically delivered until the person's psychological
    problems are "cured". In some models this means complete personality
    restructuring), more contemplative (several sessions are taken to establish
    rapport, conduct an extensive personal history, and deliver extensive

psychological testing), and person rather than population focused. This clash of ecologies produces many desynchronizes in forming a functioning team.
2.   The behavioral care provider's skill set typically is not adequate to the task. Most mental care providers have few skills in disease management, treatment adherence, general medical literacy, and psychopharmocology, for example. Thus, the skill set which mental health professionals typically have needs to be significantly supplemented in the integrated care delivery system.
3.   Of particular importance is that most mental health professionals do not know how to function in a consultation/liaison model with medical professionals. Their role is often not to take over a patient's care but to consult with the PCP in his or her management of the case.

Strosahl (1998) has provided a nice summary of the differences between his model of consultation/liaison integrated care and specialty mental healthcare.

A Second Caveat: Incomplete Integrative Care is not Successful

Integrative care is not something that can be done in a partial or incomplete way. When it is attempted in a half-hearted way, the benefits of integrative are typically not found (see Cummings, Cummings & Johnston, 1997). At times individuals parachute in one disease management program or a depression program into a fragmented medical-surgical setting. This system fails for many reasons but one of the principal reasons is that it is not set up to address the full range of behavioral health problems that the BCP will confront. One cannot just train professionals in depression because patients will also present with anxiety, substance abuse, borderline personality disorders, bereavement, etc. When the system is not integrated and the team cannot co-manage the full range of psychosocial problems the "integrative care" system does not work. Professionals feel frustrated as they may be unable to treat the full range of behavioral health problems. When these cases are referred out for treatment, the primary care professional again finds a low compliance rate, very little feedback from the specialty care mental health professional (much of which is irrelevant; see Satterfield, this volume), and the person to whom the referral was made may not have adequate training in the specialized task (e.g., medical treatment adherence).

The Context of Fragmented Care

Of course, the need to bring these services together is brought about by the fact that, traditionally, behavioral health and primary care have been separate. They have been separated historically for several reasons:

1.   Behavioral health problems have thought to have a different status then physical problems. For example, they have been thought to be "moral," "spiritual," or "problems of the will" while physical problems have been thought about in more mechanistic terms.

Dimension	Consultation	Specialty Treatment
Primary Goals	- performs appropriate clinical assessments -support PCM decision making -build on PCM interventions - teach PCM "core" mental health skills - educate patient in self management skills through exposure - improve PCM-patient working relationship - monitor, with PCM, "at risk" patients - manage cronic patients with PCM in primary provider role - assist in tea building	- deliver primary treatment to resolve condition - coordinate with PCM by phone - teach patient core self management skills -manage more serious mental disorders over time as primary provider
Session Structure	- limited to one to three visits in typical case - 15-30 minute visits	- session number variable, related to patient condition - 50 minute visits
Intervention Structure	- informal, revolves around PCM assessment and goals - less intensity, between session interval longer - relationship generally not primary focus - visits timed around PCM visits - long term follw rare, reserved for high risk cases	- formal, requires intak assessment, treatment planning - higher intensity, involving more concentrated care -relationship built to last over time - visit structure not related to medical visits - long term follow-up encouraged for most clients
Intervention Methods	- limited face to face contact - uses patient education model as primary model - consultation is a technical resource to patient - emphasis on home based practice to promote change - may involve PCM in visits with patient	- face to face contact is primary treatment vehicle - education model ancillary - home practice linked back to treatment - PCM rarely involved in visits with patient
Termination/ Follow Up	- responsibility returned to PCM *in toto* - PCM provides relapse prevention or maintenance treatment	- therapist remains person to contact if in need - therapist provides and relapse prevention or maintenance treatment
Referral Structure	- patient referred by PCM only	- patient self refers or is referred by others
Primary Information Products	- consultation report to PCM - part of medical record	- specialty treatment notes (*i.e.*, intak or progress notes) - part of a separate mental health record with minimal notation to medical record

Table 1.1 Defining Characteristics of the Consultation vs. Specialty Treatment Models.

2.   Behavioral health problems are often less understood and there has been less clarity in their definition, etiology, prevention, and treatment.
3.   Mental health problems have had different reimbursement problems and mechanisms. Epidemiologists have had less success and less precise

predictions of the rate of occurrence; insurers have had less success in pricing necessary treatment; many treatment fads have occurred (see Lilienfeld, Lohr, & Lynn, 2003) and thus the pricing for either indemnity insurance or a capitation rate has been more difficult. This has been augmented by the fact that with each new edition of the Diagnostic and Statistical Manual, more and more human behavior has been judged as problematic, requiring treatment, and is therefore reimbursable.

4. Moreover, it has not been clear whether mental health treatment is a specialty area or problems that can be better treated in primary care. There has been an interesting inconsistency here: on the one hand most behavioral health problems are currently treated in primary care (e.g., depression, anxiety and obesity), although the health system is set up as if behavioral health were a specialty domain; mental health specialists are outside primary care facilities and have treatment ready to be delivered only in a specialty setting with a specialty ecology.

5. Finally, the ecologies of the two disciplines differ dramatically. The timeframe for service delivery is slower in mental health; lower level problems are considered treatable and meriting considerable resource expenditure; more emphasis is placed on knowing the person, etc.

Training in the Skill Set to Deliver Integrated Care

In general, there are three sets of targets for training in the integrative care delivery system: 1) the behavioral care provider; 2) the administrators; 3) the physicians. Each of these will be discussed separately.

The Behavioral Care Provider

In general, the training goals of the behavioral health provider are to:

1. Increase medical knowledge/literacy
2. Increase consultation/liaison skills
3. Foster an understanding of population management
4. Increase abilities to perform in a different ecology
    a. faster
    b. more action-oriented
    c. treatment-driven
    d. team-based delivery
5. Increase knowledge of psychopharmocology
6. Increase knowledge of medically related assessments and interventions such as disease management and treatment adherence

The Programs at the University of Nevada, Reno and Forest Institute of Professional Psychology

Although currently these skills need to be taught in intensive "bootcamps" in integrated care settings, because of the lack of appropriately trained professionals the University of Nevada, Reno (UNR) and the Forest Institute of Professional Psychology in Springfield, MO have adopted specialty tracks in primary care psychology to prepare their doctoral level clinical students in the skills to practice and even manage integrated care settings. The curriculum supplements the general doctoral curriculum in the Ph.D. program at UNR and the PsyD program at Forest. The curriculum includes:

COURSE AREA: SYSTEMS OF ORGANIZED CARE

Introduction to Health Care Delivery

Topics to be included: A survey of health care economic issues appropriate for all graduate students in psychology; introduction to empirically supported treatments, integrated psychological care in primary care setting, business and administration principles, and methods of obtaining medical cost offsets.

Psychotherapy and Supervision in Organized Systems of Care

Topics to be included: The Biodyne clinical model. Consultation/liaison skills in integrated care environments. Practica in disease management, treatment adherence, treatment of psychological comorbidity involved in medical diseases, lifestyle change and other behavioral medicine/health psychology interventions.

Organized Systems of Care Practicum/ Externship

Topics to be included: 3 credits (1 semester; 20 hours/ week) will be devoted to service delivery in a managed care setting, preferably in primary care, supervised by a licensed psychologist. 3 credits (1 semester; 20 hours/ week) will be devoted to gaining administrative and management skills in a managed care setting, preferably in primary care, supervised by a licensed psychologist.

COURSE AREA: BUSINESS AND FINANCE

Economics of health Care and Health Policy
Topics to be included: Understanding the macroeconomics of health care; defining managed care and identifying managed care providers; under-standing the health care market; current policy debates with regard to the political economy of health care; risk and managed care from an actuarial standpoint.

Introduction of Business Basics

Topics to be included: Entrepreneurship, finance basics, creating a business plan, marketing techniques, and administrative skills.

COURSE AREA: PRIMARY CARE PRACTICES

Medical Psychology

Topics to be included: Basic physiology; a comprehensive introduction to clinical medicine; the role of behavioral health care in primary care medicine

Psychopharmacology

Topics to be included: Introduction to prescribing practices, understanding classes of drugs commonly prescribed for psychological problems, drug interactions, side effect profiles, and implications of the use of pharmacotherapy.

Behavioral Medicine

Topics to be included: Introduction to disease management, psychological implications of and treatments for medical problems such as chronic pain and treatment compliance.

Training the Physician

Strosahl's (1998) model also involves PCP training. He has successfully trained physicians in a number of settings. Key core competencies targeted in his model of physician training include:

1. Accurately describing and selling behavioral health services when referring patients to a behavioral health care specialist.
2. Demonstrating an understanding of the relationship of medical and psychological systems to cultural contexts of individual patients.
3. Diverting patients with behavioral health issues to behavioral health consultants.
4. Using an intermittent care strategy such that the patient is receiving services from both the physician and the behavioral health care specialist in turn.
5. Referring patients appropriately to behavioral health classes in the primary care clinic.
6. Clearly stating the referral question in behavioral health referrals.
7. Interrupting the behavioral health provider as needed.

8. Conducting effective curbside consultations with the behavioral health provider.
9. Being willing to aggressively follow up with behavioral health providers when indicated.
10. Focusing on treatment plans that reduce physicians' visits and workloads.
11. Engaging in co-management of patient care with a behavioral health provider.
12. Documenting behavioral health referrals and treatment plans in chart notes.
13. Demonstrating knowledge of the behavioral health care provider role.
14. Being comfortable orienting the behavioral health provider to the primary care environment.
15. Paging the behavioral health care provider with urgent questions.

Training the Administrators

In addition, Strosahl (1998) has developed training programs for increasing organizational readiness for integrated care. Keys include:

1. Insure senior level management ratifies strategic vision of integrated care.
2. Involve key internal stakeholders (e.g., department heads).
3. Involve internal "opinion leaders".
4. Involve key external stakeholders.
5. Gain staff investment in the change process.
6. Address resistance to integration (e.g., due to philosophical differences, etc.).
7. Provide preparatory workshops and training to increase understanding of the integration initiative.
8. Involve skeptics of integration in the design and development process.
9. Base the system of care in a well documented administrative process and structure.
10. Design a service that is seen as feasible to implement and operate by participants.
11. Embed integrated services in a team approach to health care.
12. Evaluate benefit design and identify payment mechanisms for behavioral health providers.
13. Develop a sustainable budget strategy.
14. Identify methods for risk sharing with partners.
15. Develop agreements for distribution of cost savings.
16. Create a Policies and Procedures service manual.
17. Determine reporting and supervisory relationships.
18. Determine charting and documentation requirements.
19. Develop recommended schedule templates.
20. Identify the need for skill based training for behavioral health providers and PCPs.
21. Employ structured case discussions.
22. Assess consumer and provider satisfaction with integrated services.
23. Assess program accessibility and penetration rates.

24. Develop practice profiles for individual providers and PCP teams.
25. Adopt performance indicators as a core management tool.

The Clinical Toolbox

The success of integrative care rests on the effectiveness of its clinical interventions. Psychotherapy has all too often had "psychoreligions" that were practiced independent of the evidence of the effectiveness of their interventions or in the worse cases despite the evidence of the ineffectiveness or even of evidence of their iatrogenic effects (Lilienfeld, et al., 2003). The first and second authors of this chapter once inspected an "integrated care" delivery site in which the behavioral care provider was treating patients with dance therapy and with "urethral regression therapy". All integrative care efforts can fail without an effective and more specifically a cost effective therapy model.

Cummings has developed a medically sophisticated focused psychotherapy that is brief, intermittent, and occurs throughout the life cycle (See Cummings & Sayama, 1995). It was developed in the 1980's in the Hawaii Medicaid Study and was the basis for American Biodyne's success. Each American Biodyne therapist was initially trained in this model and continually supervised for adherence and competence. It is based on an important therapeutic contract:

"My job is never to abandon you as long as you need me, never to ask you to do anything until you can do it. Your job is to join me in a partnership to make me obsolete as soon as possible."

The techniques of this therapy are focused on correctly diagnosing patients' resistances, understanding the patient's implicit contract (the often unstated but real reason for entering therapy), making an operational diagnosis (understanding the answer to the question: "Why is the patient here now?"), and understanding the patient's position in a useful heuristic: the onion/garlic chart. "The onion patient is fuiltridden and suffering. The garlic patient does not feel quilt, makes everyone else suffer, and cannot understand why everyone is bothered by his or her behavior" (Cummings & Cummings, 2000, p. 92). The onion garlic chart is a paradigm of a psychodynamic division that allows the formation of useful treatment plans. A key element of the Biodyne model of therapy is that the first session involves treatment and homework, rather than just assessment, as in more traditional psychotherapy.

Cummings' model can incorporate the empirically-validated treatments typically associated with cognitive behavior therapy. Cognitive-behavior therapy has effective short-term protocols for problems commonly encountered in intergrative care settings such as depression (see Robinson, this volume), anxiety, stress, chronic pain, child management problems, and treatment adherence. O'Donohue et al. (in press) have recently edited two books that contains leading experts describing these interventions. These can be used as resources for developing effective clinical skills in integrative care settings.

Conclusions

Integrating behavioral health services into traditional medical surgical practice appears to be the wave of the future. It may help contain escalating health care costs not by restricting the supply of health care services but rather by decreasing the demand for health care services. Clinical integration accomplishes this by recognizing the tremendous extent to which behavioral problems are involved in medical visits and thereby by appropriately and comprehensively treating the patient.

However, the road to integration is not an easy one. It is not simply dropping specialty mental health care into medical treatment settings; that is simply parachuting in a disease management program. Rather, it involves significant understanding of clinical, training, operational and administrative issues. However, there are clear demonstration projects in which these issues were handled well and integrative care realized its promise. The following chapters in this book detail these projects as well as well as some of the other major core competencies needed to successfully integrate.

References

Cummings, N.A. Somatization. In W. O'Donohue, D. Henderson, M. Byrd & N. Cummings (in press). *Treatments that Work in Primary Care*. Boston: Allyn & Bacon.

Cummings, N. A., & Cummings, J. L. (2000). *The essence of psychotherapy: Reinventing the art in the new era of data*. San Diego, CA: Academic Press.

Cummings, N.A., Cummings, J.L, & Johnson, J.N. (1997). *Behavioral health in primary care: A guide for clinical integration*. Madison: Psychosocial Press.

Cummings, N.A., & Sayama, M. (1995). *Focused psychotherapy: A casebook of brief, intermittent psychotherapy throughout the life cycle*. New York:Brunner/Mazel.

Kaplan, A. (2002). *Integrative care: The Hawaii Project*. Paper delivered to the Hawaii Psychological Association, November, 2002.

Lilienfeld, S., Lohr, J, & Lynn, S. (2003). *Science and pseudoscience in clinical psychology*. New York: Guilford.

O'Donohue, W., Fisher, J.E., & Hayes, S.C. (in press). *The techniques of cognitive behavior therapy: A step by step guide*. Hoboken, NJ: John Wiley.

O'Donohue, W., Henderson, D., Byrd, M., & Cummings, N.A. (in press). *Treatments that work in primary care*. Boston: Allyn & Bacon.

Spors, K.K. (2003). Health spending is likely to slow but still exceed economic growth. *Wall Street Journal*, 2/7/03.

Strosahl, K. (1998). *An integrative care manual*, unpublished manuscript.

Advantages and Limitations of Disease Management: A Practical Guide

Nicholas A. Cummings

Disease management and population based programs have most often yielded disappointing results, in both measures of effectiveness as well as efficiency. Seldom have these resulted in cost savings. Too often programs have parachuted a modicum of disease and population management into an otherwise traditional setting, and not surprisingly results have been elusive at best, and negative at the worst. Most programs have been medically oriented, and although the medical aspects have been sound, they lack sufficiently extensive behavioral interventions that are both highly targeted and focused, as well as being empirically derived. It is now an accepted fact that between 60% and 70% of physician visits are by patients who are manifesting a translation of stress into physical symptoms, or whose physical disease is being complicated by psychological factors, and which very often result in non-compliance with medical regimen (Follette & Cummings, 1967; Cummings, Cummings & Johnson, 1997; Katon, VonKorff, Lin, Lipscomb, Russo, Wagner & Polk, 1990; Kroenke & Mangelsdorff, 1989).

This chapter discusses effective and non-effective program characteristics as gleaned from actual experience in successful delivery systems. The emphasis is on pragmatics: transmitting concepts useful in building disease and population management programs, and research citations are kept to a minimum. Although the delivery methodologies began in the laboratory which yielded evidence-based treatments (EBTs), these often had to be modestly or even drastically modified to meet the exigencies of the real world. In making these modifications, field research was heavily relied upon (field-tested EBTs), using medical cost offset results as the criteria for effectiveness in reducing the kinds of stress and distress that lead a patient to over-utilize medical care, in both quantity and inappropriateness. The ultimate criterion of both efficiency and effectiveness, however, was the unprecedented degree of system satisfaction (both patients and physicians) that resulted in over a decade of service delivery that was absent a single malpractice suit or patient complaint that had to be adjudicated. These delivery systems began with the Hawaii HCFA Medicaid Project of 36,000 Medicaid recipients plus 92,000 federal employees (Cummings, Dorken, Pallak & Henke, 1990) and proceeded through its successor, American Biodyne, which culminated in 1992 with 14.5 million covered lives (Cummings, Cummings & Johnson, 1997). Readers wishing to explore primary research sources are referred to the extensive literature, beginning with summaries and bibliographies by Cummings, Cummings and Johnson (1997) and Cummings, O'Donohue, and Ferguson (2002). The research methodology used to measure cost-therapeutic effectiveness over more than four decades was published by Cummings (1994).

A Summary of the Hawaii Project

The 7-year Hawaii Project was an $8 million three-way contract among the Health Care Financing Administration, the State of Hawaii, and the Foundation for Behavioral Health, with HMSA (the BC/BS affiliate in Hawaii) acting as fiscal intermediary. A separate delivery system was created to serve 36,000 Medicaid recipients and 92,000 federal employees, or a total population of 128,000 on the Island of Oahu (Honolulu) randomized into 2/3 experimental and 1/3 control groups. Evidence-based programs (protocols, guidelines using individual/group models) addressed six chronic diseases: asthma, diabetes, emphysema and other airways diseases, hypertension, ischemic heart disease, and rheumatoid arthritis. Further evidence-based programs addressed several behavioral conditions: five kinds of depression, panic/anxiety states, phobias, chemical dependency, and Borderline Personality Disorder. An aggressive, sensitive and highly successful outreach program contacted the 15% highest utilizers of healthcare each month. *Medical cost offset*, or the reduction in medical/surgical/psychiatric services was measured for the year before and the three years following the behavioral care interventions. The 15% highest utilizers were defined each month by *frequency* of services, not by total dollar amount inasmuch as the latter reflects high ticket conditions such as transplants and terminal illness rather than the somatizers. Clinical services for the specially created delivery system were for three years, with tracking of outcomes for the four succeeding years. With one year of set-up, training, and partial delivery of services preceding launching of the full service/research endeavor, the Hawaii Project had a total of eight years.

Results:

- Medical cost offset savings in the experimental group were of such magnitude that the government recovered its investment within 18 months.
- Traditional behavioral services (control group) actually raised medical costs.
- Medical cost offset savings were the highest in the chronic disease and chemical dependency groups, and less (even though substantial) in the non-chronic, non-CD patients.
- Medical cost offset in disease management reflects highly organized healthcare systems and is lesser or absent in more traditional settings.

The American Biodyne Delivery System

American Biodyne was founded as a proprietary delivery system in 1985, four years after the creation of the nonprofit Biodyne Centers in Hawaii, and with the encouragement of the federal funding agency. It employed the delivery models tested and refined during the initial phases of the Hawaii Project, refinements that continued for the remainder of the HCFA research as they did also for the first seven years of American Biodyne's original founding management. Taken from two Greek words meaning: *life change,* American Biodyne sought, first, to save the hard-fought mental health/substance abuse benefit that was in jeopardy. The federal government was unable to write Diagnosis Related Groups (DRGs) for behavioral care as it had done for medical/surgical care. Whereas the inflation rate for the latter rapidly diminished, it increased dramatically for psychiatry as hospitals and health systems replaced losses of revenue in medicine and surgery with expansion of behavioral health services, particularly hospitalization. Third party payors responded by dropping the mental health benefit, a trend American Biodyne confronted with programs that reduced costs and capped them for three years, all the while increasing benefits.

Immediately prior to the advent of American Biodyne, there were two predecessor managed behavioral healthcare organizations (MBHOs) that sought to reduce costs by utilization review, case management, pre-certification, and other such restrictive measures on patient access to services. In contrast, American Biodyne was the first (and perhaps the only) national MBHO that reduced costs by increasing services. Extensive use of effective treatments provided in an efficient manner reduced patients' demand for more costly psychiatric services, and met the psychological needs that were driving up medical costs. The *Biodyne Manual* proffered 68 protocols that were based on EBTs that had been translated into effective delivery models in which clinician discretion and flexibility were permitted within wide-ranging guidelines. Thus, proven treatments were conducted without having to resort to a series of cookbooks that would never succeed in the real world of healthcare delivery. Narrative forms of the *Biodyne Manual* and its several updates are found in Cummings and Sayama (1995) and Cummings and Cummings (2000).

Originally it was the intent to give away the model to the profession. A limit of 500,000 covered lives was self-imposed so as to create a model that colleagues could emulate, assuring that the MBHO delivery system would remain under practitioner control. A do-it-yourself kit was published (Cummings, 1986), inviting psychologists and psychiatrists to come and learn the delivery system. When no one came in the first two years, the author took his foot off the brake, and American Biodyne skyrocketed to 14.5 million enrollees in 39 states in the next five years. The profession lost the opportunity to own managed behavioral care, and Cummings disappointedly sold the company in 1992, after successfully going public in an initial public offering (IPO) in 1991. A testimonial to the effectiveness of this clinically driven model is the following unprecedented record: with ultimately 14.5 million covered lives resulting in millions of treatment episodes by 10,000 psychologists, psychiatrists and social workers over seven years, there was not a single malpractice suit or patient complaint that had to be adjudicated. But it should also be pointed out that all clinicians received intensive initial and ongoing training in the model, and 15% of all their time was spent in quality assurance, predominately with extensive collegial case conferencing. American Biodyne from the onset built ongoing research into the delivery system, and continues to this day as a wellspring of data, long after the delivery system was swallowed up and drastically altered by its successors (for recent examples see Wiggins & Cummings, 1998; Cummings & Wiggins, 2001).

Lessons Learned

In the past there have not been large-scale delivery systems in which the concept of integration has been paramount, extensively translating EBTs out of the laboratory and into the field. Existing systems are difficult to change, yielding only to incremental shifts that are not sufficient for behavioral health to make an impact on primary care. This has led to the unfortunate conclusion that it is easier to create a new delivery system than to significantly alter an existing one, a concept that was espoused by HCFA and the researchers on the Hawaii Project after several fruitless years of attempting to persuade traditional systems to embark on a large-scale project of integration. American Biodyne was also founded under the same premise. Now there are several projects underway in which existing systems have retooled so as to integrate behavioral health into primary care. These include in government the U.S. Air Force, the Veterans Administration, and a number of the Community Health Centers, and in the private sector Kaiser Permanente's Northern California region with 2.4 million enrollees. Soon Kaiser Permanente will be rolling out this model to their other regions. It should be noted that these projects have been mandated from the top down, perhaps the only way such extensive retooling can proceed, although in all instances much care is being taken in the subsequent involvement of all levels of the system.

It should be emphasized that the Hawaii Project and American Biodyne, as extensive as they were, nonetheless employed the collaborative model, with no co-location of behavioral practitioners within the primary care setting. These are regarded as limitations to the concept of full integration. The new endeavors that have been recently launched espouse co-location and the concept of complete integration of behavioral and primary care rather than a collaborative model between primary care and specialty behavioral care. Hopefully these projects will yield results of a greater magnitude and even a different conceptualization. Also launched in the latter part of 2001 is Hawaii Project II in which there is co-location of behavioral health with primary care in three separate healthcare settings. Perhaps this project will shed light on what is needed to transform a traditional system into one that is fully integrated. There is federal and private foundation funding for Hawaii Project II, avoiding the nearly impossible hurdle of persuading an existing healthcare delivery system to fund its own retooling as Kaiser Permanente is solely doing.

It should also be noted that both the original Hawaii Project and American Biodyne delivered behavioral care services that go far beyond the series of brief contacts in the primary care setting. Rather, with focused, targeted individual brief therapy and highly structured group programs, they encompassed about 85% or more of the services within the collaborative setting of what in the Air Force and similar models would be referred to specialty psychiatric or psychological care. The magnitude of the targeted programs, along with the intensive outreach, increased substantially the kinds of services that resulted in the impressive medical cost offset.

The following do's and don'ts are gleaned from the experiences in Hawaii and nationally from American Biodyne, both successful, large-scale collaborative clinical delivery systems that effectively transformed the laboratory into the field, and in an ongoing fashion continued an interplay from laboratory-to-field-and-back-to-laboratory, always culminating in the real world of service delivery, with an aggregate of over ten years with millions of patients and treatment episodes rendered by thousands of practitioners.

Criteria for Success in Disease and Population Management

The eight criteria for success of integrated programs using disease/population management programs are deceptively simple. On the surface they seem straightforward, while in actuality they are difficult to implement because they are likely to meet all kinds of rationalized resistances in traditional health settings. Reluctance or inability to implement these criteria has led to incremental progress, with disappointing outcomes.

Pervasiveness. The concept of integration must pervade the entire delivery system, with at least four, and preferably five to ten (and even more) disease/population management programs. The parachuting of one or two programs into an otherwise traditional delivery system is unlikely to succeed as these become isolated and have limited impact on the system as a whole. It is tantamount to putting a few small droplets of red paint in a fifty gallon drum of white paint with the expectation it will turn pink.

System-wide acceptance. There must be a universal buy-in of the innovations. This is difficult to achieve and may require at least a year and probably two years of staff training and negotiations to accomplish. Even silently reluctant physicians can wreck the new system. The most likely detractors are from specialty psychiatry and psychology, as they perceive their domain shrinking as more and more of behavioral health is encompassed by the integrated primary care. However, all specialists may be threatened, as the trend is to push knowledge downward. In this way, nurse practitioners are doing more of the work of primary care physicians, while the latter are encroaching on the lower rungs of the ladders of specialty care.

Co-Location. The co-location of behavioral health with primary care is highly desirable and markedly increases integration through ready contacts, such as the "hallway hand-off" and the ability to walk a patient a few steps down the hall to the behavioral practitioner's office. It must be emphasized that this means the co-location of specially trained and integrated behavioral care professionals, not the co-location of specialty psychiatry or psychology. When these conditions of co-location are met, not only is there a doubling of the psychological problems recognized by primary care physicians, but of those referred, there is a 90% acceptance of behavioral treatment instead of the mere 10% that is characteristic of the system of referral to specialty psychiatric care. The resulting nine-fold increase in patient acceptance of behavioral interventions accounts for the huge surge in medical cost offset. Co-location does most to create a seamless system in which in the patients' eyes medical and behavioral care are indistinguishable, removing from their minds the fear of stigmatization that comes with treatment in specialty psychiatry.

Outreach program. An aggressive, but sensitive outreach of the 15% highest utilizers of medicine by frequency (not dollar amount) contributes greatly to the success of an integrated program. Such outreach has been shown to significantly increase those needy patients who accept behavioral interventions and subsequently reduce their over-utilization of medical and surgical services. To await physician referral of many of these patients can be problematic, or slow at best. It is important that physicians are aware and agreeable to such outreach, knowing they will be immediately informed when one of their patients is outreached.

Focused, targeted interventions. Programs should employ focused, targeted interventions, empirically derived. When treatment is proven to be both effective and efficient, services can be increased not only as preventative, but also in advance of more costly interventions that would otherwise become necessary without the early interventions. Traditional psychological services are only minimally helpful, and are likely to significantly increase costs.

Specificity of group programs. Integrated disease/population management makes extensive use of group protocols, but the programs should be limited to those patients suffering from the same condition. Groups composed of patients from mixed conditions do not form the cohesiveness and group identity that specific groups manifest, important ingredients contributing to success. One of the most frequent mistakes is in assigning depressed patients to group programs, lumping together several different kinds of depression. This is because too often depression is erroneously regarded as a unitary condition, whereas there are distinct kinds of depression requiring specific, cohesive group approaches (e.g., reactive depression, chronic depression, bipolar depression, bereavement, anniversary depression).

Special training. Both behavioral care practitioners and physicians will need extensive orientation to the new model. The term "orientation" is preferred, as professionals object to the notion that they may need training or retraining. The initial formal orientation, no matter how extensive, will not be sufficient. Regular follow-up orientation that includes case conferencing is imperative, and as previously mentioned, at least one year of such ongoing orientation is mandatory, and two years is preferable. Even then there may be at least one or two holdouts who never get it, and would be better off leaving the new system to return to more traditional practice.

Outcomes research. Ongoing outcomes research, permitting continuous refinement of the protocols and the delivery system as a whole, is important to a successful endeavor, but it is seldom given the deserved attention. Unless an unobtrusive research component is built into the delivery system itself at the outset, it is difficult to introduce at a later date. The best outcomes research is conducted in unnoticed fashion, without intrusion into the delivery of care, while enabling the continuous, rapid fine-tuning of the system and its component parts. Unfortunately, few healthcare systems possess the knowledge, capacity or the will to engage in such ongoing corrective self-evaluation beyond perfunctory and often questionable patient satisfaction questionnaires.

Caveats

Along with the foregoing eight do's, there are five don'ts that if not attended can wreck a well-meaning integrated system.

Undue reliance on laboratory findings. Just because a protocol has had demonstrated efficacy in the laboratory, do not assume it will work equally well in the real world without adaptation. This obverse error can be just as deleterious as that of using interventions that have no empirical base. The successful program uses EBTs refined and adapted to the exigencies of the delivery system. Just as drugs approved for release by the FDA do not manifest a host of side effects, and even mortality, until they are in use by the general public, EBTs also reveal flaws or unworkable aspects when they are subjected to the realities of healthcare delivery. Patients are often surprisingly different from the highly selected behavioral research subjects seen in a university setting.

Depression is not a unitary condition. That there are several kinds of depression requiring different interventions can not be overly emphasized. Because depression is found in 40% of primary care patients, it is often assumed that that a program just addressing depression will bear results. In addition to the foregoing comments (see criterion number six, above), it is important to note that the depression often accompanying chronic illness (e.g., diabetes, rheumatoid arthritic) is best treated as part of the protocol of that specific chronic disease.

Ineffective use of antidepressants. Management of depression through extensive use of antidepressants does not seem to be effective or efficient. In addition to there being several different kinds of depression with varying degrees of responsiveness to antidepressants, depression has become the "common cold" of psychiatry, with mildly depressed patients demanding antidepressants just as persons with a common cold have for decades inappropriately demanded antibiotics. Physicians are increasingly giving in to these demands, but not being able to adequately differentiate those who could benefit from antidepressants versus those who would not, these same doctors are reluctant to prescribe anything more than a small "safe" dosage. The net result is ineffective treatment: there are patients receiving antidepressants who do not need them, while those needing them are receiving insufficient dosages.

Beware the folly of increased traditional services. Traditional behavioral services are not only inappropriate in an integrated setting, research indicates they are prone to drive up costs while being ineffective. This was true in the Hawaii Project, but the Fort Bragg Champus Study (Bickman, 1996) yielded even more startling data. This latter study purported to show that all that was needed to obtain medical cost offset was unlimited access to traditional psychological services. Instead, there was an astounding ten-fold increase in costs (from $8 million to $80 million), with no increase whatsoever in treatment effectiveness. This prompted the authors to title their report, "More is not always better."

Beware the borderline personality disorder. Because of their potential to disrupt any group, patients with chronic diseases who also manifest borderline personality disorder should be assigned to programs especially constructed for them. Patients who are not borderline personalities are incapable of coping with the acting out behavior they display. Even one borderline personality in a group can prevent the other patients from benefiting from the program, and two such patients can literally wreck the group. These patients characteristically employ the psychological mechanism of splitting, and with seemingly little effort they pit the group against the staff, or half the group against the other half. Attempting to contain the splitting often merely increases the havoc. In groups composed only of borderline patients, they seem to very aggressively police each other's behavior in a manner the doctor could never do.

Components of the Ideal Protocol

Each ideal protocol has three major characteristics: *treatment, prevention, and management.* Although each is present in every protocol, the degree to which one or two characteristics prevail is a function of the condition being treated. Because the Borderline Personality Disorder and rheumatoid arthritis are chronic, management is emphasized, while in the hypertension protocol compliance with treatment regimen for prevention of heart attacks is paramount.

There is currently a plethora of disease/population management protocols, few with any real empirical basis, and many resembling pop psychology. In constructing protocols, or in choosing existing ones, it is important that they not only be evidence-based, but they also should have a number of important components.

Educational component. From the educational component the patient learns a great deal about the medical or psychological condition, as well as the interplay between one's body and emotions. Data have shown that even the understanding of one's chronic condition is beneficial.

Pain management. Since so many conditions are accompanied by chronic pain, pain management must be an integral part of the program. This includes help in reducing undue reliance on pain medication and addressing any problems of iatrogenic addiction. Available are excellent protocols stressing "skills, not pills."

Relaxation techniques. The need to learn to relax is very important in these patients, and relaxation techniques should include meditation and guided imagery.

Stress management. Stress is the universal accompaniment of any psychological problem or chronic disease, making stress management, adjusted to meet the needs of specific conditions or populations, an important component.

A support system. The group milieu is a source of support, but this is intensified by the presence of "veterans" who went through the program successfully and wish to repeat it. A useful modification of the group support system is the pairing of patients into a "buddy system" that allows them to call each other, meet for desensitization or other homework, and generally be there for each other in time of need.

Self-evaluation. There should be a self-evaluation component that not only enables the patient to assess how well he or she is doing psychologically, but also teaches the patient to monitor such critical features as blood pressure, diet, insulin, and other signs important in chronic illness.

Homework. Homework is assigned after every session. The homework is carefully designed to move the patient to the next step of self-mastery, and may include desensitization, behavioral exercises, readings, planned encounters with one's relationships or environment, and other assignments that are critical to the well-being of the patient. The homework is never perfunctory. It is tailored to each individual's needs and is always relevant to the condition being treated and well timed to enhance development. It is the homework that extends the treatment process between sessions so it covers the entire week.

Treatment of depression. For those patients whose severely altered mood is interfering with their ability to participate in the program, their depression is best addressed within the context of their own disease management program. Since depression to some degree accompanies chronic illness, every program is structured to address it.

Self-efficacy. Bandura (1977) calls self-efficacy the belief that one can perform a specific action or complete a task. Although this involves self-confidence in general, it is the confidence to perform a specific task. Positive changes can be traced to an increase in self-efficacy brought about by a carefully designed protocol that will advance self-efficacy.

Learned helplessness. Seligman (1975) established that helplessness is learned and can be unlearned. Some patients with chronic illnesses fall into a state of feeling helpless in the face of their disease. A well-designed protocol will enable a patient to confront and unlearn helplessness.

A sense of coherence. Antonovsky (1987) pointed out that a sense of coherence is required to make sense out of adversity. Patients with chronic physical or mental illnesses feel not only that that their circumstances do not make sense, but neither does their life. The ability to cope often depends on the presence or absence of this sense of coherence, and the protocol should be designed to enhance it.

Exercise. Exercise is an essential component of every protocol, and is the feature that is most often neglected by patients. Exercise helps ameliorate depression, raises the sense of self-efficacy, and promotes coping behavior. The patient should be encouraged to plan and implement a personal exercise regimen, and then stick to it.

Timing, length and number of sessions. The timing, length and number of sessions vary from protocol to protocol, reflecting the needs of each population or condition, and in accordance with research and experience. For example, the group protocol for Borderline Personality Disorder consists of twenty weekly two-hour sessions (Cummings and Sayama, 1995), while the group bereavement protocol has fourteen two-hour sessions spaced as follows: four semiweekly sessions followed by six weekly sessions and then by four concluding sessions, held monthly (Cummings, 1998). One or two individual sessions to assess, motivate and orient the patient characteristically precede assignment to a group, and some protocols make access to an individual session during the group sequence on an as-needed basis, but in such a way that it will not drain the patient's commitment to the group process.

Modular formatting. Designing the protocols with modular formatting enables them to serve different but similar populations and conditions by inserting or substituting condition-specific modules.

Market Pulse

As of this writing, the marketplace is in a state of transition from managed care as we have known it the past decade, to the second generation of the industrialization of healthcare that is yet to acquire its own morphology. Along with the turbulence that accompanies such transitions, the market is also wary and hesitant, waiting to see which way economic, legal, legislative and social pressures will take it. A number of trends and issues are emerging and need our attention.

Entrenchment of the carve-out. Although the MBHO, commonly known as the behavioral carve-out, has outlived its usefulness, it is now firmly entrenched with 175 million covered lives. It gives lip service to integration, but it is making no serious moves in that direction. It is reluctant to jeopardize its current profit base attempting integration, something it does not know how to do. The entrenchment of the carve-out is not only preventing integration, it severely hampers efforts at collaboration between the two separate systems, physical and behavioral care. The medical system has a "good riddance" attitude toward psychological problems, and characteristically dumps them on the MBHO expecting to save the cost of their care. In return the carve-out, knowing that medication is cheaper and easier than psychotherapy, prescribes drugs that under contractual arrangements are charged back to the medical system. Patient dumping is a two-way street that is being perpetuated by the carve-out arrangements.

The disappointing record of disease management. As shown in previous sections, disease and population management has more often raised costs while rendering questionable clinical results. There is a vast difference between a behaviorally driven disease management program versus what has been occurring, but the marketplace is not sophisticated enough to discern this. Having been burned by the usual disease/population management program, buyers remain wary and difficult to convince. Buyer resistance, coupled with provider opposition, are enough to seriously delay what many experts would regard as the next step in the evolution of healthcare.

Risk/reward sharing. Buyer resistance can be overcome with what might be termed "the godfather offer," otherwise known as an offer you can't refuse. A vendor that guarantees cost savings in the following manner cannot help but get the buyer's attention: if the program increases costs the vendor will make up the difference; if the program breaks even the service is provided at no cost; and if there is a cost saving it is shared 50-50 between the purchasing health organization and the integration vendor. The drawbacks to the vendor are obvious. There must be a sufficient financial reserve to cover increased costs, and the vendor must have complete confidence in the product through experience and research.

The employers' zero sum game. As the industry contemplates stepping up to the plate, it is confronted by a high stakes game. Translated into a question in which the clinical advantages are forgotten in the face of financial considerations, "How much do I have to stake up front to *possibly* save how much in the future?" Chief financial officers want to leverage a risk, and the prospect of staking $1 million to save an equal $1 million is readily rejected because there are other more attractive financial alternatives. In proposing a program, one must be able to demonstrate how the medical cost offset would be several times the dollar risk.

Arriving at reliable cost outcome measures. It would be relatively easy to demonstrate cost savings by randomizing the population. The difference in costs between control and experimental groups at the end of two years would be apparent. However, various laws and regulations require that an employer's health plan must offer the same benefits to all employees. To have a control group would result in denial of services to some (control group), while providing them to others (experimental group). Unless a method of calculating costs and savings is agreed upon at the outset, endless unsolvable arguments will ensue after the fact.

Medical cost offset begins to show in eighteen months, is discernible in two years, and is robust in three years. During any three year period in the current healthcare environment there will be a multitude of factors driving up costs, among them an increase in the nation's annual inflation rate, ascending costs of new technologies, and government and court mandates for coverage and services. Without a firm way of determining the difference in costs attributable to the integration of behavior care with primary care, the argument is endless.

Federal and state micromanaging. The laws and regulations governing healthcare can change in midstream. In addition, the courts may award services or damages that were unforeseen when capitation rates were negotiated. There is an increasing tendency for legislatures and courts to micromanage healthcare delivery, rendering the healthcare industry today very risky at best, and on the verge of collapse if there is an enactment of some pending federal and state laws that would virtually turn over healthcare to the trial lawyers. Such a crisis has first erupted in Nevada as a harbinger of what is to come in other parts of the country. In Nevada physicians are leaving the state in droves because they can no longer afford malpractice insurance.

Resistances in the public sector. Washington is gently pushing the community health centers (CHC) toward integration, but the funding structure for the CHCs mitigate any incentives for change. One of the main reasons for integration is the cost savings, but the CHCs have any budget shortfalls absorbed by the government at the end of each year. So why go through all the hassle of retooling? Furthermore, the community *mental* health centers are opposed to the integration of behavioral care and primary care in the CHCs because they fear this would reduce the number of referrals to the CMHCs, leading to shrinkage of their funding.

Resistances in the commercial sector: PCP concerns. Recent years have seen a marked reduction in capitation arrangements between payors and physician groups, mainly because physicians could not control costs and calculate capitation rates. Rather than see these groups flounder, payors have reinstated fee-for-service. Unfortunately, this also mitigates incentives for saving costs through integration. Under fee-for-service over-utilization of medical care by patients with psychological problems only increases revenue to the physicians. It is important to show and persuade physicians that even under fee-for-service, appropriate attention to behavioral problems frees up the physician to perform higher level and more costly procedures than that paid for a visit with a somatizer, thus actually increasing revenue.

Resistances in the commercial sector: specialist concerns. Specialists, and particularly specialty psychiatry, are aware of the potential loss of referrals to them if (1) most psychological problems can be addressed in primary care and without referral to specialty care, and (2) if PCPs are freed up to perform the lower levels of specialty care (office minor surgery, dermatology, prenatal care, etc.) there will be a reduction of income to specialists. Some psychiatrists and psychologists fear that referrals to specialty care may shrink by 50 to 60%, whereas in actuality specialty care will have the time and resources to attend to the more mentally ill rather than the mildly neurotic or the worried well.

Resistances in the commercial sector: payor concerns. Payors are on the defensive and they fear continued backlashes from both physicians and patients. "We want no trouble with the docs," is a statement heard over and over, while the scepter of the health insurance portability and privacy act (HIPAA) is casting a shadow of fear over the industry. Such accepted practices as outreaching the 15% highest utilizers of medical care come into question under proposed HIPAA rules, and the possibility of lawsuits increases exponentially for a number of reasons. There are recent indications that in response to complaints from physicians as well as the industry that patients will be ill-served with a plethora of unworkable rules, the administration will ease-up on HIPAA's proposed strictures. In the meantime, payors are reluctant to take chances on such innovative programs as innovation.

Summary and Conclusions

This chapter seeks to go beyond the laboratory into the difficult world of healthcare delivery. It presents findings and directions gleaned from years of experience in the two large-scale delivery systems to date, both of which were newly created in response to the seemingly insurmountable task of sufficiently changing an existing system to deliver extensive integrated or collaborative care. From these experiences a hands-on, how-to-do-it list of eight criteria for success and five caveats has emerged. Also listed are fourteen components of the ideal disease/population management protocol. These components assure the presence of sufficient behavioral interventions to overcome the deficiencies of the typical protocol in use today.

The assessment of the marketplace finds the buyers to be wary and the providers resistant. This is a time of considerable flux in healthcare delivery, with most players sitting on the sidelines waiting to see which way it will go. In the meantime, several large-scale integrated programs are underway in both the private sector as well as in government. As these are among the largest health delivery organizations in the nation, success with these will catapult interest in integration almost overnight. It should be pointed out, however, that in all of the retooled integrated programs recently launched, none reflect the degree of behavioral services found in the delivery systems under consideration in this article. In our systems, integrated care extends into, and encompasses at least 50% or more of what is customarily specialty psychiatry and psychology.

References

Antonovsky, A. (1987). *Unraveling the mystery of health: How people manage stress and stay well*. San Francisco, C A: Jossey-Bass.

Bandura, A. (1977). Self-efficacy: Toward a unifying theory of behavioral change. *Psychological Review, 84*, 191-215.

Bickman, L. (1996). A continuum of care: More is not always better. *American Psychologist, 51*, 689-701.

Cummings, N. A. (1986). The dismantling of our health system: Strategies for survival of psychological practice. *American Psychologist, 41*, 426-431.

Cummings, N. A. (1994). The successful application of medical offset in program planning and in clinical delivery. *Managed Care Quarterly, 2*, 1-6.

Cummings, N. A. (1998). Approaches in prevention in the behavioral health of older adults. In P. Hartman-Stein (Ed.), *Innovative behavioral healthcare for older adults: A guidebook for changing times* (pp. 1-23). San Francisco, CA: Jossey-Bass.

Cummings, N. A., & Cummings, J. L. (2000). *The essence of psychotherapy: Reinventing the art in the era of data*. New York, NY: Academic Press.

Cummings, N. A., Cummings, J. L., & Johnson, J. N. (Eds.) (1997). *Behavioral health in primary care: A guide for clinical integration*. Madison, CT: Psychosocial Press (an imprint of International Universities Press).

Cummings, N. A., Dorken, H., Pallak, M. S., & Henke, C. J. (1990). The impact of psychological intervention on health care costs and utilization. The Hawaii Medicaid Project. *HCFA Contract Report #11-C-983344/9.*

Cummings, N. A., O'Donohue, W. T., & Ferguson, K. E. (2002). *The Impact of Medical cost offset on Practice and Research: Making It Work for You.* Reno, NV: Context Press.

Cummings, N. & Sayama, M. (1995). *Focused psychotherapy: A casebook of brief, intermittent psychotherapy throughout the life cycle.* New York, NY: Brunner/Mazel (now Brunner-Routledge).

Cummings, N. A., & Wiggins, J. G. (2001). A collaborative primary care/behavioral health model for the use of psychotropic medication with children and adolescents. *Issues in Interdisciplinary Care, 3(2),* 121-128.

Follette, W. T., & Cummings, N. A. (1967). Psychiatric services and medical utilization in A prepaid health plan setting. *Medical Care, 5,* 25-35.

Katon, W., VonKorff, M., Lin, E., Limpscomb, P., Russo, J., Wagner, E., & Polk, E. (1990). Distressed high utilizers of medical care: DSM-III-R diagnoses and treatment codes. *General Hospital Psychiatry, 12,* 355-362.

Kroenke, K., & Mangelsdorff, D. (1989). Common symptoms in ambulatory care: Incidence, evaluation, therapy, and outcome. *American Journal of Medicine, 86,* 262-266.

Seligman, M. E. P. (1975). *Helplessness: On depression, development and death.* San Francisco, CA: W.H. Freeman.

Wiggins, J. G., & Cummings, N. A. (1998). National study of the experience of psychologists with psychotropic medication and psychotherapy. *Professional Psychology: Research and Practice, 29(6),* 549-552.

Core Competencies of the Primary Care Provider in an Integrated Team

Jason M. Satterfield

Teaching core behavioral health competencies to medical providers in an integrated health care setting is a rewarding, challenging, and frustrating experience full of important possibilities. To teach successfully requires a meaningful understanding of the medical culture and a passionate, evidence-based belief in the value of behavioral science in medical education (Armstrong, Fischetti, Romano, Vogel, & Zoppi, 1992; Bolman, 1995; Carr, 1998). This chapter will first review the importance of understanding the role of behavior in health and how integrated behavioral health interventions benefit both healthcare provider and patient. Secondly, a brief description of the medical culture will provide the context needed to design effective educational programs that match prevailing medical attitudes and values. Finally, examples of select core competencies and teaching strategies at the medical student, resident, and post-licensure levels will be used to demonstrate how essential attitudes, knowledge, and skills can be taught to a primary care team.

Behavior and the Biopsychosocial Model

Western medicine currently uses two competing models to explain health and illness – the biomedical model and the biopsychosocial model. The more traditional biomedical model argues that all illness can be explained as a result of some aberrant somatic process such as a biochemical imbalance or physiological abnormality. Regardless of the symptom, presentation, or diagnosis, one looks for a biomedical explanation and most likely prescribes a biomedical treatment. The biomedical model has been tremendously successful over the past century as evidenced by the dramatic shifts in the causes of death and the substantial increase in life expectancy. However, the biomedical model is unable to account for the roles of behavior and society in health and disease and thus misses many opportunities for meaningful treatment and prevention.

The biopsychosocial model has been growing in popularity since the term was coined in 1977 (Engel 1977, 1980). Conceptualizing illness with the biopsychosocial model requires a multidimensional analysis of three different yet dynamically interdependent areas - biology, psychology, and socio-cultural factors (see Figure 3.1). The biology includes genetics, biochemistry, physiology, and other usual biomedical variables. Psychology might include personality, cognitive style, mood, or other variables germane to health. Socio-cultural factors might include social support, community structures, ethnicity, socio-economic status, access to healthcare, traditional health beliefs, etc. The individual's health is thus impacted by a complex interaction of variables from all three dimensions. Almost by definition, an integrated healthcare team more frequently utilizes the biopsychosocial model and is better positioned to consider behavior and health. In such a model, the core competencies of the primary care provider must be expanded beyond the biological to include expertise in psychological and social factors related to health and illness.

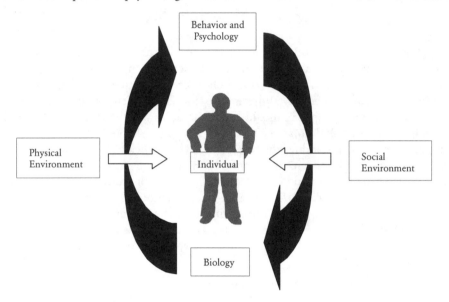

Figure 3.1. exhibits the Biopsychosocial Model.

Why Does Behavior Matter In Primary Care?

Traditional Western medicine has almost exclusively focused on the reduction of morbidity and mortality through advances in pharmacology and medical technology. However, over the past decade, there has been an increasing recognition of the role of behavior in health and disease as more attention has been directed to the actual causes of death (McGinnis & Foege, 1993). The leading causes of death are no longer infectious diseases, but rather long-term chronic diseases that often have behavior as a causative agent – e.g. heart disease, cancer, and HIV infection (U.S. DHHS, 1997). A look at the impact of specific behaviors further highlights the importance of behavior in health. Tobacco accounts for 19% of mortality in the United States each year. Diet and activity patterns account for 14%. Alcohol causes 5% of U.S. deaths per year and is implicated in more than 50% of motor vehicle accidents. All in all, 50% of deaths from the ten leading causes of death in this country are due to modifiable lifestyle factors as listed in Table 3.1 (McGinnis & Foege, 1993).

Actual Causes of Death: Estimates for the U.S., 1990	
	% of Deaths
Tobacco	19
Diet/Activity patterns	14
Alcohol	5
Microbial Agents	4
Toxic Agents	3
Firearms	2
Sexual Behavior	1
Motor vehicles	1
Illicit use of drugs	<1
Total	**50**

Table 3.1. Actual Causes of Death; Estimates for the U.S., 1990.
Data from McGinnis & Foege, 1993.

Although pharmacology and medical technology will continue to make dramatic improvement in both the quality and quantity of our lives, it is clear that the essential skills of a physician must include expertise in understanding and changing patient behaviors. Experts in behavior clearly have an important opportunity to profoundly impact the health and well-being for most patients over many different diseases either through direct delivery of clinical services or through developing these competencies within primary care clinicians. Many emerging new models of integrated healthcare delivery have begun to demonstrate how this potential may become a reality in both the fields of preventive health and chronic disease management (Belar, 1997; Blount, 1998; Cummings, Cummings, & Johnson, 1997; Cummings, O'Donohue, Hayes, & Follette, 2001).

Mental and Physical Health

Although the links between behavior and health are more than enough to support the need for an integrated behavioral healthcare system, it would be remiss to overlook the additional impact of mental health on morbidity and mortality. Although most primary care providers will not directly deliver psychological services, many will be solely responsible for the pharmacologic treatment of their patients with mental illness. For this and both epidemiologic and systemic reasons, primary care should be a critical target for education and dissemination. It is estimated that between 20-33% of all primary care patients have a psychiatric disorder and for half of these patients, the primary care setting is the only place they will seek help (Higgins, 1994; Leon et al., 1995). These patients also show higher healthcare utilization rates and greater medical morbidity and mortality hence are more expensive to treat and have poorer medical outcomes (Chiles, Lambert, & Hatch, 1999; Cummings et al., 1997). Systemically, as healthcare continues to evolve, primary care providers are increasingly seen as the gatekeepers for access to all specialty services, including mental health and behavioral medicine, further fueling the need for accurate screening and appropriate referrals (Shortell, Gillies, & Anderson, 1994). Unfortunately, 33-79% of psychiatric disorders are not recognized and hence not treated or referred for appropriate treatment (Higgins, 1994).

Although many mental illnesses may not be considered terminal illnesses, they can be among the most disabling of medical diagnoses. Disability Adjusted Life Years (DALY) represent the number of healthy, productive life years a person loses as a consequence of their disease. All cardiovascular diseases are the number one cause of DALY accounting for 18.6% of all lost years of productive life. The number two cause, or 15.4% of all lost years of productive life, is mental illness (not including alcohol or drug abuse which contribute an additional 6.2%) (Murray & Lopez, 1998). By improving the psychiatric skills of primary care providers, integrated health systems could substantially impact one of the greatest causes of disability and lost quality of life worldwide.

A large body of research has furthermore demonstrated the impact of psychiatric illness on co-morbid medical illnesses such as cardiovascular disease, diabetes, and perhaps cancer. Individuals who are depressed, anxious, or abusing substances are more likely to engage in health compromising behaviors and less likely to adhere to needed medical treatments (e.g. Stoudemire,1998; Wedding, 2001). Detecting and treating these psychiatric disorders thus impacts both psychiatric and medical morbidity and mortality. The core competencies of a primary care physician in an integrated team should therefore include the accurate detection and treatment or referral of psychiatric conditions and an understanding of how co-morbid psychiatric conditions might impact other medical diseases and health-related behaviors.

Given the need for new ways of thinking about health and disease and the substantial roles of behavior and mental illness in most medical illnesses, the field of medical education has many important and immediate opportunities. Primary care providers in an integrated health team should be able to perform the following: 1) conceptualize health and disease from a multidimensional biopsychosocial model, 2) understand the role of behavior as a major contributor to many leading causes of morbidity and mortality and be able to effectively facilitate patient lifestyle modification, 3) effectively screen for and treat a wide variety of mental illnesses and manage the complex interactions between mental illnesses and medical co-morbidities. In order to accomplish these goals in such a rapidly changing and time-pressured environment it also seems essential that primary care providers also develop effective ways of working in multidisciplinary teams and working with increasingly diverse patient populations.

Integrating Behavioral Health in Primary Care

Meaningful and long-lasting integration must include education, clinical applications, and basic research. Preliminary suggestions have been offered to improve integration of clinical services (Gunn et al., 1997; Haley et al., 1998; Pace, Chaney, Mullins, & Olson, 1995; Satterfield, 2000). A strong, persuasive case for integrated service delivery models has been made on the grounds of improved medical outcomes, medical cost-offset, and improved patient and provider satisfaction (Blount, 1998; Bray & Rogers, 1995; Chiles et al., 1999; Cummings et al., 1997; Cummings et al., 2001). Entities such as the Office of Behavioral and Social Science Research at the National Institutes of Health have begun to make compelling arguments for the inclusion of the social sciences in medical research (Anderson, 1997). Integrating behavioral health into medical education has only recently been identified as an important need in both undergraduate and graduate medical education with innovative and promising models only just emerging (Gaufberg et al., 2001; Jones, Higgs, de Angelis, & Prideaux, 2001; Makoul & Curry, 1998; Makoul, Curry, & Novack, 1998; Rabinowitz et al., 2001; Steele & Susman, 1998).

The Emergency Department Case Management Project at San Francisco General Hospital provides a good example of these three interactive types of integration at work. This community hospital primarily serves low income and indigent individuals with complex medical, psychiatric, and social problems. About 10% of patients who visited the emergency room accounted for 50% of all emergency room visits costing the hospital hundreds of thousands of dollars. In response to this problem, a team of physicians, behavioral scientists, and social workers designed an educational intervention for health care workers on how to best meet the biopsychosocial needs of these patients, an integrated clinical intervention using a case manager/behavioral health expert, and an integrated research project to demonstrate the clinical and financial utility of this integrated model. Looking at 53 patients over the course of 12 months, this group was able to demonstrate substantial decreases in ER utilization, decreased inpatient costs, decreased homelessness, decreased alcohol and drug abuse, and a $1.44 return on each $1.00 invested in integrated education, treatment, and research (Okin et al., 2000).

Medical Culture

In order to effectively teach and deliver integrated care in a medical setting, it is essential to be familiar with the medical culture or the set of values, norms, beliefs, attitudes, behavior styles, and traditions that comprise the medical mindset. "Culturally-competent" medical education requires a familiarity with traditional medical teaching methods (e.g. grand rounds, case conferences), selecting highly practical and empirically-based content with an understanding of the appropriate depth and pacing, careful attention to medical language and terminology, and a special empathy for the stressors of medical practice that might impact learning and retention.

In general, physicians prefer concrete, action-oriented, symptom-focused interventions with clearly operationalized outcomes and specific recommendations of what they should do with a particular patient. Evidence-based practice and algorithmic thinking is strongly preferred (e.g. Pace et al., 1995). Exhaustive literature reviews and extensive explanations of the theoretical underpinnings of behavioral or other theories are not likely to be useful. Given the severe time constraints placed on primary care providers, anything or anyone that assists them with time efficiency and patient care is likely to be strongly embraced. Specific recommendations, clear treatment plans, and regular brief treatment updates are likely to be most valuable although further supportive, empirical literature should be available (Grol & Grimshaw, 1999; Gunn et al., 1997; Haley et al., 1998; Pace et al., 1995; Satterfield, 2000).

The general approach to teaching in medicine is "see one, do one, teach one" meaning education is often based on observation and experiential learning. In contrast, graduate school education involves a greater reliance on synthesizing original writings and research to develop and debate different abstract theories – a very different way of thinking and learning. Optimally integrated medical education would match the pre-existing expectations of medical education then perhaps make slight yet important modifications. For example, when educating primary care providers about depression, the providers need to see a screening instrument being used, use it themselves, then demonstrate their grasp of the material by teaching others how to use the screening instrument. Providers need to observe smoking cessation counseling or other behavior change interventions then actively practice and teach those techniques. Although these interventions are experientially based, it is essential that the demonstrated skills be evidence-based whenever possible. Medical providers will rarely have the time or inclination to go back to the original evidence but building and maintaining credibility rests on being able to prove the utility of the skills in question.

In medical education, there is substantial pressure to summarize and distill essential information. This process could produce some discomfort in non-MD instructors who are wary of "spoon feeding" their learners and reinforcing memorization rather than active, good thinking. However, it is important to have an appreciation for the volume of information that daily deluges the primary care provider. Most medical professionals, on any given day, are like people who are trying to drink from a fire hose. There is no possible way to keep up with so many sources of information if that information is not summarized and distilled. This information overload is a substantial source of stress, frustration, and insecurity and shouldn't be amplified by overzealous non-physician teachers.

Language is an important part of the medical culture and requires a non-physician teacher to be "bilingual". Table 3.2 shows the full text of a mental health referral written by a primary care physician and an excerpt of a six page reply written by a mental health provider. The differences in language and focus emphasize the potential for miscommunication and "cultural" confusion. The primary care provider's referral in non-medicalese should read, "Patient is a 52 year old African-American female status post motor vehicle accident secondary to alcohol with a history of major depression, non-insulin dependent diabetes mellitus and hypertension, now complaining of increased anxiety. Mental status is within normal limits and there is no acute crisis. Please evaluate for substance abuse, post-traumatic stress disorder, and psychiatric medications." As seen in Table 3.2, the reply does not use any similar language and does not fully address the primary reasons for the referral. The primary care physician did not find much of the information useful and is less likely to make similar referrals in the future. More effective clinical services and teaching would match the language, pacing, and focus already present in the primary care setting.

Effective teaching also requires accurate empathy for the learner. Even the most ideal content and the most innovative and powerful teaching techniques will fail if the emotional and/or physical state of the learner does not support learning. In most top training programs, medical interns and residents routinely work 80-90 hours per week. Every third to fourth day they may work a 36-hour shift, often with no sleep. If their salary were calculated on an hourly basis, most would barely make minimum wage. In the midst of this physically demanding job, these trainees, most in their mid to late twenties, are also vicariously experiencing a great deal of pain,

Referral to Mental Health from Primary Care
Pt is a 52yo AAF s/p MVA 2° etoh c hx of MDE, NIDDM, HTN, c/o anxiety. MSE WNL, ø acute crisis. Pls eval for SA, PTSE, Y meds.
Response from Mental Health Provider
Thank you for this interesting and challenging referral. This 59 year old twice divorced woman's recent car accident has likely precipitated a new episode of mood distrubance... Her longstanding issues of emotional dependency, lack of ego resilience, and poor social supports have prevented her from accommodating this substantial insult to the integrity of her body and psyche...

Table 3.2. Medical Language and Miscommunication.

suffering, and death with their patients and their patient's families. When designing educational programs for these trainees, it is thus important to attend to their state of wellness and perhaps include supportive interventions to supplement their behavioral health education (Quill & Williamson, 1990).

Finally, it is important to understand the workload and time pressures faced by most physicians on all levels in training. Most outpatient primary care physicians see 5-6 patients per hour some of whom are of high complexity. They must meet rigorous and demanding productivity standards and often spend many unreimbursed hours per day filling out various forms, navigating insurance bureaucracies, answering phone messages, or returning pages. Most are required to be available in some capacity 24 hours per day, 7 days per week (Schroeder, 1992; Shortell, Gillies, & Anderson, 1994). Even so, there is often a lingering sense of guilt about not doing enough, doubt about whether something essential was missed, and an exaggerated sense of personal responsibility (Gabbard, 1985). Unfortunately, it is in this difficult maelstrom that most medical education must be delivered.

Designing An Educational Program

After developing the necessary understanding of the medical culture and an appreciation for the stressors of being a medical provider, it is important to next identify the level of the learner and the relevant needs to be targeted. Levels of medical education for physicians may range from undergraduate medical education (years 1-4 of medical school) to graduate medical education (internship, residency, and some fellowships) to continuing medical education programs for licensed physicians. Interdisciplinary teams of healthcare providers are becoming increasingly common and could create opportunities for behavioral health education with nurses, pharmacists, social workers, psychologists, counselors, and others. The level and discipline of the learner will obviously dictate the depth and pacing of any materials presented and will likely provide very different infrastructures to support any educational endeavor.

For undergraduate medical education, the traditional model is to focus primarily on basic science education in the first two years - physiology, biochemistry, anatomy, etc. In the third and fourth years, students begin to learn clinical applications in a variety of clerkships. Clinical training tends to be highly experiential and often depends greatly on the personality of the attending physician and/or the resident leading the medical team. UCSF and several other medical schools have recently launched new curricular models that integrate clinical, basic, and social science education starting with the first year of medical school (Jones et al., 2000; Rabinowitz et al., 2001). The ultimate goal is to prepare students to think and act more integratively during their challenging clinical training years in medical school, residency, and beyond.

After targeting the level of learner, it is imperative to identify needs and objectives. A formal or informal needs assessment is a common way to start and can involve questionnaires, focus groups, or any other informal means of surveying provider and patient needs. Given the usual time and resource limitations a good needs assessment helps pinpoint the type of educational interventions that are likely to produce the highest yield (Hodges et al., 2001; Russell & Potter, 2002). A deficit-based needs assessment focuses on what populations or conditions are not being adequately diagnosed or treated. An epidemiology-based needs assessment identifies the most common behavioral health conditions being seen in primary care and would allocate teaching resources accordingly. Institutional priorities or special funding opportunities may also dictate the focus of your behavioral health education program.

Teaching Methods

Evidence-based medicine has become a mainstay of medical education and practice and has begun to gain popularity in the field of mental health. Unfortunately, "evidence-based teaching" hasn't gained wide acceptance despite several decades of sound educational research. There is a significant body of literature concerned with what teaching methods are most effective in changing provider attitudes, knowledge, and skills. The following teaching recommendations have evolved from an integration of the available literature and from the experiences of both psychologists and primary care providers who have grown accustomed to working and teaching side-by-side in a large university primary care clinic (Bray & Rogers, 1995; Grol & Grimshaw, 1999; Gunn, Seaburn, Lorenz, Gawinski, & Mauksch, 1997; Haley et al., 1998; Halpern, Lee, Boulter, & Phillips, 2001; Hodges, Inch, & Silver, 2001; Pace et al., 1995; Sachdeva, 2000).

In general, the passive dissemination of information alone (e.g. the standard didactic lecture) isn't likely to have a significant impact on professional practice (Grol & Grimshaw, 1999). More effective teaching strategies use multimodal teaching methods such as talking, videos, small groups with active practice, and using written, verbal, and visual electronic media. Actively training and interacting with primary care providers while providing competent and visible services from the student level and up could impact a culture that has traditionally separated mind from body. Effective dissemination through education requires creating new training opportunities and insinuating behavioral health education into currently existing teaching forums. Teaching can take the form of didactic presentations, case conferences, grand rounds, CME training, provider and patient brochures, print media, medical student courses or rotations, behavioral medicine seminars, online resources, individual or group supervision for medical and psychiatric residents, clinic shadowing/joint patient appointments, referral and diagnostic information in reference and precepting rooms, providing free access to APA journals online with email notification of relevant articles, and making treatment guidelines easily available. Multiple other "micro-teaching" opportunities can be created simply by being present and participating in various medical meetings.

While it is important to emphasize evidenced-based medicine, the salience of personal experience cannot be ignored. UCSF medical students surveyed at the end of their first year rated applied case examples as one of the most memorable and important aspect of their learning. Residents typically remember vivid cases long after they have forgotten empirical studies. It is thus important to build educational case materials in a way that grows from an empirical knowledge base but still retains enough real and memorable details to enhance salience.

Core Content and Teaching Examples

A full review of all core behavioral competencies for the primary care provider in an integrated team is beyond the scope of this chapter. Several introductory texts provide useful overviews of these topics (Feldman & Christensen, 1997; Russell, 1999; Sierles, 1993; Stoudemire, 1998; Wedding, 2001). Illustrative teaching examples will be provided in three broad categories – basic "doctoring" skills, mental health, and behavioral health – and will reflect a wide range of teaching methods and learner levels. Examples of important competencies in each category are listed in Table 3.

Basic Doctoring Skills	Mental Health	Behavioral Health
Empathy	Detection and screening for psychiatric disorders	Assessing medical adherence
Active listening	Assess severity and triage	Medical adherence interventions
Communication	Basic psychopharmacology	Facilitating health-promoting behaviors
Negotiation	Making appropriate referrals	Preventing health-compromising behaviors
Emotional management	Familiarity with non-pharmacologic treatments	
Rapport-building		
Setting boundaries		

Table 3.3. lists examples of "Core Compentencies".

Doctoring Skills: Empathy and Communication

Basic doctoring skills must include effective communication and empathy. Although these skills have traditionally been downplayed by most medical curricula, good doctor-patient communication and accurate empathic attunement have been shown to increase patient and provider satisfaction, improve medical adherence, and improve medical outcomes (Girón et al., 1998; Noble, 1998; Roter et al., 1995; Smith et al., 1995; Stewart, 1995; Suchman, Markakis, Beckman, & Frankel, 1997). While these skills are important in nearly every encounter, they become especially critical when dealing with patients in psychological distress or from different cultural or linguistic backgrounds. The growing attention to "medical professionalism" and "humanism" have generated several solid skill-building programs which include empathy and communication and promise to integrate these skills further into mainstream medical education (Branch et al., 2001; Feldman & Christensen, 1997; Lipkin, Putnam & Lazarem 1995).

Empathy is an essential skill that includes the accurate perception and response to an emotion in another. Since the physician's job is primarily about action – finding a cause and prescribing a treatment – we encourage our learners to conceptualize empathy as an active and sometimes healing intervention. To the uninitiated, the statement, "I'm so sorry that happened" seems like weak and ineffectual response to someone's tragic life story. Students learn to shift their expectations from curing to caring for patients and experience firsthand the power of a well-placed empathic statement. (Spiro, 1992; Suchman et al., 1997).

When training students to communicate and respond to difficult patient issues, it is essential to concurrently teach students a broad range of emotional management skills that extend beyond empathy. Students need to have some idea of how to manage the emotions that patients may share and the emotions that may be invoked in themselves. Many medical providers dread opening "Pandora's Box" for fear of losing control of the visit length or opening intense emotional issues that they might feel unable to handle. They may feel ill-equipped and poorly trained to manage some of the intense emotional reactions presented by their patients and are consequently afraid to ask about these important and relevant issues.

We address these and similar fears by introducing the concept of emotional intelligence and how it might be used in a doctor-patient encounter. Active teaching exercises help physicians to perceive emotions in themselves and others, to recognize them as important sources of data in order to develop empathy and understanding of these feelings, and to manage emotions in themselves and their patients (Salovey & Mayer, 1990). The goal in training is the give the learner an active experience of identifying an emotion, developing an understanding of its cause and meaning, and thinking of ways to respond as demonstrated in Exercise 1.

Exercise 1:
Recognizing, Understanding, and Responding to Emotions

An emotionally charged stimulus video of a patient sharing her desperation and pleading for assistance is shown to a group of primary care providers who are instructed to assume she is speaking directly to them. After watching the video, learners complete the form found in Appendix A to assist them in identifying their feelings, understanding the origin of their feelings, and developing helpful responses. Group discussions help normalize the learner's experience and iterations of different videos provide important skill practice.

While training in empathy and emotional intelligence may help providers to feel more competent to recognize and manage emotions in themselves and others, their concern about losing precious time by opening emotionally-charged issues still remains. To address this and other fears, a study of "emotional clues" analyzed the content of patient visits to primary care providers and to surgeons (Levinson,

Gorawara-Bhat, & Lamb, 2000). Emotional clues were identified, coded by content, and the response (if any) they elicited from the physician. There was a mean of 2.5 emotional clues per primary care visit and 2.0 clues for surgical visits. The response rate, or when the physician detected and responded to the clue, was 38% in surgeons and 21% in primary care. More importantly, when visit length was analyzed, responding to emotional clues predicted shorter visits. When clues were not attended to, the patient lengthened the visit by continuing to bring up the clue in different ways (Levinson et al., 2000).

Negotiation and Dealing with Difficult Encounters

In the current health insurance environment, patients and providers often seem to be at odds with one another. Patients may attribute their suboptimal care to the negligence or greed of their managed care physician (Pantilat & Lo, 1997). Patients may make inappropriate or excessive requests for medical interventions based on the burgeoning media and internet coverage of health and medicine. Physicians feel more time and financial pressures than ever and run even greater risks of burning out and losing the sense of meaning and connection they once enjoyed with their patients. The potential consequence of these and other factors is greater conflict, more difficult patient visits, and a strong need to be competent in negotiating with patients while maintaining the integrity of the doctor-patient relationship (Balint & Shelton, 1996; Levinson et al, 1999; Lipkin et al., 1995).

Even without the growing stressors of managed care, the intimate nature of the doctor-patient visit is often a potent emotional trigger for both patient and provider. Family of origin issues, insecurities triggered by being ill, power dynamics, or unresolved relationship issues may all contribute to the potency of a medical encounter and create misunderstanding and conflict. Teaching providers the skills of negotiation and conflict resolution first requires a high degree of emotional awareness and personal insight into why the encounter may have a special charge. Empathy and communication skills plus special negotiating styles – e.g. confrontations, collaborative alliances, identifying common goals – are then integrated into a dynamic methodology of effective patient care (Fisher & Ury, 1981).

Exercise 2:

A Difficult Patient Encounter: The Experience of the Provider

In this active exercise, providers are asked to recall and write about an actual difficult patient encounter (see Appendix B). With the aid of stimulus questions, the provider is encouraged to think about the interplay of emotion, cognition, behavior, and the consequences of their reactions to this patient before, during, and after the visit. Participants then role play their patient while a partner role plays the provider. Participants thus have the experience of what it is like to be their patient and how another provider might respond differently to the same set of circumstances. It may be important for the teacher to ask the learner to explore why a patient may push that learner's buttons and how the learner can change his or her behavior to change the dynamic. In an effort to model cognitive balance and positive reinforcement, stimulus prompts often include positively and negatively framed questions.

It is also important to instruct the learner to clearly define goals and develop personal and patient outcome measures. Goals might include improved healthcare utilization or elimination of an unhealthy behavior for patients or less anger and burnout for providers. Objective measures for these goals can be particularly useful when emotion may cloud the assessment of progress. Physicians are used to tracking biomedical patient outcomes, however, most providers are less familiar with objective ways to measure psychosocial or behavioral health issues. When positive changes are detected with objective measures, the changes can serve as important motivational tools for both patients and providers. When no change or negative changes are noted, important adaptations can be made in order to make interactions more effective.

Mental Health: Screening, Management, and Treatment

Given the high prevalence of psychiatric disorders in primary care and their substantial impact on morbidity, mortality, and co-morbid medical diseases, another essential core competency should include the detection, treatment, and management of mental illness. The volume and time constraints in primary care require any screening instrument to be quick and have a high degree of sensitivity and specificity. If a possible psychiatric disorder is detected, an appropriate referral and/or treatment should be initiated. Finally, patients with psychiatric disorders sometimes require special empathy, support, education, and encouragement that can be provided by the educated primary care provider (Hodges, Inch & Silver, 2001; Kroenke, Taylor-Vaisey, Dietrich & Oxman, 2000).

For the purposes of detection, students are first taught to look for clues that a psychiatric problem might be present – e.g., a patient has a problem-list longer than five different items, substantial medical non-adherence, complex family issues affecting treatment, multiple phone calls or messages, or any unusual change in utilization. Students are also taught to look for verbal and nonverbal clues that are often packed into a patient encounter. The active and accurate use of these clues is taught by having a group of students view videos of patient encounters to collaboratively identify the clues that a psychiatric disorder might be present. Students may also look at their schedule for the day and predict which of their patients might have some psychiatric distress and why. Those predictions are then tested by asking brief diagnostic questions to the selected patients. After multiple iterations, students often begin to develop an intuition which helps them predict what sorts of patients may need more time or at least a few screening questions about possible psychiatric problems.

In the interest of time and efficiency, it is important to have great familiarity with specific screening questions that have the greatest sensitivity and specificity. Sample questions can be found in the DSM-IV, the SCID, and the PRIME-MD (APA, 1994; Spitzer, Williams, Kroenke, & Linzer, 1994). Providers will adapt these questions to their own style but may appreciate hearing concrete examples of how these questions are worded and asked. Role plays can provide early practice while taped patient encounters can validly assess if and when these screeners are used appropriately.

Other Psychosocial Issues

The detection of stress and an appreciation for how it affects patients' lives is another core competency required for an integrated team. Although stress isn't always associated with a psychiatric disorder, it often substantially impacts a patient's quality of life and may be the primary reason for seeking medical attention. Stress can likewise contribute to a number of chronic diseases either throughout a direct pathophysiologic link or by causing patients to engage in behaviors that are harmful to their health (e.g. smoking, excessive drinking). Common stressors seen on a daily basis in primary care include bereavement, physical and sexual abuse, parenting problems, or problems with housing, finances, and employment.

Behavioral Health: Facilitating Behavior Change

Recall that 50% of premature deaths are caused by modifiable lifestyle factors (McGinnis & Foege, 1993). Assisting patients in modifying their lifestyles or changing their behaviors is thus an essential core competency for successful medical providers. Being able to facilitate behavior change effectively requires a mixture of many skills including communication, empathy, and an understanding of how to enhance motivation in patients who may be at very different degrees of readiness for change. One method for teaching these skills is outlined in Exercise 3.

Exercise 3:

Teaching Behavior Change Skills:

An Example of Smoking Cessation

The Transtheoretical Model or "Stages of Change Model", is first introduced with a brief didactic summary. This is followed by "seeing one" in a video demonstration of motivational interviewing - the clinical application of the Stages of Change Model (Miller & Rollnick, 1991; Prochaska, Johnson, & Lee, 1998). Participants "do one" using role plays of multiple case vignettes reflecting patients at different stages of readiness for change for a wide range of behaviors. After discussion of what it was like to "see one" and "do one", participants "teach one" by watching a video of a student assisting a patient with smoking cessation. Appendix C provides the instructions and prompts for this final exercise where participants are asked to provide a critique, develop learning objectives, and role play how they would achieve these objectives. By continuing to visit issues of behavior change throughout the year in a variety of teaching venues, learners eventually acquire the necessary number of repetitions to internalize these important skills.

Special Teaching Methods

The potential power of direct, constructive feedback regarding patient encounters or interactions with other professionals often gets overlooked. Skills in delivering effective feedback often go undeveloped. Before giving feedback, it is important to have your primary teaching objectives and evidence-based teaching principles in mind. In this case, the general goals are to teach core competencies including mental health/mental illness, health behavior/behavior change, and doctor-patient skills such as empathy and communication. When giving feedback, it is important to first assess the learner's ability to listen – e.g., degree of fatigue, time pressure, defensiveness – then to maintain that openness during the feedback session. One strategy is to always start with a positive comment or have the learner share what he/she did well. Rather than focusing on "weaknesses", learners can discuss areas for further practice and improvement. Feedback is generally more effective when it comes from a respected authority figure and is seen as concrete, immediate, and personally relevant.

The "curbside consult" and precepting sessions are other important vehicles for teaching with strong and direct clinical applications (Ferenchick, Simpson, Blackman, DaRosa, & Dunnington, 1997). Residents initially see their patients alone and develop an initial diagnosis and plan. While the patient is left waiting in the exam room, the resident will seek out a faculty supervisor or preceptor in order to discuss the case. While this supervisor is usually another physician, it can include a behavioral health practitioner who covers specific areas of clinical competence. The preceptor's goal is to check the accuracy and quality of the resident's medical care but also to assist the resident in learning the most effective and efficient process of arriving at a diagnosis and treatment. Socratic questioning is the most common methods of eliciting the resident thought processes and guiding the resident in helpful directions without simply telling them what to do (e.g., Furney et al., 2001). While biomedicine often takes precedence, these "curbside consults" or precepting sessions are often a good way to help the resident learn about mental health screening, behavior change, and doctoring skills such as communication and empathy.

Exercise 4:

Doing a Precepting Session

Active role-plays are an important teaching tool that requires learners to have more than just basic knowledge and attitudes. Although there is usually some initial discomfort, embarrassment, or resistance, these sessions are often rated as having the highest impact on clinical practice. Appendix D describes a role play for two participants with one playing the resident and one the preceptor. By discussing a real case, both the resident and the preceptor can practice important skills and try variations in their style. Classmates and/or teachers can observe the role plays and provide feedback. Further guidance on how to effectively precept can be found in Furney et al. (2001).

Optimal medical education includes teaching both the science and art of medicine. The behavioral health educator may need to teach the science of mental health, behavior change, and communication skills but the artful management of relationships, finding meaning, and developing as a mindful practitioner may also fall within the realm of behavioral health expertise. For example, a learner doing a curbside consult may need to be educated about anxiety disorders and the role of stress in cardiovascular disease. However, they may also need to learn how to educate and motivate their patients, how to "sell" a referral, or how to inspire hope in an anxious, grieving widow while maintaining a sense of personal integrity, boundaries, and connection to their personal values.

Exercise 5:

Writing an Action Plan

The most effective teaching strategies not only impart knowledge but assist the learner in moving this knowledge into regular practice. This is more likely to happen if the learner can immediately reflect on how this information is directly relevant to his/her personal and professional lives. An action plan is one common strategy that helps learners make the sometimes difficult leap between learning and actually changing their behavior. Action plans or similar exercises often provide important ways to summarize and end a particularly rich teaching experience including a workshop or reading a journal article or book chapter. A sample action plan designed to facilitate personal reflection and practical applications can be found in Appendix E and can be personally used after the completion of this chapter.

Teaching Evaluations

The effectiveness of teaching strategies should be just as rigorously evaluated as any medical or psychiatric treatment. Learner outcomes can be compared with initial learning objectives to assess the effectiveness of that educational intervention. Objectives can include changes in attitudes, knowledge, or behaviors and should be shared with learners at the beginning of any educational session. Sample objectives and their relevant assessment instruments can be found in Table 3.4. Other evaluation tools to measure changes in attitudes and knowledge can include pre-post questionnaires, short answer questions which pose clinical problems or require the learner to demonstrate integrative skills, essays, case stems which pose complex medical and psychosocial dilemmas, peer evaluations, and problem-based learning cases where students must demonstrate both knowledge of medical content and familiarity with the ideal process of collaboratively finding answers to difficult questions.

Assessing skills or other behavioral changes is more challenging but ultimately most important. Classroom-based assessments can include role plays, stimulus videos which present clinical materials and require learner responses, live patient interviews, and viewing previously taped learner-patient clinic visits. Clinic-based assessments often include standardized patients, clinicial OSCE (objective struc-

Learning Objective	Assessment Tool
1. Students will be able to describe the role of behavior in contributing to many of the leading causes of disability and death.	1. Written multiple choice or short answer exams.
2. Students will be able to create a basic biopsychosocial formulation of a patient's presenting complaint incorporating elements or culture, race, diversity, and family/social environment.	2. Clinical case write-up drawn from an observed patient encounter and a review of the patient's medical records.
3.Students will successfully perform a preliminary screening and diagnostic workup for Major Depressive Disorder including assessing relevant psychosocial stressors and issues pertinent to age and gender.	3. Simulated patient interview with student rated by the patient and/or an expert observer.

Table 3.4. lists sample learning objectives and assessment instruments.

tured clinical exams), preceptor ratings, peer ratings, and patient surveys (Epstein & Hundert, 2002). Changes in patient outcomes such as utilization, adherence, disease, and symptom measures are ultimately most important but difficult to measure and often not dependent on any single educational intervention.

In summary, the core competencies of a primary care provider in an integrated team can be divided into three important categories – basic doctoring skills, behavioral health, and mental health. Behavioral health providers are perhaps ideally trained to teach these competencies in an empirically-supported and psychologically-mindful way. Careful attention to the medical culture and innovative teaching strategies are likely to improve educational outcomes and could ultimately impact both patient and provider well-being. The current trend to review and revise medical education makes now the ideal time to move toward a true, multidimensional integration including clinical work, research, and, most importantly, medical education.

References:

American Psychiatric Association. (1994). *Diagnostic and Statistical Manual of Mental Disorders, 4ᵗʰ Edition*. Washington, D.C.: American Psychiatric Association Press.

Anderson, N. B. (1997). Integrating behavioral and social sciences research at the National Institutes of Health, U. S. A. *Social Science and Medicine, 44*(7), 1069-71.

Armstrong, P., Fischetti, L. R., Romano, S. E., Vogel, M. E., & Zoppi, K. (1992). Position paper on the role of behavioral science faculty in family medicine. *Family Systems Medicine, 10,* 257-263.

Balint, J., & Shelton, W. (1996). Regaining the initiative: Forging a new model of the patient-physician relationship. *JAMA, 275*(11), 887-891.

Belar, C. D. (1997). Clinical health psychology: A specialty for the 21st century. *Health Psychology, 16*(5), 411-416.

Blount, A. (1998*). Integrated Primary Care: The Future of Medical and Mental Health Collaboration.* New York: W.W. Norton.

Bolman, W. M. (1995). The place of behavioral science in medical education and practice. *Academic Medicine, 70*(10), 873-878.

Branch, W. T., Kern, D., Haidet, P., Weissmann, P., Gracey, C. F., Mitchell, G., et al. (2001). Teaching the human dimensions of care in clinical settings. *JAMA, 286*(9), 1067-1074.

Bray, J. H., & Rogers, J. C. (1995). Linking psychologists and family physicians for collaborative practice. *Professional Psychology: Research and Practice, 26*(2), 132-138.

Carr, J. E. (1998). Proposal for an integrated science curriculum in medical education. *Teaching and Learning in Medicine, 10*(1), 3-7.

Chiles, J. A., Lambert, M. J., & Hatch, A. L. (1999). The impact of psychological interventions on medical cost offset: A meta-analytic review. *Clinical Psychology: Science and Practice, 6*(2), 204-220.

Cummings, N. A., Cummings, J. L., & Johnson, J. N. (1997). *Behavioral Health in Primary Care: A Guide for Clinical Integration.* Madison, CT: Psychosocial Press.

Cummings, N. A., O'Donohue, W., Hayes, S. C., & Follette, V. (Eds). (2001). *Integrated Behavioral Healthcare: Positioning Mental Health Practice with Medical/ Surgical Practice.* San Diego: Academic Press.

Engel, G. L. (1977). The need for a new medical model: a challenge for biomedicine. *Science, 196,* 129-136.

Engel, G. L. (1980). The clinical application of the biopsychosocial model. *Am J Psychiatry, 137,* 535-544.

Epstein, R. M., & Hundert, E. M. (2002). Defining and assessing professional competence. *JAMA, 287*(2), 226-235.

Feldman, M., & Christensen, J. (1997). *Behavioral Medicine in Primary Care: A Practical Guide.* Stamford, CT: Appleton & Lange.

Ferenchick, G., Simpson, D., Blackman, J., DaRosa, D., & Dunnington, G. (1997). Strategies for efficient and effective teaching in the ambulatory care setting. *Academic Medicine, 72*(4), 277-80.

Fisher, R., & Ury, W. (1981). *Getting to Yes: Negotiating Agreement without Giving In.* Boston: Houghton-Mifflin.

Furney, S. L., Orsini, A. N., Orsetti, K. E., Stern, D. T., Gruppen, L.D., & Irby, D. M. (2001). Teaching the one-minute preceptor. A randomized controlled trial. *Journal of General Internal Medicine, 16*(9), 620-4.

Gabbard, G. O. (1985). The role of compulsiveness in the normal physician. *JAMA*, *254*, 2926 -2929.

Gaufberg, E. H., Joseph, R. C., Pels, R. J., Wyshak, G., Wieman, D., & Nadelson, C. C. (2001). Psychosocial training in U.S. internal medicine and family practice residency programs. *Academic Medicine, 76*, 738-742.

Girón, M., Manjón-Arce, P., Puerto-Barber, J., Sánchez-García, E., & Gómez, M. (1998). Clinical interview skills and identification of emotional disorders in primary care. *American Journal of Psychiatry, 155*(4), 530-535.

Grol, R., & Grimshaw, J. (1999). Evidenced-based implementation of evidence-based medicine. *Journal on Quality Improvement, 25*(10), 503-513.

Gunn, W. B., Seaburn, D., Lorenz, A., Gawinski, B., & Mauksch, L. B. (1997). Collaboration in action: Key strategies for behavioral health providers. In N.A. Cummings, J. L. Cummings, & J. N. Johnson (Eds.), *Behavioral Health in Primary Care: A Guide for Clinical Integration*, (pp.285-304). Madison, CT: Psychosocial Press.

Haley, W. E., McDaniel, S. H., Bray, J. H., Frank, R. G., Heldring, M., Johnson, S. B., et al. (1998). Psychological practice in primary care settings: Practical tips for clinicians. *Professional Psychology: Research and Practice, 29*(3), 237-244.

Halpern, R., Lee, M. Y., Boulter, P. R., & Phillips, R. R. (2001). A synthesis of nine major reports on physicians' competencies for the emerging practice environment. *Academic Medicine, 76*, 606-615.

Higgins, E. S. (1994). A review of unrecognized mental illness in primary care; Prevalence, natural history, and efforts to change the course. *Archives of Family Medicine, 3*, 908-917.

Hodges, B., Inch, C., & Silver, I. (2001). Improving the psychiatric knowledge, skills, and attitudes of primary care physicians, 1950-2000: A Review. *Am J Psychiatry, 158*, 1579-1586.

Jones, R., Higgs, R., de Angelis, C., & Prideaux, D. (2001). Changing face of medical curricula. *Lancet, 357*, 699-703.

Kroenke, K., Taylor-Vaisey, A., Dietrich, A., & Oxman, T. E. (2000). Interventions to improve provider diagnosis and treatment of mental disorders in primary care. *Psychosomatics, 41*(1), 39-52.

Leon, A. C., Olfson, M., Broadhead, W. E., Barrett, J. E., Blacklow, R. S., Martin, B. K., et al. (1995). Prevalence of mental disorders in primary care: Implications for screening. *Archives of Family Medicine, 4*, 857-861.

Levinson, W., Gorawara-Bhat, R., Dueck, R., Egener, B., Kao, A., et al. (1999). Resolving disagreements in the patient-physician relationship: Tool for improving communication in managed care. *JAMA, 282*(15), 1477-1483.

Levinson, W., Gorawara-Bhat, R., & Lamb, J. (2000). A study of patient clues and physician responses in primary care and surgical settings. *JAMA, 284*(8), 1021-1027.

Lipkin, M., Putnam, S. M., & Lazare, A. (Eds.). (1995). *The Medical Interview: Clinical Care, Education, and Research*. New York: Springer-Verlag Inc.

Makoul, G., & Curry, R. (1998). Patient, physician & society: Northwestern University Medical School. *Academic Medicine, 73*(1), 14-24.

Makoul, G., Curry, R. H., & Novack, D. H. (1998). The future of medical school courses in professional skills and perspectives. *Academic Medicine 73*(1), 48-51.

McGinnis, M., & Foege, W. (1993). Actual causes of death. *JAMA, 270*, 2207-2212.

Miller, W. R. & Rollnick, S. (1991). *Motivational Interviewing: Preparing people to change addictive behavior*. New York: Guildford.

Murray, C. J. & Lopez, A. D. (1998). The global burden of disease, 1990-2020. *Nat Medicine, 4*(11), 1241-3.

Noble, L. M. (1998). Doctor-patient communication and adherence to treatment. In Lynn Myers & Kenny Midence (Eds.), *Adherence to Treatment in Medical Conditions* (pp. 51-82)., London: Harwood Academic.

Okin, R. L., Boccellari, A., Azocar, F., Shumway, M., O'Brien, K., Gelb, A., Kohn, M., et al. (2000). The effects of clinical case management on hospital service use among ED frequent users. *American Journal of Emergency Medicine, 18*(5), 603-8.

Pace, T. M., Chaney, J. M., Mullins, L. L., & Olson, R. A. (1995). Psychological consultation with primary care physicians: Obstacles and opportunities in the medical setting. *Professional Psychology: Research and Practice, 26*(2), 123-131.

Pantilat, S. Z., & Lo, B. (1997). Advocates or adversaries: Is managed care changing the physician-patient relationship? *Ophthalmology Clinics of North America, 10*(2), 155-163.

Prochaska, J. O., Johnson, S., & Lee, P. (1998). The transtheoretical model of behavioral change. In S. A. Shumaker, E.B. Schron, J. K. Ockene, & W. L. McBee (Eds.), *The Handbook of Health Behavior Change* (pp. 59-84). New York: Springer Publishing Co.

Quill T. E., & Williamson P. R. (1990). Healthy approaches to physician stress. *Archives of Internal Medicine, 150*, 1857-1861.

Rabinowitz, H. K., Babbott, D., Bastacky, S., Pascoe, J. M., Patel, K. K., Pye, K. L., et al. (2001). Innovative approaches to educating medical students for practice in a changing health care environment: The national UME-21 project. *Academic Medicine, 76*, 587-597.

Russell, G: *Essential Psychology for Nurses and Other Health Profession*als. New York: Routledge 1999.

Russell, G., & Potter, L. (2002). Mental health issues in primary healthcare. *Journal of Clinical Nursing, 11*, 118-125.

Sachdeva, A. K. (2000). Faculty development and support needed to integrate the learning of prevention in the curricula of medical schools. *Academic Medicine, 75*(7), S35-S42.

Salovey, P., & Mayer, J. D. (1990). Emotional Intelligence. *Imagination, Cognition, and Personality, 9*, 185-211.

Satterfield, J. M. (2000). Disseminating empirically-supported psychological treamtents in primary care settings. *The Behavior Therapist, 23*(5), 93-97.

Schroeder S. A. (1992). The troubled profession: is medicine's glass half full or half empty? *Annals of Internal Medicine, 116*, 583 -592.

Shortell S. M., Gillies R. R., & Anderson, D. A. (1994). The new world of managed care: creating organized delivery systems. *Health Affairs*, 13(5), 46-64.

Sierles, F. S. (Ed.). (1993). *Behavioral Science for Medical Students*. Baltimore, Maryland: Williams and Wilkins.

Spiro, H. (1992). What is empathy and can it be taught? *Annals of Internal Medicine, 116*(10), 843-6.

Spitzer, R. L., Williams, J. B., Kroenke, K., & Linzer, M. (1994). Utility of a new procedure for diagnosing mental disorders in primary care: The PRIME-MD 1000 study. *JAMA, 272* (22), 1749-1756.

Steele, D. J., & Susman, J. L. (1998). Integrated clinical experience: University of Nebraska Medical Center. *Academic Medicine, 73*(1), 41-47.

Stewart, M. A. (1995). Effective physician-patient communication and health outcomes: A review. *Canadian Medical Association Journal, 152*(9), 1423-1433.

Stoudemire A: *Human Behavior: An Introduction for Medical Students*. Philadelphia: Lippincott-Raven 1998.

Suchman, A., Markakis, K., Beckman, H. B., & Frankel, R. (1997). A model of empathic communication in the medical interview. *JAMA, 277*(8), 678-682.

U.S. Department of Health and Human Services. (1997). *Atlas of United States Mortality*. (DHHS Pub No. PHS 97-1015). Hyattsville, MD: Author.

Wedding, D. (2001). *Behavior & Medicine*, 3rd Ed. Seattle, WA: Hogrefe & Huber.

Appendix A

Exercise 1: Recognizing, understanding, and responding to emotions
Instructions:

• Imagine you are a primary care provider in your outpatient clinic seeing an acute drop-in patient. You are having the usual busy day and are already somewhat behind in your schedule.

• Watch the stimulus video of how this patient opens your visit.

• What do you immediately think and feel?

My thoughts:

My feelings:

• What is the first thing you would do for yourself? What is the first thing you would do for her? Please be concrete and specific.

• What is the first thing you say to her? Write this down verbatim.

- How would your inward and outward thoughts, feelings, and behaviors affect this situation? What recommendations would you give a colleague who was seeing this patient?

Appendix B

Exercise 2: A difficult patient encounter; The experience of the provider

- Recall a patient encounter you found difficult or challenging to manage effectively. With this patient in mind, answer the below prompts.
- Find a partner and exchange write-ups. Review your partner's description of his/her difficult encounter and consider how you would recommend working with this patient.
- Begin a role play where one person plays the patient they have written about. The partner will play the provider interacting with this patient. The provider should model how he/she would recommend interacting with this patient.
- Discuss the experience for both patient and provider. What were the treatment obstacles? Was your partner's experience of this patient the same as your own? What was the provider's main teaching points? What interventions for the provider or for the patient might improve your next encounter with the patient?

1. Describe a patient encounter you found difficult or challenging to manage effectively.

2. What about this patient was difficult? (What *exactly* does the patient *do* or *express* that makes him/her difficult?) What about the encounter was difficult?

3. What was your response? What were your thoughts, feelings, and behaviors? (How did you know you were in a difficult situation)? How did your response vary before, during, and after the visit?

4. What was the impact of your response on the patient or the encounter? In what ways was your response helpful? Not so helpful?

Appendix C

Exercise 3: Facilitating behavior change: An example of smoking cessation

- Watch the video of a primary care resident encouraging his patient to change her behavior.
- Immediately write down any observations, strengths, areas for improvement, or other teaching objectives you might want to use with this resident. Be sure to draw on what you have learned about the Stages of Change and Motivational Interviewing.

- Consider how you would go about achieving these teaching objectives (e.g., teaching strategies and teaching process)
- Find a partner and role play how you would teach this resident.
- Discuss how this felt from the perspective of both the teacher and the resident

Video Notes:

Learning Objectives:

Appendix D

Exercise 4: Doing a precepting session
A Role Play for 2 participants

Instructions:
- One participant will play the part of the resident/student who has just seen a patient and is presenting his/her findings to a preceptor for validation and advice.
- One participant will play the role of the consultant/preceptor who hopes to insure appropriate care for the patient and to educate the resident about his/her style, knowledge, and process of thinking.

Participants will role play the following scenario: The resident quickly presents the patient's case to the consultant (case below) looking for a "rubber stamp". The consultant worries about the patient's psychosocial environment and/or a possible psych disorder. It seems that the resident has not addressed these issues with the pt. Using teaching methods amenable to this venue, the consultant wants to teach the resident the importance of empathy, how to elicit reports of psychosocial stressors, and how to screen and triage a possible anxiety disorder. Try to use Socratic questioning, active learning (i.e. having the resident practice what to say to the pt), and other evidence-based teaching strategies.

Should the consultant accompany the resident back to the exam room and see the patient together? What would you do or say? Would you model how to ask about psychosocial issues? How to screen for a psych disorder? Try out several strategies as time permits.

The Case (Resident's perspective)
Pt is a high functioning 35yo married female in for her 4th primary care appt with you in the past year. She complains of unresolved GI discomfort and constipation. She requests a colonoscopy although this is not medically indicated. You believe she is experiencing mild dyspepsia (indigestion) and possible GERD. The indicated medical treatment is acid suppression and a mild laxative or diet modification. You are frustrated she keeps coming back with such minor medical

issues. You go to your preceptor/colleague for a quick curbside consult although it seems more of a formality than a necessity.

Appendix E

Exercise 5: Writing an action plan

1. Reflect on areas where your clinical and educational activities may change as a result of what you have learned from reading this chapter and actively practicing the exercises.

2. In what ways could these training ideas (both content and process) be applied to your work setting? Brainstorm a list of ideas.

3. How will you implement these ideas and how will you evaluate their impact? What obstacles do you forsee and how will you address them?

4. Create a time-line for each step to be completed over the next several months.

Implementing a Primary Care
Depression Clinical Pathway

Patricia Robinson

There are many opportunities for population-based care of behavioral health conditions in the primary care setting, and depression is an ideal initial target for pathway attention. Among the many conditions troubling primary care patients, depression ranks high (Riegier, Goldberg, & Taube, 1978; Reiger et al., 1993). Depression in medical patients has been linked to increased functional disability, increased medical utilization, negative perceptions of health status, and non-adherence to disease management regimes, as well as increased risk of morbidity and mortality (Katon, 1992; Katon, Von Korff et al., 1994; Wells, Steward, Hays, Burnam, Rogers et al., 1989). Use of a clinical pathway approach to depressed primary care patients may result in improvement in clinical outcomes and patient and provider satisfaction (Katon et al., 1996, Robinson, 1996b; Robinson, Wischman & Del Vento, 1996a; Mynors-Wallace, Gath, Lloyd-Thomas, & Tomlinson, 1995). Further, cost effectiveness analyses suggest that expenditure of behavioral health resources results in greater value (i.e., degree of clinical improvement relative to the cost of delivering treatment services) in the primary care as compared with the mental health setting (Von Korff et al., 1998).

Since health care resources are limited and the greatest improvement opportunities appear to be in the primary care context, behavioral health providers must begin to partner with primary care providers and work as team members to improve outcomes for depressed primary care patients. In this chapter, I provide information to help behavioral health providers make this endeavor a creative and successful undertaking. Pathways need to reflect the needs and resources within individual clinics, and, therefore, I encourage you to create pathway committees and to study the patient population and unique resources in your clinic. I provide information on the prevalence of depression and the opportunities inherent in targeting sub-groups of depressed primary care patients. I present a brief review of empirical studies conducted in an effort to define effective treatments that primary care patients accept and complete at high rates. Behavioral health providers need to understand population-based care and principles of evidence-based medicine in order to create a model of integrated care that will support implementation of a pathway for treating depressed patients. I present these briefly and introduce the Primary Care Behavioral Health (PCBH) model (Robinson, Wischman, & Del Vento, 1996; Strosahl, 1996a; 1996b; 1997; 1998). The PCBH Model incorporates these important changes in perspective and provides a great deal of structure to support inclusion of behavioral health providers on primary care treatment teams.

Medication treatments are common among primary care providers, and behavioral health providers have expertise that can improve outcomes when patients and providers decide to use medicines in treatment. I offer specific ideas for improving outcomes for this popular primary care treatment approach. In the final section, I make suggestions about pathway committee membership and tools that will support members in their work. I also define possible team members in a clinical pathway program and suggest tasks for each. There are many possible pathways, and I provide a list of examples to inspire you to be original in designing a pathway that improves outcomes for depressed patients in your unique setting. The first step is to begin, and the second is to continue your effort. It is my hope that this chapter will help you plan initial steps or go a little further on the road toward improving care to this large and growing group of patients.

Prevalence and Impact

Depressed individuals suffer a great deal. Symptoms of depression are the leading reason for pursuit of mental health services (Zimmerman, M., & Mattia, 2000). However, most depressed individuals do not seek mental health treatment, and, in part, they do not seek treatment because it is not available in the current mental health delivery system, whose resources are inadequate for serving the seriously mentally ill population. Depressed patients go to primary care clinics because primary care is accessible. They fill primary care waiting rooms on a daily basis, and primary care physicians focus on their medical complaints and prescribe antidepressants when depression is identified. Providers often lose control over their busy schedules in an effort to support depressed patients, and depressed patients often fail to adhere to the antidepressant medications regimes as well as other medical regimes associated with management of chronic conditions. It is no wonder that depressed patients and the primary care providers who care for them often feel dissatisfied with the process.

This is a big problem, in that as many as 1 in 4 primary care patients report significant depressive symptoms (Katon & Schulberg, 1992; Narrow, Reiger, Rae, Manderscheid, & Locke, 1993; Barrett, Barrett, Oxman, & Gerber, 1988, Katon & Schulberg, 1992). In some primary care settings (e.g., a women's public health care clinic), one out of three patients in the waiting room may be experiencing clinically significant symptoms of depression, and these troubling symptoms impact multiple outcomes. If the depressed individual receives care, it is most likely to be initiated in the primary care setting (Regier, Narrow et al., 1993), and the clinical pathway offers opportunities for improving detection, diagnosis, treatment, follow-up, and relapse prevention. Treatments integrated into the primary care setting may be more effective than traditional treatments delivered in mental health clinics (Katon, Von Korff, Lin, Walker, Simon, et al.; 1995; Katon, Robinson, Von Korff, Lin, Bush et al., 1996; Mynors-Wallace, Davies, Gray, Gath, & Barbour, 1997; Mynors-Wallis, Gath, Day, & Baker, 2000; Mynors-Wallis, Gath, Lloyd-Thomas& Tomlinson, 1995), and several of these studies will be discussed at length in the next section.

The presence of depressive symptoms impacts the individual's functioning in many ways, all of which are negative, and the costs of depression are staggering. Direct and indirect costs of depression in the United States approach $43 billion annually. Prior to identifying sub-populations of depressed patients where cost savings are most promising, the term cost-offset needs attention. It can be applied to the medical or mental health dollar. When providing mental health services to patients suffering from depression leads to a decrease in their use of medical services, medical researchers and economists refer to this as a medical cost-offset effect. The cost of providing mental health services is offset by reductions in the cost of general medical services. Medical cost-offsets have the potential to occur when use of health care services is driven in part or whole by psychological or psychiatric factors and when patient management of chronic conditions improves and reduces medical utilization, particularly more expensive procedures. The mental health cost-offset occurs when providing mental health services in the primary care context results in a decrease in the cost of providing mental health services in a mental health setting.

In addition to health care costs, depression exerts a cost to employers (Birnbaum, Greenberg et al., 1999). Depression causes more disability than do many chronic medical disorders (Spitzer, Kroenke, Linzer, Hahn, Williams et al., 1995; Hays, Wells, Sherbourne, Rogers, & Spritzer, 1995). This is felt dramatically in worker productivity, absenteeism and disability claims. Some clinics will be able to partner with employers in forming steps in a pathway for depression.

Based on the literature on cost-offset effects, several specific patient groups have high potential for generating cost-offset effects. These include medical inpatients, patients with somatization disorder, and alcoholic adults (Olfson, Sing, & Schlesinger, 2001). Additionally, improved treatment of patients with chronic medical disease and psychologically distressed adults presenting to the primary care setting may contribute to development of a medical cost offset (Robinson, 2002). Finally, making improvements to the care of older adults who are demoralized or depressed by health problems is a fertile area for clinics that serve a large group of older adults.

Major depression may go undetected in primary care patients who present to the clinic for treatment of chronic conditions and when they are hospitalized for medical problems. Unfortunately, providers may see depression as a normal reaction to serious illness, such as cancer, myocardial infarction, stroke, dementia and Parkinson's disease. While the risk of depression is higher for these patients, depression is not a normal response and it may worsen patient outcomes (Cassem, 1995). Mumford (1984) reviewed 58 controlled trials involving general medical patients and found that delivery of psychosocial interventions to inpatients was associated with 10 percent reduction in inpatient medical care costs.

Nearly half of the people in the United States are currently living with chronic conditions (Hoffman, Rice, & Sung, 1996), and many experience depression at the time of their initial diagnosis or later in the course of their disease condition. Up to 25% of diabetic patients experience clinically significant symptoms of depression. These symptoms often compromise patient abilities for successful adherence to disease management plans. Four conditions that are ideal for combined depression treatment and self-management skill training are diabetes, heart disease, arthritis, and asthma, as these collectively cost the nation an estimated $457.6 billion a year (National Institutes of Health, 1995).

Depression often co-occurs with other conditions that are common in primary care patients. These include patients with somatization disorder, drug and alcohol problems, chronic pain and domestic abuse problems. Somatization disorder is a chronic (although fluctuating) disorder and these patients receive a great deal of time from primary care providers, who work diligently to explore their many vague complaints (e.g., dizziness, headaches, and abdominal pain). Individuals with somatization disorder may be at increased risk for depression secondary to medical procedures that inadvertently result in medical problems with an organic basis. Smith, Rost, & Kashner (1995) found that delivery of psychiatric consultation services to patients with somatization disorder resulted in lowered medical charges. From a population care perspective, it is important to note that there are roughly 100 additional adult patients with symptoms of this disorder for every single patient meeting diagnostic criteria for somatization disorder (Robins & Regier, 1991), and this large group contributes generously to the problem of health care accessibility.

Symptoms of depression and mood instability are among the most common psychiatric symptoms seen in individuals with substance use disorders. Data from the ECA study indicated that among people with any affective disorder, 32% had a co-morbid addictive disorder (Robins & Regier, 1991). Among individuals with major depression, 16.5% had a co-morbid alcohol-use diagnosis. Medical cost savings can be realized by treatment of alcoholic patients, particularly during the early stages of alcohol-use disorders (Holder & Blose, 1986). One HMO study found that changes in co-pay structures designed to improve access to an alcohol treatment program resulted in increased use of alcohol treatment services, longer periods of abstinence and greater participation in non-drinking activities (Hayami & Freeborn, 1981).

Many opportunities for prevention of chronic pain and related depression and disability are missed in today's primary care health care system (Robinson, unpublished). Chronic pain patients often obtain referrals to expensive specialists and remain in their care for years. Chronic pain patient functioning usually improves when depression receives effective treatment. The mere presence of behavioral health staff in the primary care clinic may boost recognition and treatment of domestic abuse and support treatment of depression in perpetrators as well as victims.

Psychologically distressed primary care patients are also a group worthy of targeting in a depression pathway. The growing discipline of mind-body medicine is defining a causal link between mental/emotional problems and physical illnesses (see, for example, Ornstein & Sobel, 1988; 1990). Pautler (1991) reported that as many as 25 percent of all outpatients visits can be accounted for by psychological factors that cause physiological disturbance with no permanent organ damage (e.g., migraines, functional bowel disease, types of chronic pain). This rate increases to 50% when the definition of psychosomatic illness is broadened to include conditions where actual physiological changes occur (e.g., hypertension, hyperthyroidism, asthma, and chronic skin disorders) (Paulter, 1991). Brief psychotherapy reduces patients' stress levels, related physical symptoms, and overall medical costs (Cummings, 1993; Cummings & VandenBos, 1981).

There are many reasons to target older adults in a primary care depression pathway. Older primary care patients with depression visit the doctor and emergency room more often, use more medication, incur higher outpatient charges, and stay longer when in the hospital (Callahan, Hui, Nienaber, Musick, & Tierney, 1994; Cooper-Patrick et al., 1994; Callahan & Wolinsky, 1995; Unutzer, Katon, Simon, Walker, Grembowski et al., 1996). Older adults with symptoms of depression also accrue greater average diagnostic test charges than their non-depressed cohorts (Callahan, Kesterson, & Tierney, 1997). Diagnosis of depression in older adults is more difficult, as symptoms tend to be less severe than in younger adults. Additionally, older persons with depression may not present with typical symptoms of depression, such as sadness, and may present with somatic complaints for which no apparent medical etiology can be found (Gallo & Rabins, 1999). With the segment of the population of older adults growing rapidly, clinical pathway developers may consider targeting older adults in assessment efforts and in development of specific interventions. Older adults, unlike younger adults, have time to participate in group or class programs. Life Satisfaction Classes and programs that integrate medical and behavioral treatment in a group format are acceptable to many older adults, and such may re-shape utilization patterns of frail older adults, while improving satisfaction with care (See Robinson, Del Vento & Wischman, 1998 for curriculum).

Finally, a depression pathway development committee needs to take note of the reality that some medical conditions may cause depression. These include endocrine disorders (hypothyroidism, Cushing's disease) and neurological disorders (multiple sclerosis, Parkinson's disease, migraine, various forms of epilepsy, encephalitis, and brain tumors). Additionally, some medications (e.g., reserpine, glucocorticoids, anabolic steroids) may result in depression. In the busy context of primary care practice, on-going screening of these vulnerable patients may be easily overlooked (Perez-Stable, Miranda, Bunoz, & Ying, 1990). In designing a primary care clinical pathway for depression, designers need to assess the patient population in their specific clinic and to use pertinent information about the patient population (e.g., age distribution, prevalence of various chronic conditions, etc.) and provider mix (family practice, internal medicine, etc.) to further define specific sub-populations for pathway targeting.

Depression: Effective Treatments

The purpose of delivering health care services to all patients, including depressed patients, is to improve their health status by using available resources cost effectively (Eddy, 1996). This requires providers, administrators, and patients to develop clinical policies based on evidence about treatment benefits, harms, costs, and patient preference concerning use of the collective health care dollar. In addition to defining a population of concern, a clinical pathway identifies new, empirically supported treatments and providers that will deliver these to the population of concern. The delivery of the new treatments needs to result in an improvement over current treatments on several outcomes (clinical, patient and provider satisfaction) and/or a better use of resources available for treatment of the identified condition among the entire group of patients suffering from that condition. A number of studies are available to inform the definition of treatments for depression that will meet these criteria. First, it appears that that primary care treatment of depression is improved by models of care that bring behavioral health providers into the primary care clinic to work as team members with primary care providers (Miranda, Hohmann, Attkisson, & Larson, 1994; Mynors-Wallace et al., 1997; Mynors-Wallis, Gath, Day, & Baker, 2000; Mynors-Wallis, Gath, Lloyd-Thomas & Tomlinson, 1995). Studies have explored a range of models, including primary care psychiatry treatment (Katon et al., 1995); primary care behavioral health brief treatment (Katon et al., 1996); problem solving therapy (Mynors-Wallis, Davies, Gray, Gath, & Barbour, 1997; Mynors-Wallis, Gath, Day, & Baker, 2000; Mynors-Wallis, Gath, Lloyd-Thomas, & Tomlinson D., 1995) and cognitive behavioral group therapy (Miranda, Hohmann, Attkisson, & Larson, 1994; Munoz, Ying, Bernal, Perez-Stable, Sorensen et al., 1995).

A second concern in treatment design is that of patient acceptability, which must be high if a pathway is to succeed in impacting a high percentage of depressed patients. Primary care patients expect brief treatments that emphasize self-management strategies, and studies employing such report better treatment completion rates than those involving delivery of mental health setting-sized interventions. Schulberg evaluated the effectiveness and feasibility of providing empirically supported treatments to primary care patients at intensity levels characteristic of mental health treatment settings (Schulberg, Block, Modonia, Scott, Rodriquez et al., 1996). While 70% of treatment completers in the pharmacotherapy or interpersonal psychotherapy protocols were judged as recovered at eight months (in comparison with 20% of the usual care patients), only 33% of the pharmacotherapy and 42% of the psychotherapy patients completed treatment. In contrast to this effort, Katon and colleagues (1996) designed an intervention involving team treatment of depression by a primary care provider and an on-site behavioral health provider that was about ¼ of the intensity of traditional behavioral treatment of depression. Patients participated in 4 to 6 educational sessions with a psychologist for a total of 2.5 to 3.5 hours of direct contact over a 6 week period and a series of 4 phone call follow-ups over the following 6 months. Primary care providers prescribed antidepressants for patients taking medications and supported patient implementation of quality of life improvement plans and relapse prevention plans, which were included in the patient's medical chart. Psychologists consulted with liaison psychiatrists on medication issues. In the primary care-sized intervention, 94% of patients who began the program completed it (Katon et al., 1996). Other primary care behavioral health interventions of similar intensity report similar rates of patient retention (Mynors-Wallace, Gath, Lloyd-Thomas, & Tomlinson 1995).

This brief intervention that relied on an integrated model of care resulted in significant improvements over usual care. Usual care involved routine care by primary care providers and patient ability to self-refer or be referred by their primary care providers to a mental health clinic that provided cognitive behavioral therapy in group and individual formats and antidepressant therapy directed by a psychiatrist. In comparison with usual care, the intervention was shown to (1) improve short-term clinical outcomes for major depression, (2) increase patient satisfaction with treatment, and (3) increase the percent of patients receiving antidepressant treatment at or near levels recommended by the Agency for Health Care Policy and Research (AHCPR) (AHCPR, 1994). For major depression, the extent of improvement in depressive symptoms was comparable to that obtained in randomized controlled trials evaluating the efficacy of pharmacotherapeutic and psychotherapeutic treatments. For patients with minor depression, results were not consistently significant, but a positive trend was suggested. Instructional materials for primary care clinical providers and behavioral health providers working in primary care are available on this model (Robinson, Wischman, & Del Vento, 1996; Robinson, 1996).

Von Korff and colleagues (1998) pooled information from the Katon study (Katon, et a., 1995) with that of another study (Katon et al., 1995) to explore the cost effectiveness of collaborative treatment by behavioral health and primary care providers in the primary care setting. The method of using patients exposed to treatment or usual care conditions on a randomized basis avoids the potential bias of the before-after design employed in some cost-offset studies (Mumford, Schlesinger, Glass, Patrick, & Cuerdon, 1984). For each of the 332 study patients included in the cost analysis, cost data were summed for the one-year period beginning with the date of the initial primary care visit during which depression treatment was initiated. Costs (not charges) were derived from the HMO cost information system. Since mental health services provided by study personnel were not entered into this system, the price of obtaining comparable services in the local community were used to derive estimates. Patients ranged in age from 18 to 80. The costs of specialty mental health services were significantly lower among patients with major depression assigned to integrated care than among those assigned to usual care ($123 versus $317; p = .027). Because of this cost-offset in specialty mental health service use, the added cost of providing integrated behavioral health care for patients with major depression was less than it would have been otherwise. The added cost of mental health treatment in the psychiatric model (Katon, 1995) was $487 and the added cost in the psychologist model (Katon, 1996) was $264.

The total costs of providing mental health treatment for major and sub-threshold depression were higher in both studies than the costs of delivering mental health services in the usual care model. The additional cost of providing integrated care for patients with minor depression was relatively more expensive (an additional cost of $641 and $520 per patient, respectively), as patients with minor depression who received usual care tended to use less traditional mental health services and to improve without more intensive mental health treatment.

In addition to choosing a model for integration that supports a pathway and designing specific interventions to improve clinical and cost outcomes and that are acceptable to patients, clinical pathway designers need to improve patient and provider satisfaction. In the Katon study (Katon, 1996), 88% of the intervention patients with major depression rated their treatment for depression as good or excellent compared with 56% of the usual care patients. Among patients with minor depression, 97% of the intervention patients, compared with 71% of the usual care patients rated their treatment of depression as good or excellent. One hundred percent of the primary care providers preferred the integrated treatment to usual care.

Treatment selection in the pathway development process is a balancing act. At times, the choice is between a more costly treatment that is more effective and a less costly treatment that is less effective but beneficial to a larger group of patients. Patient/consumer involvement in pathway development efforts is critical to decision-making. A stepped care program may help in solving some of the controversial issues that pathway developers face in making use of limited resources. For example, in the health care organization where the Katon study (1996) was conducted, planners decided to treat patients with sub-threshold depression at a lower intensity level than patients with major depression. Specifically, the pathway suggested that a patient in this large group (almost half of the patients identified by primary care providers as having probable major depression) receive a brief psychoeducational intervention from their primary care provider and a follow-up visit one month after diagnosis. Additionally, providers were encouraged to follow a policy of watchful waiting in regards to use of antidepressant medications with this group. Health care companies adopting policies such as this will want to evaluate provider adherence to the guideline and the long-term economic impact, as prevention of episodes of major depression among patients with minor or sub-threshold levels of depression may result in significant cost savings and improved consumer loyalty.

There are several more recent research directions that warrant ongoing attention from clinical pathway developers. The first concerns prevention of relapse, as relapse rates are high for depressed primary care patients. Acceptance and Commitment Therapy techniques (Hayes, Strosahl, & Wilson, 1999) and mindfulness techniques are newer treatments, and they may be particularly effective in increasing the robustness of state-of-the art, psychological treatments for depression. Teasdale and colleagues (Teasdale, Segal, Williams, Ridgeway, Soulsby, & Lau, 2000) found that participation of recovered patients in a brief, mindfulness group intervention resulted in lower relapse rates. A second line of research that may have implications for pathway development is that of using exercise as a treatment. In a recent study, 156 patients with major depressive disorder aged 50 to 77 years were assigned randomly to a program of aerobic exercise, sertraline or combined exercise and medication (Blumenthal et al., 1999). Subjects attended three supervised exercise sessions per week for 16 consecutive weeks. All three groups exhibited a significant decline in depression symptoms. The percentage of patients who were no longer clinically depressed at the end of the four-month treatment period did not differ across treatment groups. Patients in the exercise and combination group showed significant improvement in aerobic capacity, while patients in the medication group did not show this much improvement. Pathway development is an on-going process, and committee members will need to stay current on new interventions and to incorporate them as evidence warrants change to the pathway.

In the clinical pathway development process, committee members often choose to conduct mini-studies to inform the decision-making process. Many research studies use measures that are not feasible in daily clinical practice, so pathway developers need to think through their options and to select feasible measures. I encourage pathway developers to select both a clinical measure (e.g., the PHQ-9) and a functioning measure (e.g., the Duke Health Profile, see Parkerson, Broadhead, & Tse, 1990) at the outset, so that these clinical data are consistently available for informing policy development. I also recommend that they identify data that are already available from billing encounters to avoid any duplication in effort. Various data elements are often already available to help providers self-manage and improve their performance in the new pathway. Satisfaction data are important, and pathway developers are smart to obtain pre-guideline data on provider and patient satisfaction to serve as a baseline. Research studies often fail to collect data related to patient harm, yet this is very helpful in making pathway decisions. Finally, developers need to decide on an approach to measure provider buy-in concerning new treatments, baseline skill levels for delivering new pathway treatments, impact of training on skills, and provider fidelity to the pathway (once it is implemented). Ultimately, a clinical pathway is only as effective as the provider who delivers it. Provider buy-in and adequacy of training in new treatments are critical to the success of a pathway.

Models for Improving Depression Outcomes

A clinical pathway for depressed primary care patients needs to evolve from the models of population based care and evidence-based medicine. While these models are familiar to most primary care providers, behavioral health providers may be less familiar with them. Therefore, I will review them briefly before introducing the Primary Care Behavioral Health Model (PCBH) (Strosahl, 1998, 1997, 1996a, 1996b, 1994; Strosahl et al., 1997). The BCBH model supports close integration of primary care and behavioral health services by bringing behavioral health providers into the primary care clinic setting where they become new team members.

It has a great deal in common with the Depression Collaborative and differs primarily in the level of integration of medical and behavioral health services supported by the model and the resulting opportunities for improving the behavioral health care of patients attending the clinic.

Population based care is grounded in public health concepts that may be unfamiliar to many behavioral health providers. This approach is designed to help the health care system achieve satisfactory levels of basic preventive care, accessibility to acute care and effective chronic disease management. It uses public health and epidemiological principles to describe a population, analyze care for problems of highest priority, and design and modify services to deliver that care and monitor results. The population based care approach has been applied to community-oriented primary care, as well as to age group and chronic disease group populations. There are two basic principles of population based care that are critical to building a depression pathway. First, population care is effective only to the extent that basic clinical services are accessed by a large percentage of the medical population. This involves providing limited services to many members of the population, instead of providing intensive services to very few members of the population. Second, population based care interventions work best when they accommodate consumer preferences. When consumer acceptance of interventions is high, consumers are more likely to seek the service and to follow the required steps of an intervention. Population-based care principles can support clinical pathway development in multiple health care settings, ranging from health care systems with numerous large clinics to the individual primary care physician practice.

Evidence based medicine is often confused with using empirically validated treatments that are supported by clinical practice guidelines. It should be noted that the growing emphasis on empirically supported treatments in the behavioral health industry has developed in relative isolation from the principles guiding evidence-based medicine. Evidence-based medicine is far more complicated than simply looking at the results of clinical trials and implementing a procedure based upon the empirical results alone. When implemented properly, this approach to medicine integrates cost considerations, risk-benefit to the consumer, existing variability in costs and outcomes, strength of empirical evidence, as well as consumer preferences.

Like population-based care, evidence-based medicine is rooted in clinical epidemiology and public health concepts. It involves the conscientious, explicit and judicial application of current best evidence in making decisions about patient care. Practice of evidence-based care requires integration of clinical expertise with the best available external clinical evidence from systematic research. Within the context of everyday patient care, the provider that practices evidence-based medicine seeks to balance the factors of research evidence, clinical expertise, and patient preference in providing care to the individual patient (Sackett, 1996). A major product of evidence-based medicine is the development of a practice guide suggesting a quality hierarchy for guideline development (Eddy, Hasselblad, & Shachter, 1992; Eddy, 1996a). This hierarchy for guideline development moves from the most basic level of global subjective judgment to the level of having an evidence base. The highest level in Eddy's quality hierarchy is a research based practice guideline that is sensitive to patient preference. The Agency for Health Care Policy and Research (AHCPR) has created 19 practice guidelines and established a group of evidence-based practice centers around the country to develop guidelines on a contractual basis (Practice Trends, 1997). AHCPR also created a national guideline clearinghouse on the Internet.

Behavioral health providers in primary care need to understand the principles of population-based care and evidence-based medicine prior to sitting down at the clinical pathway development table. This involves becoming proficient in applying a large group of decision rules to the problem of depression, as it exists in a population. For most behavioral health providers, this involves a steep learning curve, but most learn quickly when a model of integration that encourages a fresh view supports them.

The Primary Care Behavioral Health Model. The Primary Behavioral Health Model involves managing the psychosocial aspects of chronic and acute diseases (i.e., behavioral medicine) and addressing lifestyle and health risk issues (i.e., health psychology) through brief consultative interventions and temporary co-management of certain behavioral health conditions. (Strosahl, 1998, 1997, 1996a, 1996b, 1994; Strosahl et al., 1997). In this model, there is an emphasis on early identification and treatment, as well as long-term prevention and support of healthy lifestyles. Primary behavioral health services are delivered with a goal of increasing the effectiveness of primary care providers in addressing the behavioral health needs of patients. Behavioral health providers see patients in exam rooms or in offices nested in the primary care clinic. Behavioral health providers do not take charge of the patient's care, as would be the case in a specialty mental health approach. The goal is to manage the patient within the structure of the primary care team, with the behavioral health provider functioning as an integral member of this team. For patients, care feels seamless. When a patient fails to respond to primary behavioral health care, or obviously needs specialized treatment, the patient is referred to a specialty mental health service (Strosahl, 1994). The Primary Behavioral Health Care model relieves patient concerns about receiving a mental health service. Consequently, many patients that have historically been reluctant to receive specialty mental health services (i.e., the elderly, male adults, ethnic and cultural minorities) accept care more readily.

There are two distinct but complementary approaches to providing integrated behavioral health care. These have been described as horizontal and vertical models of integration (Strosahl, 1997). Horizontal integration is the most basic form of integrative care because almost any behavioral health problem can benefit from a well-organized general behavioral health service. Horizontal integration programs are designed to serve all referred patients. The goal is to deliver a large volume of brief psychosocial services that systematically improve the health of the entire primary care population. Only small numbers of patients are referred to specialty treatment centers and hospitals. A primary goal in this approach is to raise the skill level of primary care team members for treating behavioral health problems. Over time, primary care providers learn to handle routine behavioral health concerns more effectively in the context of the 10-minute medical visit. Primary care providers learn quickly in a model that involves both consultation and the co-management of cases. The behavioral health of the primary care population improves as care delivered by primary care providers improves. The primary behavioral health consultant works himself or herself out of the job of seeing less complex patients. Then, he or she has time to take a lead role in the development of vertical behavioral health programs. In this sense, the horizontal integration provides a framework from which a clinical pathway for depression can be implemented successfully. While the development of a pathway for depression can occur prior to the development of the horizontal platform, a clinic needs to have a combination of targeted clinical pathways or vertical program that address the needs of high frequency and/or high impact sub-populations and a highly accessible horizontal integration service that serves as an easy access point for other patients.

In the Primary Care Behavioral Health Model, a secondary approach involves development of vertical integration programs. Vertical integration involves providing treatment according to a specific protocol to a defined sub-population, for example, depressed primary care patients. Vertical integration programs are developed to serve highly prominent populations. Primary care populations may be prominent because they are prevalent, as is the case with depressed patients, or because they are high profile patients, as may be the case with chronic pain patients. Common vertical integration targets are high prevalence conditions, such as depression, panic disorder or high impact conditions, such as somatization and chronic pain. Vertical integration programs may be linked to clinical treatment pathways or practice guidelines. Vertical programs typically have both an acute and preventive treatment foci. This allows the program to accommodate patients needing different levels of care and to prevent relapse. Successful vertical integration programs are developed through application of the principles of population-based and evidence-based medicine.

Improving Medication Treatment Outcomes

In the medical setting, interview strategies and level of care assignments are made quickly, and the tendency is toward ruling out medical conditions and attempting to describe presenting complaints in biomedical terms. This reflects preparation and training for primary care providers, who can readily explain the medical basis of psychological symptoms (e.g., depression related to hypothyroidism) and assess the physical symptoms related depression more thoroughly than the psychological ones. Primary care providers are trained to evaluate the whole person. Predictably, they are more likely than psychiatrists to give physical exams, neurology exams and to obtain multiple lab tests (Epstein, 1995) and to prescribe psychotropic medications differently from their psychiatrist colleagues (Beardsley, Gardocki,

Larson & Hdalgo, 1988). However, they do provide brief behavioral counseling to depressed patients, and this seems to be associated with patient use of more specific coping strategies to improve mood and with better adherence to medications (Robinson, Bush, Von Korff, Katon, Lin et al., 1995).

Pharmacological treatments for depression are common in primary care, and primary care providers prescribe the vast majority of antidepressants in the United States. There are a number of opportunities for improving outcomes related to this very common primary care treatment. One concerns the adoption of a watchful waiting strategy with patients with mild symptoms and minor impairments in functioning. Many of these patients would recover without use of antidepressant medications, and providers might feel more comfortable with not picking up the prescription pad when they are provided quantitative information about the severity of depression prior to the visit and training in using a behavior change prescription pad. Clinical pathway builders are strongly encouraged to pursue this possible intervention, as recent re-analysis of studies evaluating use of anti-depressants suggest that depressed patients who never use antidepressants are less likely to have relapse episodes of depression than patients who use antidepressant solely or in combination with psychotherapy (Zeiss, 2002).

When a patient elects to use antidepressant medications and symptom severity is consistent with medication treatment, the issue of patient adherence may be a quality improvement issue for pathway developers. Reasons for non-adherence are many. Many patients cannot afford prescribed medications. Others stall out in the pharmacy line, as they struggle privately with anxiety-producing beliefs about medication use (e.g., I should be able to get better without using drugs). Others experience side effects, stop the medicine, and fail to return to the prescriber to discuss a new plan until they are more seriously impaired by their depression. Others misunderstand provider directions, fail to refill their prescriptions, or take the medicine at inconsistently or at variable doses.

Behavioral health providers may help prescribers help patients to adhere to antidepressant treatments in several ways. Medication adherence relies on patient use of effective behavior change strategies, and behavioral health providers who provide clinical pathway services in primary care need to be the experts in behavior change technology and to share this expertise with the primary care team. Behavioral health providers can conduct functional analyses to assist with development of adherence programs for medication, as well as medical regimes. As a part of a pathway, behavioral health providers may conduct medication risk assessments and determine the level of support necessary for successful treatment.

The Medication Assessment Questionnaire is a structured interview that provides quantifiable information about risk related to patient history, preference, concern for symptoms, beliefs about medication, and reservations about side effects (Robinson, Wischman, & Del Vento, 1996). Available information suggests that use of behavioral health providers in this role and with minimal support from a liaison psychiatrist (concerning medication doses, switches, etc.) results in significant improvement in medication adherence relative to usual primary care (Katon, et al., 1996). Behavioral health consultants can also provide phone call follow-ups to depressed patients prescribed medications. Phone call follow-up may increase the probability of adherence, as well as timely switches and restarts.

Liaison psychiatrists may provide highly valuable consultation and supervision services. For behavioral health providers, they provide helpful supervision concerning medication issues. For primary care providers as well as behavioral health providers, they can provide ongoing education and training experiences. A team involving a behavioral health consultant working alongside a primary care provider (with off-site support from a liaison psychiatrist) can manage medication issues for more than 90% of depressed primary care patients. Hopefully, this team approach, along with use of empirically supported procedures that streamline the work, will lesson the burden on psychiatry, so that more of their time is available for consultation and education activities concerning primary care patients and providers.

Construction Tools

In order to build and maintain a pathway, a clinic or health care system needs to identify a group of individuals that have enthusiasm for improving care to the identified population. Hopefully, this group will include one or more opinion leaders from provider groups (behavioral health and primary care), a patient, a researcher or program evaluator, and an administrator. With this in place, the next step is to know the literature and to have tools available for the building process. The tool bag needs to include measures for many things, variation factors that are potential pathway targets, a methodology for decision-making, and training techniques.

Table 4.1 provides a list of measurement areas. The first measurement issue concerns identifying strong candidates for membership in the pathway development committee. I recommend use of a sociometric nomination method, where all clinic staff members are asked to list three coworkers they would like to see in this role. Nominations are given anonymously, and the respondent can nominate him or herself. The next step involves assessing the level of enthusiasm among providers for developing a pathway, and this information can be obtained in a satisfaction survey that is specific to depression and solicits opinions about the need for improvement. Screening is a measurement issue, and one that is often controversial (Perez-Stable, Miranda, Bunoz, & Ying, 1990; Simon & Von Korff, 1995). Many clinics will want to conduct a pilot to assess the hit rate and the impact of screening on patient flow, as well as acceptability of screening by patients and providers. Symptoms and functioning can be assessed in numerous ways. I recommend that the selected method be free, brief, simple, and sensitive to change. While a new endeavor, an attempt to anticipate and measure treatment harms is important. Preventing relapse in a recovered patient saves time, money and suffering, so measures related to development of relapse prevention plans, occurrence of support

Pathway Issue	Purpose	Specific Suggestion
Population Description	Identify Prevalence of potential high impact sub-populations of depressed patients	System Specific
Pathway Committee Membership	Identify enthusiastic and capable candidates that are recognized by peers	Sociometric nomination method
Provider Buy-in	Assess level of enthusiasm for change	Satisfaction Survey specific to providing care to depressed patients
Screening	Improve Detection	PHQ-9 Screener
Assessment of Symptoms	Improve diagnosis Improve matching of treatment to diagnosis	PHQ-9
Assessment of Functioning	Improve matching of treatment to impairment	Duke Health Profile
Treatment Effectiveness	Evaluation Decision-making concerning intensification of treatment	PHQ-9
Treatment Harms	Weigh relative risk to potential benefit	Unique to treatment
Relapse	Prevent Relapse	Measure of process variable (e.g., rate of using specific mood management skills, adherence of relapse prevention plan)
Provider Fidelity to Pathway	Assess buy-in Assess need for/impact of training	System Specific

Table 4.1. Clinical Pathway for Depression Measurement Areas.

to relapse prevention plans, and presence of relapse prevention plans in medical charts is important. Provider fidelity measures are critical to accurate pathway evaluation, and these will necessarily be system specific.

Table 4.2 provides a list of sources of variation that are possible targets for pathway intervention. Sources of variation of concern in pathway decision-making derive from providers (both primary care and behavioral health), patient, and health care system factors. For providers, sources of variation include attitudes and interests, skills, use of patient education materials and screening/assessment approaches, follow-up timelines, and rates of developing relapse prevention plans. Pathway interventions need to accommodate varying levels of interest and enthusiasm among providers. One strategy is to allow less interested primary care providers to make greater use of behavioral health consultation services and to allow more interested primary care providers to deliver more intensive behavioral interventions to depressed patients. Clinic or system-wide use of patient education materials, screening/assessment approaches, and relapse prevention formats help build consistency among providers. Depressed patients may see written materials about behavior change and medicines helpful (Robinson, Bush et al., 1997). I recommend that primary care providers be the only provider that prescribes antidepressants, even when the behavioral health consultant has prescriptive authority. The primary care provider needs to be the hub of the wheel for a pathway patient, and the behavioral health consultant needs to remain highly accessible to patients served by multiple primary care providers. System level sources of variation include the feasibility of between the primary care clinic and external mental health service delivery systems and the clinical governance structure operating in the clinic. In many cases, there will be very little service readily available from external mental health services for depressed patients. Referral to community mental health centers usually mean months of waiting for depressed patients, unless they are suicidal or homicidal. However, community mental health providers are starting to link with primary care clinics in some states, and there is potential for collaboratively developed pathway statements about use of external mental health services. In some cases, primary care clinics have staff model mental health clinics within the health care system. Formal linkage in pathway statements is more easily developed in these practice settings.

Patients themselves are tremendous sources of variation, and levels of need and depression severity are several important ones. For example, a pathway might direct patients in an initial episode who do not have strong preferences of medication treatment to the behavioral health consultant for programmatic psychological treatment. This is a reasonable decision, as patients who receive psychological treatments without adjunctive medication are less likely to have reoccurrences of depressive episodes than patients treated with medication, in solo or combined treatment. Symptom severity and functional impairment in combination with patient preference may be useful in making pathway decisions about referral of patients to the primary care behavioral health provider. Older adults may have significant functional impairment, even with more mild symptoms. Interpersonal support is a protective factor, and systematic assessment of such may be useful for decision-making, as well as for development of behavioral plans designed to

Source	Factor
Primary Care Provider and Behavioral Health Consultant (PCP and PCBHC)	Attitudes and interest in depression
PCP and PCBHC	Use of screening/assessment method
PCP and PCBHC	Skills for diagnosing and treating depression
PCP and PCBHC	Use of standardized patient education materials
PCP and PCBHC	Provision of written homework assignments
PCP and PCBHC	Buy-in to system or clinic guideline
PCP and PCBHC	Rate of developing relapse prevention plans
PCP and PCBHC	Assessment and follow-up timelines
Primary Care Provider	Rate of prescribing antidepressants
System/Clinic	Link between primary care clinic and external mental health services
System/Clinic	Clinical governance structure
Patient	Level of need (new acute, chronic)
Patient	Symptom severity
Patient	Functional impairment
Patient	Interpersonal/social support
Patient	Socioeconomic status
Patient	Attitudes toward mental health treatment
Patient	Locus of control
Patient	Level of comorbidity

Table 4.2. Sources of Variation.

improve mood. Socioeconomic status is an important factor, and many patients may be experiencing depression secondary to almost catastrophic levels of daily stress. For these patients, the pathway may suggest provider use of specific community resources. Attitudes toward mental health treatment are an important aspect of patient preferences and warrant systematic attention and thought, and language may be an important consideration. For example, many older adults will accept referral to the behavioral health consultant for discussion of life satisfaction issues, but refuse a referral for depression evaluation and treatment. Patients with greater internal locus of control tend to be more accepting of self-management strategies and more successful in using them, while patients with less internal locus of control experience more struggles with such. Co-morbidity is usually the case with depressed primary care patients, and many have multiple diagnoses on Axis I. In most cases, depression is the first diagnosis in need of treatment, and, often, other symptoms improve when depression is effectively treated.

I recommend that committee members use Eddy's principles of evidence-based medicine to guide decision making (Eddy, 1996b, pp. 252-65). These include the following.

1. Consider financial costs of interventions.
2. Set priorities.
3. It is not feasible to provide every treatment that might have some benefit.
4. The objective of health care is to maximize the health of the population served with available resources.
5. Priority of a treatment should not depend on whether a particular individual is our personal patient.
6. Priority setting relies on estimates of benefits, harms, and costs.
7. Empirical evidence takes priority in assessing benefits, harms, and costs.
8. A treatment must meet 3 criteria before being promoted for use:
   a. Compared with no treatment, treatment is effective in improving health outcomes.
   b. Compared with no treatment, benefits outweigh harms of outcomes.
   c. Compared with next best alternative treatment, the treatment is a good use of resources for the population served (principle 5).
9. Patient preferences should be sought in making judgments of benefits, harms, and costs of a treatment.
10. In determining whether a treatment satisfies principle 8, the burden of proof is on those promoting its use.

The committee will need to specify procedures for training and for evaluating training efforts. It is critical that behavioral health providers receive training that will enable them to make the numerable shifts in orientation required to embrace population-based care and primary care behavioral health. Often, behavioral health providers benefit from observing behavioral health providers working in fully integrated primary care clinics. Additionally, they benefit from mentoring experiences with more experienced primary care behavioral health providers. It is imperative that the clinic not under-train the primary care behavioral health provider because much on the success of the guideline depends not only on their ability to deliver treatments that are often new to them but to provide ongoing consultative learning experiences for the primary care providers.

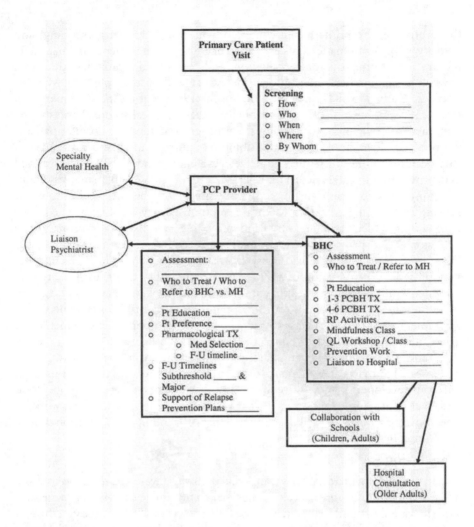

Figure 4.1. Primary Care Depression Pathway Worksheet.

Figure 4.1 is a worksheet that will help the committee systematically address some of the who, what, when, and by whom issues. In most clinics, the pathway team will include a primary care clinical provider, a primary care behavioral health consultant, a nurse or nursing assistant, and a medical receptionist. Some systems will be able to access psychiatry services by phone and/or receive educational presentations on medications from psychiatrists at the clinic or through tele-medicine presentations. In most pathways, primary care clinical providers will deliver all ongoing clinical management services, including assessment, patient education, brief behavioral interventions (e.g., behavioral activation, problem-solving), and prescribing. Behavioral health provider services may include all of those provided by primary care clinical providers (other than prescribing) and delivery of programmatic services, adherence-related assessment and planning, registry monitoring, outcome evaluation, and primary care provider education. Several programmatic interventions are available (For example, see Mynors-Wallace, Gath, Lloyd-Thomas, & Tomlinson, 1995; Robinson, Wishman, Del Vento, 1996; Robinson, 1996). Additionally, behavioral health consultants may be requested to collaborate with schools, employers and medical hospital patients (particularly older adults). The responsibilities of nurses and nursing assistants will vary from site to site. Nurses may be active in evaluation and training efforts, as well as in providing clinical services (Hunkeler, Meresman et al., 2000). In many systems, screening for depression and ongoing assessment will be the responsibility of nursing and nursing assistants. Medical receptionists may assist with scheduling, maintaining a depression registry, and providing call sheets for primary care behavioral health providers and for primary care providers (concerning, for example, failed prescription refills). Liaison psychiatrists or psychiatric nurse practitioners may provide a combination of off-site and on-site consultation to primary care providers and behavioral health consultants and provide regular educational presentations and/or materials on antidepressant treatments. This is by no means a complete list of the various tasks that are involved in support and implementation of a guideline. It is intended to help the reader get started.

Table 4.3 provides a list of possible recommendations for pathway treatment of depressed primary care patients. In order to select the best options from this table, pathway developers may need to obtain data that describe their clinic population and to conduct simple pilots to see what is feasible in their clinic. What works in one clinic may not work well in another. This list is intended to be inspirational, not comprehensive.

Conclusion

In conclusion, there are a few things that pathway developers need to avoid and a few they need to be sure to seek out in order to maximize successful experiences. Both lists are short, and I will start with the things to avoid. First, the greatest mistake a clinic can make in developing a clinical pathway for depressed patients is that of failing to start. Without starting, one cannot learn from successes or mistakes. Once started, other factors come into play. If support from clinic and medical group leadership is only lukewarm, the pathway will have a bumpy course (Fischer, 2001). Ideally, clinicians will perceive an almost urgent need for a new care system for depressed patients prior to the start of the pathway. The pathway committee can help create this by their initial educational efforts and pilot studies. Another predictor of poor pathway performance is the development of initiatives that are seen as too complex (Fischer, 2001) and that impede patient flow. Finally, a disconnect between the pathway committee and other clinical providers will result in implementation problems. The committee wants to avoid being seen as a bunch of cheerleaders that do not understand the front line, and the best insurance for this is thoughtful selection of committee members (using methods mentioned earlier).

1. This clinic will screen passively for depression in primary care by displaying exam room posters that educate patients about symptoms of depression and encourage discussion with the primary care provider.
2. Providers in this clinic will use the same interview (or screening or assessment) approach (e.g., SPACE DIGS, PHQ-9).
3. Primary care providers will refer patients preferring medication treatment to the behavioral health consultant for a structured antidepressant adherence risk assessment prior to start of antidepressant therapy.
4. All depressed patients presenting to this primary care clinic will be treated here unless they prefer external treatment for fail to respond to clinic pathway treatments.
5. This clinic will provide brief primary care behavioral health programmatic service of a psychological nature to patients with major depression who prefer bahavioral treatment to medication treatment.
6. This clinic will offer frail elderly patients who are demoralized by health problems and loss of quality of life the option of a group model of care that combines medical and behavioral health care.
7. This clinic will provide a brief, psychoeducational Quality of Life on an ongoing basis class for primary care patients with mild symptoms of depression, particularly patients with chronic medical illnesses.
8. This clinic will use the Geriatric Depression Inventory to screen hospitalized older adults for depression prior to discharge.
9. Providers in this clinic will offer older medical inpatients that screen positive for depression a consultation visit with the primary care behavioral health consultant.

Table 4.3. Examples of depression pathway statements.

Beyond having the courage to start and persist in this daunting process, several other factors enhance the likelihood of successful pathway development and implementation. Reorganizing to a model of care that supports pathway implementation is of critical importance. The model that is most likely to provide optimal support and to be sustainable is that of the Primary Care Behavioral Health Model (Strosahl, 1996; 1997). In this model, part of the burden associated with pathway implementation can be shifted to the on-site behavioral health consultant that works as an auxiliary primary care team member. This greatly enhances the feasibility of providing more psychological interventions for primary care patients, and this is a critical part of improving outcomes. Providers also need ongoing training in the new model of care and in all aspects of implementing the clinical pathway. There is a tremendous tendency for all providers—primary care and behavioral health—to return to what is familiar, even if it works poorly. Additionally, selected process and outcome variables need ongoing monitoring, and providers need to hear about findings on a regular basis. Another factor is that of the form of clinical governance operating in the clinic. There is a significant variation in governance, and some forms are more supportive of pathway development and implementation than others. McColl and Roland, M. (2000) offer guidance on developing optimal clinical governance systems. A final must is that of involving one or more patients in the pathway design and implementation process—after all, this is really all about the patient.

References

Agency for Health Care Policy and Research. National Guideline Clearinghouse. See www.guideline.gov. Barrett, Barrett, Oxman, & Gerber (1998)

Beardsley, R, Gardocki, G., Larson, D., & Hidalgo, J. (1988). Prescribing of psychotropic medication by primary care physicians and psychiatrists. *Archives of General Psychiatry, 45*, 1117-1119.

Birnbaum, H. G., Greenberg, P. E., Barton, M., Kessler, R. C., Rowland, C. R., & Williamson, T. E. (1999). Workplace burden of depression: A case study in social functioning using employer claims data. *Drug Benefit Trends, 11 (8),* 6BH-12BH.

Blumenthal, J. A., et al. (1999). Effects of exercise training on older patients with major depression. *Archives of Internal Medicine, 159*, 2349-2356

Callahan, C. M., Hui, S. L., Nienaber, N. A., Musick, B. S., & Tierney, W. M. (1994). Longitudinal study of depression and health services use among elderly primary care patients. *Journal of the American Geriatrics Society, 42*, 833–838.

Callahan, C. M., Kesterson, J. G., & Tierney, W. M. (1997). Association of symptoms of depression with diagnostic test charges among older adults. *Annals of Internal Medicine, 126*, 417-425.

Callahan, C. M., & Wolinsky, F. D. (1995). Hospitalization for major depression among older Americans. *Journals of Gerontology. Series A, Biological Sciences and Medical Sciences, 50*, M196–M202.

Cassem, E. H. (1995). Depressive disorders in the medically ill: An overview. *Psychosomatics, 36*, S2-S10.

Cooper-Patrick, L., Crum, R. M., & Ford, D. E. (1994). Characteristics of patients with major depression who received care in general medical and specialty mental health settings. *Medical Care, 32*, 15–24.

Cummings, N. (1993). Somatization: When physical symptoms have no medical cause. In Goleman, D. & Gurin, J. (Eds.), *Mind Body Medicine*. New York: Consumers Union.

Cummings, N., & VandenBos G. (1981). The twenty years Kaiser-Permanent experience with psychotherapy and medical utilization: Implications for national health policy and national health insurance. *Health Policy Quarterly, 1*,159-175.

Depression Guideline Panel. *Depression in primary care. Clinical practice guideline, No. 5.* Rockville, MD: U.S. Department of Health Human Services, Public Health Service, Agency for Health Care Policy and Research; April, 1993. AHCPR publication no. 93-0551.

Eddy, D. M., Hasselblad, V., & Shachter, R. (1992). *Meta-analysis by the confidence profile method: The statistical synthesis of evidence.* Boston: Academic Press.

Eddy, D. M. (1996a). *Clinical decision making from theory to practice: A collection of essays from the Journal of the American Medical Association.* Sudbury, MA: Jones and Bartlett.

Eddy D. M. (1996b). Benefit language: Criteria that will improve quality while reducing costs. *Journal of the American Medical Association, 275(8)*: 650-657.

Epstein R. M. (1995). Communication between primary care physicians and consultants. *Archives of Family Medicine, 4(5)*:403-9.

Gallo, J. J., & Rabins, P. V. (1999). Depression without sadness: Alternative presentations of depression in late life. *American Family Physician,* http://www.aafp.org/afp/990901ap/820.html

Hayami, D. E., & Freeborn, K. K. (1981). Effect of coverage on use of an HMO alcoholism treatment program, outcomes, and medical care utilization. *American Journal of Public Health, 71,* 1133-1143.

Hayes, S., Strosahl, K., & Wilson, K. (1999). *Acceptance and commitment therapy: An experiential approach to behavior change.* New York, NY: The Guilford Press

Hays, R. D., Wells, K. B., Sherbourne, C. D., Rogers, W., & Spritzer, K. (1995). Functioning and well-being outcomes of patients with depression compared with chronic general medical illnesses. *Archives of General Psychiatry, 52,* 11-9.

Hoffman, C., Rice, D., & Sung, H. Y. P. (1996). Persons with chronic conditions. *Journal of the American Medical Association, 276,* 1473-1479.

Holder, H. D., & Blose, J. O. (1986). Alcoholism treatment and total health care utilization and costs: A four-year longitudinal analysis of federal employees. *Journal of the American Medical Association, 2567,* 1456-1460.

Hunkeler, E., Meresman, J., Hargreaves, W., Fireman, B., Berman, W. H., Kirsch, A., et al. (2000). Efficacy of nurse telehealth care and peer support in augmenting treatment of depression in primary care. *Archives of Family Medicine, 9*:700-708

Katon, W., Von Korff, M., Lin, E., Bush, T., Lipscomb, P., & Russo, J. (1992). A randomized trial of psychiatric consultation with distressed high utilizers. *General Hospital Psychiatry, 14,* 86-98.

Katon, W., Von Korff, M., Lin, E., Walker, E., Simon, G., Bush, T., et al. (1995). Collaborative management to achieve treatment guidelines: Impact on depression in primary care. *Journal of the American Medical Association, 273,* 1026-1031.

Katon, W., Robinson, P., Von Korff, M., Lin, E., Bush, T., Ludman, E., Simon, G., & Walker, E. (1996). A multifaceted intervention to improve treatment of depression in primary care. *Archives of General Psychiatry, 53*, 924-932.

McColl, M. R., & Roland, M. (2000). Clinical governance in primary care: Knowledge and information for clinical governance. *British Medical Journal, 321*, 871-874.

Miranda, J., Hohman, A. A., Attkisson, C. C. & Larson, D. B. (Eds.). (1994). *Mental disorders in primary care*. San Francisco: Jossey-Bass.

Mumford, E., Schlesinger, H., Glass, G., Patrick, C., & Cuerdon, T. (1984). A new look at evidence about reduced cost of medical utilization following mental health treatment. *American Journal of Psychiatry, 141*, 1145-1149.

Munoz, R. F., Ying, Y. W., Bernal, G., Perez-Stable, E. J., Sorensen, J. L., Hargreaves, et al. (1995). Prevention of depression with primary care patients: A randomized controlled trial. *American Journal of Community Psychology, 23*, 199–222.

Mynors-Wallace, L., Gath, D. H.., Lloyd-Thomas, A. R., & Tomlinson, D. (1995). Randomized controlled trial comparing problem solving treatment with amitriptyline and placebo for major depression in primary care. *British Medical Journal, 310,* 441-446.

Mynors-Wallis, L. M., Davies, I., Gray, A., Gath, D. H., & Barbour, F. (1997). Randomised controlled trial and cost analysis of problem-solving treatment for emotional disorders by community nurses in primary care. *British Medical Journal, 170*: 113-119.

Mynors-Wallis, L. M., Gath, D. H., Day, A., & Baker, F. (2000). Randomised controlled trial of problem solving treatment, antidepressant medication, and combined treatment for major depression in primary care. *British Medical Journal, 320*: 26-30.

Narrow, W. Reiger, D., Rae, D., Manderscheid, R. & Locke, B. (1993). Use of services by persons with mental and addictive disorders: Findings from the National Institute of Mental Health Epidemiologic Catchment Area Program. *Archives of General Psychiatry, 50*, 95-107.

National Institutes of Health. (1995). *Disease-specific estimates of direct and indirect costs of illness and NIH support*. Bethesda, MD: Office of the Director.

Olfson, M., Sing, M., & Schlesinger. (2001). Mental health / medical care cost offsets: Opportunities for managed care. http://www.projhope.org/HA/bonus/180209.htm; 12/30/00, 1-9.

Ornstein, R., & Sobel, D. (1988). *The Healing Brain*. New York: Simon & Schuster.

Ornstein, R., & Sobel, D. (1990). *Healthy Pleasures*. Reading, Mass: Addison-Wesley.

Parkerson, G. R. Jr., Broadhead, W. E., Tse, C.-K.J. (1990). The Duke Health Profile, a 17-item measure of health and dysfunction. *Medical Care, 28*, 1056-1072.

Pautler, T. (1991). A Cost-effective mind-body approach to psychosomatic disorders. In Anchor. K. N. (Ed.), *Handbook of medical psychotherapy: Cost-effective strategies in mental health*. New York: Hogrefe & Huber.

Perez-Stable, E. J., Miranda, J., Bunoz, R. J., & Ying, Y. W. (1990) Depression in medical outpatients: Underrecognition and misdiagnosis. *Archives of Internal Medicine, 150*, 1083-1088.

Practice Trends. (1997). AHCPR moves on. *Family Practice News*, April 15, 70.

Reiger, D. A., Goldberg, I. D., & Taube, C. A. (1978). The de facto US mental health services system: A public health perspective. *Archives of General Psychiatry, 41*, 934-941.

Regier, D. A., Narrow, W. E., Rae, D. S., Manderscheid, R. W., Locke, B. Z., & Goodwin, F. K. (1993). The de facto US mental and addictive disorder service system: Epidemiologic Catchment Area prospective 1-year prevalence rates of disorders and services. *Archives of General Psychiatry, 50*, 85-94.

Robins, L. N., & Regier, D. A. (1991). *Psychiatric disorders in America: The epidemiologic catchment area study*. New York: Free Press, 1991.

Robinson, P., Bush, T., Von Korff, M., Katon, W., Lin, E., Simon, G.E., & Walker, E. (1995). Primary care physician use of cognitive behavioral techniques with depressed patients. *Journal of Family Practice, 40 (4)*, 352-357.

Robinson, P. (1996). *Living life well: New strategies for hard times*. Reno, NV: Context Press.

Robinson, P., Wischman, C., & Del Vento, A. (1996). *Treating depression in primary care: A manual for primary care and mental health providers*. Reno, NV: Context Press.

Robinson, P., Bush, T., Von Korff, M., Katon, W., Lin, E., Simon, G. E., & Walker, E. (1997). The education of depressed primary care patients: What do patients think of interactive booklets and a video? *Journal of Family Practice, 44*, 562-571. (Add in text)

Robinson, P., Del Vento, A., & Wischman, C. (1998). Integrated treatment of the frail elderly: The group care clinic. In Blount, S. (Ed.), *Integrated Care: The Future of Medical and Mental Health Collaboration*, (pp.), New York: Norton.

Robinson, P. (2002). Treating depression in primary care: What are the cost-offset opportunities? In Cummings, N. A., O'Donohoe, W. T., & Ferguson, K. (Eds.), *Impact of medical cost offset on practice and research: Making it work for you*. Reno, NV: Context Press.

Robinson, P. (unpublished manuscript). Acceptance and commitment therapy with chronic pain patients.

Sackett D. L., Rosenberg, W. M. C., Muir Gray, J. A., Haynes, R.B., & Richardson, W. S. (1996). Evidence-based medicine: What it is and what it isn't. *British Medical Journal, 312*, 71-72.

Schulberg, H. C., Block, M. R., & Madonia, M. J. (1996). Treating major depression in primary care practice. Eight-month clinical outcomes. *Archives of General Psychiatry, 53*, 913-919.

Simon, G. E., & Von Korff, M. (1995). Recognition, management, and outcomes of depression in primary care. *Archives of Family Medicine, 4*, 99-105.

Smith, G. R., Rost, K., & Kashner, T. M. (1995). A trial of the effect of a standardized psychiatric consultation on health outcomes and costs in somatizing patients, *Archives of General Psychiatry, 52*, 238-243.

Spitzer, R. L., Kroenke, K., Linzer, M., Hahn, S. R., Williams, J. B., & deGruy, F. V. (1995). Health-related quality of life in primary care patients with mental disorders. Results from the PRIME-MD 1000 Study. *Journal of the American Medical Association, 274*, 1511-7.

Strosahl, K. (1994). New dimensions in behavioral health primary care integration. *HMO Practice, 8*, 176-179.

Strosahl, K. (1996a). Primary mental health care: A new paradigm for achieving health and behavioral health integration. *Behavioral Healthcare Tomorrow, 5*, 93-96.

Strosahl, K. (1996b). Confessions of a behavior therapist in primary care: The Odyssey and the ecstasy. *Cognitive and Behavioral Practice, 3*, 1-28.

Strosahl, K. (1997). Building primary care behavioral health systems that work: A compass and a horizon. In N. Cummings, J. Cummings & J. Johnson (Eds.), *Behavioral health in primary care: A guide for clinical integration* (pp. 37-68). Madison, CN: Psychosocial Press.

Strosahl, K., Baker, N., Braddick, M., Stuart, M., & Handley, M. (1997). Integration of behavioral health and primary care services: The Group Health Cooperative Model (pp. 61-86). In N. Cummings, J. Cummings & J. Johnson (Eds.), *Behavioral health in primary care: A guide for clinical integration.* Madison, CN: Psychosocial Press.

Strosahl, K. (1998). Integration of primary care and behavioral health services: The Primary Mental Health Care Model. In A. Blount (Ed.), *Integrative primary care: The future of medical and mental health collaboration* (pp. 43-56). New York: Norton, Inc.

Teasdale, J. D., Segal, Z. V., Williams, M. G., Ridgeway, V. A., Soulsby, J. M., Lau, M. A. (2000). Prevention of Relapse/Recurrence in Major Depression by Mindfulness-Based Cognitive Therapy. *Journal of Consulting and Clinical Psychology, 68*, 615-623.

Unutzer, J., Katon, W. J., Simon, G., Walker, E. A., Grembowski, D., & Patrick, D. (1996). Depression, quality of life, and use of health services in primary care patients over 65: A 4-year prospective study. *Psychosomatics, 37*, 35.

Von Korff, M., Katon, W., Simon, G., Lin, E., Bush, T., & Ludman, E. (1998). "Treatment Costs, Cost Offset, and Cost-Effectiveness of Collaborative Management of Depression." *Psychosomatic Medicine, 60*, 143-149.

Wells, K., Steward, A., Hays, R.., Burnam, M., Rogers, W., Daniels, M., et al. (1989). The functioning and well being of depressed patients: Results from the Medical Outcomes Study. *Journal of the American Medical Association, 262*, 914-919.

Zeiss, A. (2002). Moderator on panel discussion of new data on depression treatments. *Association for the Advancement of Behavior Therapy*, Reno, NV.

Zimmerman, M., & Mattia, J. I. (2000) Principal and additional DSM-IV disorders for which outpatients seek treatment. *Psychiatric Services, 51(10)*, 1299- 1304.

Integrated Care and The High Utilizer:
An Explication of Medical Usage Patterns
and the Role in the Healthcare Crisis

Michael A. Cucciare & William O'Donohue

Spiraling health care costs are arguably the largest problem facing the U.S. health care system. Our nation is currently facing an economic health care crisis consisting of escalating costs, limited access to resources, and the prospect of an aging segment of the population suffering from multiple chronic medical conditions that will result in even a larger demand for health care services (Friedman, Sobel, Myers, Caudill, & Benson, 1995).

One of the major factors contributing to increasing cost of health care is revealed when examining utilization patterns. More specifically, what has become overwhelmingly evident is that medical expenditures are highly concentrated in a relatively small segment of individuals (Ash, Zhao, Ellis & Kramer, 2001; Anderson & Knickman, 1984; Liptzin, Regier, & Goldberg, 1980). Berk & Monheit (2001) reported that the most costly 1% of the population accounted for 27% of health care costs in 1996; the most costly 5% consumed 55%; and the top 10% consumed 69%. Ash et al. (2001) remind us that these costly subgroups do not necessarily consist of the same individuals consuming large amounts of health care resources year after year. In contrast, individuals can move in and out of high cost groups.

As a general rule, 20% of the population is consuming 80% of the health care resources. However, these figures differ among surveys. Ash and colleagues reported that the top (most expensive) 20% accounted for 88% of the total health care expenditures in 1998. Of the 2 ½ million people taken into consideration, the top 7% cost more than $5,000 each, the top 3% cost more than $10,000, and the top .8% cost more than $25,000 for 1998. In addition to a relatively small subset of the population using a greater proportion of health care resources, Berk & Monheit (2001) report that the top 10% of U.S. health care consumers are using more services every year. For example, the top 10% in 1969 accounted for 59% of total medical expenditures with that number increasing to 69% in 1996.

The percentages presented above translate into enormous costs for our health care system. Historically, this increase in costs has resulted in the use of incentives (by some managed care companies) that place limits on the availability of certain types of health care services (e.g., MRI). Logically, it would then make sense to find that the individuals in the top percentages, covered by these organizations, would demonstrate less consumption of certain health care services when compared to the top groups in more traditional indemnity health plans. However, this is not the case. More specifically, there appears to be no statistically significant differences in whether an individual belongs to an HMO or other managed care plans, and those in traditional indemnity plans with regard to both the percentages of spending by the top groups and their average yearly expenditures (Berk & Monheit, 2001). For example, Berk & Monheit reported that the most costly 5% spent an average of $17,828; the top 10% spent $11,274; and the top 30% spent $5,071 in 1996 when averaged across plan type with no statistically significant differenced across plan type. With the double digit rises in health care costs in each of the last several years, the actual dollar costs of these highest utilizers are much higher than these 1998 figures.

Furthermore, when compared to the least expensive 50% of health care consumers these numbers become even more striking. Specifically, the same study reported that the bottom 50% of health care consumers accounted for approximately 5% of total health care expenditures with an average yearly cost of $165/year per individual.

Who are High Utilizers: Issues in Definition and Chronic Conditions?

Where is the money being spent or more specifically, who are the high utilizers and what services do they utilize the most? Epidemiological research consistently demonstrates a strong positive correlation between health care service utilization and the presence of many chronic psychological and medical conditions (Liptzin et al., 1980). For instance, a variety of affective, anxiety, somatoform, psychotic, and substance abuse disorders have been linked to the amount and types of health care an individual uses (Schmitz & Kruse, 2002; Kapur, Young, & Murata, 2001). Furthermore, chronic medical conditions such as diabetes, asthma, and Alzheimer's disease have been associated with high consumption of health care services (Ash et al., 2001; Fredericks, Fisher, Buchanan, & Luevano, 2002).

Ash et al. (2001) examined the prevalence of diabetes, congestive heart failure (CHF), asthma, and chronic obstructive pulmonary disease (COPD) in a group of high utilizers. They found that 28% had diabetes, 20% had CHF, and 16% had asthma and/or COPD. Furthermore, these prevalence rates translated into substantial proportions of the total health care expenditures for those in the high utilizer group. Those diagnosed with diabetes accounted for 20% of the total health care expenditures associated with this group. Furthermore, individuals in these disease groups were observed to incur yearly health care costs of as much as 15 to 21 times the population average of $1,651.

Age has been associated with high medical utilization. In one study, the elderly made up 46.3% of the top 1% of high utilizers (Monheit & Berk, 2001). One explanation for this finding is that elderly patients suffering from chronic medical conditions often require more extensive and costly treatment than younger individuals. For example, per capita U. S. health care costs in 1997 were $1,286 for individuals under 65, $5,360 for individuals between 65 and 85, and $9,000 for those over 85 (Butler, Lewis, & Sunderland, 1998). In addition, individuals over the age of 85 have the highest incidence of Alzheimer's disease (AD), which is the third most expensive disease (cancer and cardiac disease are more expensive) to treat in the U.S. (National Alzheimer's Association). The treatment of AD results in $80 to $100 billion in annual costs and the number is expected to double over the next twenty years (Butler et al., 1998).

The presence or absence of a chronic psychological condition has been shown to be strongly associated with high utilization of expensive health care services. Several researchers have examined medical usage patterns and have found that inpatient treatment services account for a large portion of health care costs. Kapur et al. (2000) examined health care expenditure patterns of a group of high utilizers between the ages of 18 and 64. The study presented utilization data for the years of 1992 and 1993. Individuals presented in the study were considered to be high utilizers if they fit two criteria: (1) their cost for the previous 5 years had to average over $30,000 in health care expenditures per year and (2) they had to be among the most costly 15%. The researchers found that of the 1956 individuals examined, 83% were found to use some form of mental health and substance abuse treatment service (e.g., inpatient and/or outpatient treatment) with a mean cost per individual of $25,294 per year. The mean inpatient cost was reported to be $22,852 with mean outpatient costs reported to be $2,755 per year per individual. The distribution of health care expenditures presented in this study demonstrates that a large proportion of health care dollars are being used to pay for inpatient services. Furthermore, individuals with mental health needs tended to be the highest users of inpatient services.

Other research has supported the link between the presence of chronic psychological conditions and emergency room visits. Hu and Rush (1995) examined expenditure patterns of 8,348 individuals in an inpatient facility that had depression (e.g., dysthymia, bipolar, etc.) as their primary diagnosis. The researchers found that among individuals diagnosed with major depression, one out of 10 episodes of treatment involved an emergency room visit with the number doubling among those diagnosed with bipolar disorder. Inpatient treatment episodes ranged from $2,501 for those diagnosed with major depression to $2,971 for those diagnosed with bipolar disorder. Clearly, inpatient services account for a large proportion of health care expenditures among those diagnosed with chronic psychological conditions, particularly, depressive disorders.

What Can Result in High Utilization: Pathways to Unnecessary Utilization?

The presence and absence of symptoms alone plays a small role in an individual's decision to seek help from a health care provider (Friedman et al., 1995). The presence of psychosocial factors has been found to contribute greatly to an individual's decision to seek contact with a health care provider. Friedman et al. discuss several psychosocial pathways that contribute to an individual's decision to seek medical attention.

1. Information and decision support pathway. This pathway is predicated upon the fact that many patients are passive consumers of medical services. Historically, the medical community has fostered a dependency on the part of the patient to find a provider who will then diagnose and treat their condition. This has resulted in many unnecessary physician visits. Many of these unnecessary visits are due to a lack of information regarding self-management and of the appropriate use of the health care system. Many medical conditions can be self-managed without the assistance of a health care provider. Therefore, teaching patients how to effectively discriminate between conditions requiring medical assistance and those that can be self-managed is becoming increasingly important. Informing patients about their medical problems, appropriate self-management of these problems, and treatment options can result in less costly (and more appropriate) utilization of the health care system.

2. Psychophysiological pathway. There is a growing literature documenting the relationship between stress and the development and maintenance of many chronic medical conditions (Lorig, Mazonson, & Holman, 1993). Teaching patients how to effectively cope with everyday stress can have profound effects on managing chronic illness, medical procedures, and a variety of other life problems.

3. Behavior change pathway. There is no doubt that an individual's lifestyle habits can contribute to the development of many chronic medical conditions. How individuals eat, drink, use prescribed and illicit drugs, and engage in regular physical activity can have a major impact on their health. Changing behavioral habits related to these issues can have important and long-lasting effects on a person's health and subsequent medical utilization. Psychosocial interventions such as psycheducational groups that teach skills focused on lifestyle changes, smoking cessation, and substance abuse treatment can have an important impact on how a person consumes health care services.

4. Social support pathway. It is common for many patients confronting medical problems to do so without sufficient social support. Also, many patients with a social support network feel isolated when confronting certain medical problems. This results in many of these patients entering the health care system to not only gain access to medical services but to access social support from medical providers. Providing social support through peer-led groups, and teaching skills to maximize natural support can result in improved overall health and more appropriate use of many health care services.

5. Undiagnosed psychological problem pathway. Many patients presenting with physical symptoms have undiagnosed psychological conditions such as depression and anxiety. Because of high prevalence rates, failure to appropriately diagnose and treat these conditions can have a profound economic impact on our health care system. Increased training on appropriate diagnosis and treatment such as the use of many relatively less expensive psychological treatments (e.g., groups, individual psychotherapy, etc.) can result in less utilization of medical services.

6. Somatization pathway. Many patients presenting with frequent bodily complaints may be suffering from significant emotional distress. This emotional distress can be expressed through physical symptoms. These individuals often consume high amounts of physician visits that result in expensive diagnostic and treatment procedures that fail to provide any relief from emotional distress. Psychological consultation along with development and training of quick and useful diagnostic procedures that identify this psychological condition can result in less utilization of health care services.

There are several additional factors that may play a substantial role in impacting high health care utilization. Some of these include:

1. One's beliefs/skills regarding seeking medical services. An individual's beliefs regarding when to see a medical professional can play a role in when they feel it is appropriate to seek medical services. For example, some individuals may respond to physical symptoms by "toughing it out". This might translate into a person feeling that it is only appropriate to see a medical professional when their physical symptoms have worsened, which can result in making some medical conditions more difficult (and expensive) to treat. Others may have problems denoting the level/intensity of care they need or timing their visits so that they are less expensive (e.g., urgent care vs. emergency room).

2. Time availability. A person's daily routine and work schedule can impact their decision to seek medical services. For example, individuals who work inflexible (e.g., find it difficult to leave the office) and large amounts of hours each week may be less likely to seek medical services than someone who works in a more flexible environment.

3. Disease management. The management of chronic medical conditions is likely to play a crucial role in high health care consumption. Some of these factors may include monitoring and engaging in exercise, appropriate dietary decisions, and early symptom detection associated with many chronic conditions.

Can Unnecessary High Utilization be Treated: A Review of the Outcome Literature?

A number of recent studies have examined the impact of psychosocial interventions on health care utilization (Guthrie et al., 1999; Simon et al., 2001; McLeod, Budd, & McClelland, 1997). Commonly, these research programs focus on reducing the cost of health care utilization via the development of psychosocial intervention programs (e.g., individual psychotherapy, psycheducational groups, bibliotherapy concerned with disease management, etc.) for a variety of psychological conditions.

For example, integrated health care programs that effectively identify and treat the somatizer have been shown to significantly reduce the use of medical services among individuals presenting with medically unidentified physical complaints. Cummings (in press) argues that somatization commonly skews health care utilization and therefore, developing appropriate programs for the somatizer is becoming increasingly important. It is important to note that Cummings (1997b) defines the somatization as the "translation of emotional problems into physical symptoms, or the exacerbation of a disease by emotional factors or stress (p. 4)." This definition is not to be confused with the DSM-IV diagnosis of Somatoform Disorder.

Cummings, Kahn, and Sparkman (1962) investigated the impact of psychotherapy on the utilization of outpatient and inpatient medical services (e.g., visits
to health care clinics, outpatient laboratory visits, x-ray procedures, and number of
days hospitalized). The researchers hypothesized a reduction in medical service
utilization upon patients receiving psychotherapy. Psychotherapy included any
contact with the Department of Psychiatry at Kaiser Permanente. The investigators
found that medical utilization was reduced by as much as 62% over the 5 years
following the introduction of the intervention.

Cummings has continued to examine the impact of psychosocial interventions
on health care utilization. In the 1980's, Cummings was awarded an 8 million dollar
federal grant to investigate these effects on the entire Medicaid population on the
Island of Oahu (also known as the Hawaii Medicaid Study) (Cummings, 1997b;
Cummings (in press); O'Donohue, Ferguson, & Cummings, 2002). 36,000 Medicaid eligible participants and 90,000 federal employees were randomly assigned to
an experimental and control group. The experimental group received behavioral
health care through Biodyne Centers. These centers were developed specifically for
the study and provided focused psychotherapy interventions. Participants in the
control group were eligible for 52 annual sessions by community practitioner of
their choice.

Prior to the beginning of the study, psychotherapists participated in 6 months
of training with the objective of standardizing treatment delivery. Psychotherapists
participated in ongoing quality assurance and supervision to monitor adherence in
the delivery of empirically supported interventions.

High utilizers were chosen every month. Criteria for high utilization consisted
of being in the top 15% of users of health care services that accounted for 80% of
Medicaid's costs for that month. High utilizers were chosen based on their frequency
of visits to a health care professional. The high utilizer group consisted of those
suffering from a variety of chronic medical conditions including diabetes, hypertension, and rheumatoid arthritis. High utilizers were recruited into psychosocial
programs through an aggressive outreach protocol consisting of mail, telephone, and
house calls by registered nurses.

Treatment consisted of focused psychotherapy. An intake appointment was
conducted to identify the psychological problem. Participants were then assigned
to one of 68 treatment protocols focusing on different psychological problems (e.g.,
somatization). The treatment protocols were psychosocial in nature and for the most
part, run in groups consisting of 5 to 12 individuals. For example, somatizers entered
a group treatment program consisting of 20 group sessions over a 6-month period.
Participants were required to attend every session and to complete any assigned
homework. Treatment groups consisted of a combination of psychotherapy and
psycheducational information pertaining to the particular problem of the individual. For example, for somatizers, information about how stress can manifest as
physical symptoms was provided. Homework was tailored to the individual needs
of the client. Homework often consisted of readings, charting events associated with

the urge to see medical professional, and practicing alternatives to seeking medical attention in response to stress.

The results of the study demonstrated that the costs of developing the behavioral health care system were offset by the reduction in medical service utilization within 18 months. In addition, Cummings (1997b) found a continued reduction in health care service utilization without the continued use of the behavioral health care program. In contrast, an increase of 17% in service utilization was observed in the control group and a 27% increase in the control group who received no services at all.

As said earlier, a large proportion of patients utilization high amounts of medical services present with physical complaints that have no identifiable medical etiology. These individuals commonly utilize large amounts of expensive medical services; therefore, developing adjunctive (to primary care) programs has grown increasingly important. McLeod et al. (1997) conducted a randomized controlled study to evaluate the effectiveness of a 6-week behavioral medicine intervention designed to provide adjunctive treatment to primary care for individuals experiencing physical symptoms with no identified medical etiology.

A total of 81 participants were included in the study 38 participated in the treatment group and 44 were placed in a wait-list control group. Participants were recruited from a behavioral medicine program at a large health care organization. Primary care physicians referred participants to the study whom they believed were experiencing physical symptoms at least partially due to their emotional status.

The 6-week behavioral intervention consisted of weekly classes that included homework assignments, readings, meditation, classroom exercises and coaching, and out-of-class discussions with study partners. Trained leaders led the group from a variety of fields including: nursing, social work, psychology, and medicine. The main objectives of the group were to assist participants in building skills to better recognize their recurrent moods and physiological states. This was accomplished by engaging in meditation and a variety of class exercises. More specifically, by intervening on problematic behaviors and physiological states, emotional distress and physical distress was observed to diminish. Participants would then be able to engage in more adaptive ways of behaving and feeling. The wait-list control group began treatment approximately one month after the treatment group completed the 6-week course.

Participants were required to complete the Symptom Checklist 90 revised, which assesses levels of distress associated with a variety of both physical and psychological symptoms (e.g., somatization, depression, and anxiety). These three scales were of particular interest to the authors given that high utilizers of health care services often report high levels of symptoms in these domains. Assessments were conducted one-week prior and one-week after the completion of the 6-session class. Follow-up assessment was conducted 6 months post treatment completion.

Results showed that the 38 individuals in the treatment group had significantly lower scores on the depression, anxiety, and somatization subscales of the SCL-90-R when compared to the 44 individuals in the wait-list control group. Furthermore, for those in the treatment group, the significant decreases in these anxiety, depression, and somatization were maintained at 6 month follow-up.

Guthrie et al. (1999) conducted a randomized controlled trial to compare the effectiveness of a brief psychodynamic-interpersonal therapy plus treatment as usual to a control group receiving treatment as usual among patients who are high utilizers of psychiatric services. Specifically, they compared the impact of these two treatments on psychological symptoms, health status, quality of life, and health care costs.

The study took place in two large hospitals and included 110 patients. Patients who had been receiving treatment for longer than 6 months were invited to participate in the study by their psychiatrists. Participants were eligible who were (1) between the ages of 18-65 and (2) had not experienced any improvement in psychological symptoms during the duration of psychiatric treatment. Persons suffering from schizophrenia, dementia, brain damage, and learning difficulties were excluded from the study.

Upon entry into the study, psychological symptoms were assessed using the Schedules for Clinical Assessment in Neuropsychiatry that are based on the criteria set forth in the International Classification for Diseases, 10th Revision (ICD-10). Several self-report assessments were used as outcome measures including: the Global Severity Index and depression subscale of the Symptom Checklist-90-Revised were used to assess symptomology (patients scores of $< .75$ were considered to have mild depression; .75 to 1.75 moderate depression; and 1.75 to 4.0 severe depression) and the 36-item Short-Form Health Survey and The EuroQol 5D were used to assess quality of life. Participants in the study were required to complete these measures at the start, end, and at 6 months following the end of treatment.

Each participant provided health care utilization data (i.e., self-report) at 3 months prior to entry into the study, at the 8-week intervention period, and at a 6-month follow-up appointment. Health care utilization data included inpatient and day patient stays, outpatient visits, and accident and emergency visits. Additionally, primary and community care services including visits to the family physician and in-home care services, day centers, alternative therapy, and medication were collected.

The psychotherapy intervention consisted of 8 weekly sessions of a manualized brief psychodynamic-interpersonal therapy. A clinical psychologist or psychiatric trainee conducted each psychotherapy session. Participants in the treatment-as-usual condition continued to receive outpatient treatment from their psychiatrist. This included continued monitoring of medication effectiveness, risk assessment, simple problem solving techniques, and advice about other support agencies.

The results of this study showed that participants in the psychotherapy (plus treatment as usual) group (1) reported greater reduction (than controls) in symptomology and (2) reported significantly improved social and psychological functioning (i.e., a decrease in symptoms) at a 6-month follow-up. In addition, there were no differences reported between the two groups on service utilization during the time of treatment. However, results demonstrated that participants in the psychotherapy group showed a significant reduction in in-patient days, family physician contacts, practice nurse contacts, and number of medications at a 6-month follow-up. Furthermore, costs associated with both primary and secondary care were significantly lower in the group receiving psychotherapy (approximately $2,100 for control vs. $2,600 for experimental group) at 6 months following the end of treatment. Lastly, the cost associated with attending psychotherapy once a week was offset by the reduction in primary and secondary care costs at 6-month follow-up.

This study has several important findings that should be further researched. First, this study demonstrated that a psychological intervention could impact health care utilization as early as 6 months following treatment. In light of this finding, it would be interesting to examine the impact of this intervention on utilization in longer time intervals (e.g., 1, 2, 5 years post intervention). Second, the cost of the intervention was offset by the decrease in utilization. This is an important finding in that it demonstrates that a psychological intervention can be a cost-effective option for treating high utilizers in a primary care setting.

Research examining psychological correlates of health care use, consistently report a strong association between depression and high utilization of health care resources (Katon et al., 1990). An obvious implication of this finding is that by developing cost-effective assessments and treatments for individuals exhibiting symptoms of depression, we can decrease their utilization of health care resources. This hypothesis has been examined in a recent study conducted by Simon et al. (2001). The researchers conducted a randomized controlled trial to examine the cost-effectiveness and incremental cost associated with an organized depression management program designed to systematically identify and treat high utilizers of general medical care.

The study was conducted in several primary care clinics throughout the U.S. Participants between the ages of 23-63 with continuous coverage over the past 2 years were eligible to participate in the study. Participants receiving depression treatment (e.g., individual psychotherapy or antidepressants at a therapeutic dose for a minimum of 1 month) 90 days prior to treatment entrance and/ or those whom the depression treatment was inappropriate (e.g., diagnosis of bipolar I, psychotic disorder, substance abusers, or near-terminal medical conditions) were excluded from the study.

Health care utilization data was collected through an examination of visitation data at each site. Individuals whose number of outpatient visits exceeded the 85th percentile (either 7 or 8 visits per year) for each of the 2 years prior to the publication of the study were considered eligible for participation. Health care utilization costs included all health services paid for by the health plan 12 months prior to and 12 months following entry into the study. Health care costs calculated by examining all outpatient visits (e.g., all contacts with medical and secondary providers, prescribed medications, and medical procedures).

Eligible participants were contacted via phone screening consisting of the Structured Clinical Interview for DSM-IV. Individuals meeting current criteria for major depression and those reporting a recent episode (i.e., prior two years) of major depression in remission were eligible for a second telephone assessment consisting of the Hamilton Depression Rating Scale and a substance abuse screen. Those determined to suffer from the latter were excluded from participating in the study.

Participants in the study (both DMG and Usual Care Group) were assessed at 6 weeks, 3 months, and 12 months upon entry into the study. All assessments (e.g., Hamilton Depression Rating Scale , HDRS) were conducted via phone interviews. In addition, the number of "depression free days" was estimated using the HDRS. Estimations of the number of depression free days were calculated between any two assessments periods using designated cut-off scores of the HDRS.

Participants in the depression management program (DMP) (n = 218) received a primary care based intervention consisting of telephone contact, educational materials, antidepressant pharmacotherapy, and psychiatric consultation. Educational materials included mailed written and videotaped materials providing information on depression, the relationship between depression and medical conditions, and the effectiveness of treatments for depression. Physicians providing services in the DMP received a 2-hour training on the assessment of depression and the introduction of antidepressant medication. Upon entry into the study, participants were invited to participate in a 30-minute meeting with their physician. The purpose of the meeting was to confirm the diagnosis of depression, assess any prior treatment history, and to identify any complicating variables (e.g., mania and psychotic) and/or concerns regarding the use of antidepressants. Antidepressants were used when no complicating factors were identified. In addition to medication, participants in the DMP were asked to schedule at least two positive activities (e.g., exercise) per week. In contrast, participants in the treatment as usual (TU) group (n = 189) received no additional services. Participants in the TU group were given access to normally available services, such as, medication treatment and referral to specialty health care.

Their findings showed that the participants in the depression management group experienced approximately 48 additional depression-free days when compared to the treatment as usual group. However, the findings did not support the hypothesis that improved depression treatment results in a reduction in health care costs during the 12-months following entry into the study. In contrast, an increase of $1008 per year in outpatient health costs and $1974 for total health care costs per year was observed for participants in the DMP.

The findings reported in this study demonstrate that systematically identifying and treating depression in a sample of high utilizers of medical services can increase the number of depression free days (as measured by the HDRS). However, the contention that treating depression results in a reduction in health care utilization was not supported. In contrast, a significant increase in health expenditures over a 12-month period was observed in the treatment condition. One reason for the lack of cost offset may be in the fact that depression is often treated as a unitary concept and not in the context of the specific problems associated with the depression. For example, depression associated with a myocardial infarct may be different than depression associated with asthma or diabetes.

In terms of this last finding, it is important to consider that the 12-month period examined may underestimate the long-term (e.g., 1-5 years post-treatment) effectiveness and overestimate the long-term costs associated with programs such as the DMP. It is possible that the long-term effectiveness of such a program might be captured after a period of 1, 2, or 5 years post-treatment. Additionally, the incremental costs associated with such a program may be observed to decrease after a similar time period.

An increase in medical utilization has been associated with the first year or two following the death of a spouse. Cummings (1997a) studied 140,000 older adults receiving Medicare benefits through a large health care organization. Many of these older adults were experiencing an increase in medical service utilization following the death of their spouse. These individuals were outreached shortly after the death of their spouse to screen for depression and severe (but not pathological) mourning. Individuals screening positive for signs of depression were referred to psychotherapy while individuals in the latter group were referred to a group for bereavement.

The bereavement group consisted of 5-8 individuals. Individuals participating in this group received 14 sessions lasting 2 hours each. The 14 sessions were spaced in the following order: 4 semi-weekly sessions, 6 weekly sessions, and 4 monthly sessions. The 14 sessions were spaced over 6 1/2 months. The bereavement program focused on instructing the members on the process of mourning, supporting members to experience mourning as painful healing, and using teaching relaxation strategies and imaginary exposure to manage the most painful periods. Also, each group member was paired with a "buddy" to provide support on an as-needed basis.

A comparison of medical utilization was conducted between the experimental (N=323) and control group (N=278). The latter group consisted of widowed adults receiving health care services (but not the bereavement program) from a different section of the same organization. Utilization data were tracked for two years following entry into the study. Results demonstrated that after two years, medical service utilization remained 40% higher in the control group when compared to the experimental group. Furthermore, a medical cost savings of $1,400 per individual in the experimental group was observed over the two years utilization data was tracked.

Methodological Issues Relevant to Examining the Impact of Psychosocial Interventions on Health Care Utilization

Studies examining the impact of medical cost offset on an organization will differ depending on their specific goals. Identifying the appropriate dependent measures requires careful analysis of several issues. Wendel (2002) discusses eight issues that should be considered when attempting to measure medical cost savings.

1. What do you want to measure? The specific goals of a study should determine the appropriate dependent measures. When determining the appropriate dependent measures, the following questions may be relevant. First, will the health care organization absorb the costs of psychosocial intervention? Will possible costs incurred by the patient or patient's employer be considered? Second, how will cost savings interact will incentive arrangements? For example, will both the primary care physician and the psychologist benefit from medical cost savings? How will the physician be impacted financially for any reduction in demand for services? Third, is "cost" the only relevant dependent measure of interest? The impact of a psychosocial intervention on revenue may also be of importance. Revenue is impacted by enrollee turnover or employer willingness to contract with an organization, which are in turn, impacted by patient satisfaction. Therefore, measuring patient satisfaction may be of importance if variables impacting revenue are of interest.

2. Will you focus on intermediate process variables or final health outcome measures? The next question to consider is how the impact of the intervention will be measured. That is, will the targeted effects of your intervention be measured directly or indirectly? For example, will you directly measure the medical cost savings of an intervention program on the organization or will you look to the literature (if possible) to estimate reductions in cost? Both methods have advantages and disadvantages. For example, direct measures of cost savings have the advantage of being relevant to a specific organization. However, the use of small samples sizes can lead to underestimating the costs of infrequent adverse outcomes.

3. How will you measure your target variable? Relevant statistics need to be decided upon to measure the target impact of an intervention. The first issue in deciding on appropriate statistics is whether the data are qualitative or quantitative. Averages are commonly used when the data are quantitative, while proportions can be used for qualitative data. However, there are caveats to using these statistics. For example, if data are bimodal, highly skewed, or contain outliers, the average may not be a useful statistic. When decreases in variability are of interest, examining the standard deviation or proportion of observations within an acceptable range may be more appropriate.

In addition, outliers are often part of observed data sets and require consideration. Several considerations are relevant when considering the inclusion or exclusion of outliers. For example, do the outliers represent observations that are inappropriate for the study? An example of this might be the inclusion of participants with multiple comorbidities (this may result in the decision to exclude the outliers). Alternatively, outlier observations may be useful in analyzing causes of variability within a data set.

4. Are you committed to the use of statistical significance as a decision criterion? Statistical significance is a standard criterion for drawing scientific conclusions. However, its relevance for measuring medical cost offset requires careful consideration. First, should an intervention program that yields non-significant cost savings be discarded? What if the program demonstrates particular promise for future savings? What criteria will be decided upon when determining "promise"? Second, using statistical significance as the criterion for program evaluation can impact the amount of effort allocated toward specifying, collecting, and analyzing data sets. For example, large and/or complex data sets may require consultation with a statistician, development of computer programs, and/or cost accounting information systems.

5. How will you control for confounding variables? Outcomes of psychosocial programs may be influenced by a variety of confounding factors. There are at least two major methods for appropriately addressing this issue. First, the use of randomized control trials may diminish the influence of factors thought to impact the outcome of intervention by allowing the researcher to match participants on variables (e.g., age, sex, medical and/or psychological conditions, etc.) thought to influence outcome. Second, the use of regression analysis provides an alternative to matching participants on possible confounding variables by including these variables directly in the statistical analysis.

6. Will you continue to measure the intervention's impact to provide a foundation for continued improvement? Researchers examining cost offset may be interested in the continued assessment of improvements. One method for measuring continued improvements is through the use of control charts (see Ferguson in the present volume for an in-depth discussion of control charts). Control charts can provide a useful way for examining ongoing programs by determining when statistically significant changes have occurred. More specifically, control charts can differentiate between expected variations in participants' characteristics and changes that are statistically significant. Control charts require an estimate of the process mean, standard deviation, and time interval (e.g., days, weeks, or months) of interest. The chart consists of three horizontal lines. The middle line represents the historic mean. The upper and lower lines represent the region for indicating no significant changes from the historic mean. When an observation falls outside this region, the researcher must determine if it is due to chance or that some significant change has occurred.

7. Are the data readily available? Several issues deserve consideration. First, are accurate and appropriate data readily available in electronic format? Second, are the data available from within the organization or is it stored somewhere else? Data that are readily available in electronic format from within the organization are going to make the process of data collection and analysis more cost efficient than if they reside in another location (e.g., patient charts). Third, are the available data accurate? Errors may exist in databases that were not originally designed for the purpose of examining medical cost. For example, certain fields may not be widely used and therefore, contain undetected errors. Fourth, the development of a computer infrastructure that allows for cost efficient data collection and analysis may be cost efficient in the long term but require substantial cost in the short term. For example, electronic databases may require substantial investments in computer expertise, hardware, and software.

8. Which types of costs are relevant? It is important to examine the impact of an intervention on cost. For example, the impact of an intervention will have a different impact on fixed and variable costs. If the intervention impacts (e.g., reduces) the amount of services required to treat a group of patients, variable costs are relevant. However, fixed (or overhead) costs may not be impacted. Furthermore, analyzing costs associated with an intervention can be simplified by focusing on marginal costs and asking the following question, "precisely which costs will be affected by the reduction in services?" Consider the example of an intervention that reduces a patient's hospital stay by one day. The cost savings of this type of reduction is often calculated by examining the average daily cost (e.g., $2,000) of a hospital stay and then concluding that a savings by that much was produced by the intervention. However, using average costs to estimate cost savings can be problematic. This is because closer examination of patterns of costs associated with hospital visits (e.g., a 5-day visit) may indicate that proportions of costs are not divided equally among the days of a hospital stay. For example, more of the cost may be associated with the initial day or a day when a particular procedure was conducted. Therefore, estimating costs in terms of average daily costs may not be an inaccurate method for examining cost savings.

Summary and Recommendations for Future Research

The asymmetries involved in medical service utilization are having an enormous impact on both rising costs of health services and the utilization of those services. Researchers need to focus on this problem by (1) identifying pathways that lead to high utilization and (2) developing innovative ways to remedy unnecessary utilization. Certain clinical situations have been linked to the increased likelihood of high utilization. For example, high utilization has been linked with chronic psychological (e.g., depression) and/or medical (e.g., diabetes) conditions, particularly in the elderly. Furthermore, researchers have hypothesized and demonstrated a link between psychosocial factors and medical services usage. Factors such as inadequate information and social support, poor lifestyle management, and undiagnosed psychological problems can impact a person's decision to seek medical attention. For example, Cummings (in press) demonstrated that treatments such as psychosocial groups could lead to a decrease in medical service utilization in somatizers. However, this effect is not invariant. Some studies have been unsuccessful in demonstrating an impact on health care service utilization following treatment implementation. Cummings (1997b) discussed several factors that influence the empirical demonstration of medical cost offset in organized settings. The demonstration of cost offset is greater in settings that:

- Are able to integrate behavioral health and primary care
- Deliver standardized and innovative behavioral health interventions
- Employ psychotherapists who have been standardized through training and continued supervision
- Employ powerful data management information systems. These systems should reliably collect, classify, store, retrieve, and disseminate the relevant data

Researchers have argued psychosocial factors impact service utilization and treatments focusing on psychosocial issues have been linked with decreases in service utilization. Therefore, future research needs to be oriented toward developing treatment programs that focus on psychosocial factors such as disease management, social support, and education. Developing treatments that focus on these factors may require skill sets that many primary care physicians and traditional specialty care professionals lack. Therefore, initial training and continued supervision of necessary skills are needed. In addition, more controlled effectiveness studies are needed that focus on: the development of manualized treatment programs; the continued monitoring of adherence to these programs; and that examine the effects of their interventions over useful time periods (e.g., to examine recidivism). Prospective studies should consider the following methodological issues: (1) include a careful cost analysis so that the dissemination of findings can be enhanced by a clear return on investment analysis; (2) the development of algorithms that better identify high utilizers from claims data; (3) the development of successful outreach and screening procedures; (4) employ training and ongoing monitoring of necessary skills involved in treatment delivery; and (5) include empirical evidence for decisions regarding (a) the types of staff needed to do particular jobs (e.g., screening and treatment delivery) and (b) the types of specialized training required to achieve successful outcomes.

References

Anderson, G., & Knickman, J. R. (1984). Patterns of expenditures among high utilizers of medical care services. *Medical Care, 22,* 143-149.

Ash, A., Zhao, Y., Ellis, R. P., & Kramer, M. S. (2001). Finding future high-cost cases: comparing prior cost versus diagnosis-based methods. *Health Services Research, 36,* 194-206.

Berk, M. L., & Monheit, A. C. (2001). The concentration of health care expenditures, revisited. *Health Affairs, 20,* 9-18.

Butler, R. N., Lewis, M. I., & Sunderland, T. (1998). *Aging and mental health: Positive psychosocial and biomedical approaches.* Boston: Allyn & Bacon.

Cummings, N. A. (1997a). Approaches in prevention in the behavioral health of older adults. In P. Hartmann-Stein (Ed.), *Innovative behavioral healthcare for older adults: A guidebook for changing times* (pp. 1-23). San Francisco, CA: Jossey-Bass.

Cummings, N. A. (1997b). Behavioral health in primary care: dollars and sense. In N. A. Cummings, J. L. Cummings, & J. N. Johnson (Eds.), *Behavioral health in primary care: A guide for clinical integration* (pp. 3-31). Connecticut: Psychosocial Press.

Cummings, N. A. (in press). Identifying and treating the somatizer: integrated care's penultimate intervention. In W. O'Donohue, D. Henderson, M. Byrd, & N. A. Cummings (Eds.), *Treatments that work in primary health care.* Boston: Allyn & Bacon.

Cummings, N. A., Kahn, B. I., & Sparkman, B. (1962). *Psychotherapy and medical utilization: A pilot study.* Oakland, CA: Annual Reports of Kaiser Permanente Research Projects.

Fredericks, D. W., Fisher, J. E., Buchanan, J. A., & Luevano, V. (2002). Preventing excess disability in dementia care. In N. A. Cummings, W. T. O'Donohue, & K. E. Ferguson (Eds.), *The impact of medical cost offset on practice and research: Making it work for you* (pp. 201-218). Reno, NV: Context Press.

Friedman, R., Sobel, D., Myers, P., Caudill, M., & Benson, H. (1995). Behavioral medicine, clinical health psychology, and cost offset. *Health Psychology, 14,* 509-518.

Guthrie, E., Moorey, J., Margison, F., Barker, H., Palmer, S., McGrath, G., et al. (1999). Cost-effectiveness of brief psychodynamic-interpersonal therapy in high utilizers of psychiatric services. *Archives of General Psychiatry, 56,* 519-526.

Hu, T. W., & Rush, A. J. (1995). Depressive disorders: treatment patterns and costs of treatment in the private sector of the United States. *Social Psychiatry and Psychiatric Epidemiology, 30,* 224-230.

Kapur, K., Young, A. S., & Murata, D. (2000). Risk adjustment for high utilizers of public mental health care. *The Journal of Mental Health Policy and Economics, 3,* 129-137.

Katon, W., Von Korff, M., Lin, E., Lipscomb, P., Russo, J., Wagner, E., et al. (1990). Distressed high utilizers of medical care: DSM-III-R diagnoses and treatment needs. *General Hospital Psychiatry, 12,* 355-362.

Liptzin, B., Regier, D. A., & Goldberg, I. D. (1980). Utilization of health and mental health services in a large insured population. *American Journal of Psychiatry, 137,* 553-558.

Lorig, K., Mazonson, P. D., & Holman, H. R. (1993). Evidence suggesting that health education for self-management in patients with chronic arthritis has sustained benefits while reducing health care costs. *Arthritis and Rheumatism, 36,* 439-446.

McLeod, C. C., Budd, M. A., & McClelland, D. C. (1997). Treatment of somatization in primary care. *General Hospital Psychiatry, 19,* 251-258.

O'Donohue, W. T., Ferguson, K. E., & Cummings, N. A. (2002). Introduction: reflections on the medical cost offset. In N. A. Cummings, W. T. O'Donohue, & K. E. Ferguson (Eds.), *The impact of medical cost offset on practice and research: Making it work for you* (pp. 11-25). Reno, NV: Context Press.

Schmitz, N., & Kruse, J. (2002). The relationship between mental disorders and medical service utilization in a representative community sample. *Social Psychiatry and Psychiatric Epidemiology, 37,* 380-386.

Simon, G. E., Manning, W. G., Katzelnick, D. J., Pearson, S. D., Henk, H. J., & Helstad, C. P. (2001). Cost effectiveness of systematic depression treatment for high utilizers of general medical care. *Archives of General Psychiatry, 58,* 181-187.

Wendell, J. (2002). Measuring medical cost. In N. A. Cummings, W. T. O'Donohue, & K. E. Ferguson (Eds.), *The impact of medical cost offset on practice and research: Making it work for you* (pp. 115-123). Reno, NV: Context Press.

Preliminary Results from the
Hawaii Integrated Healthcare Project II

Ranilo Laygo, William O'Donohue, Susan Hall,
Aaron Kaplan, Reginald Wood, Janet Cummings,
Nicholas Cummings, & Ian Shaffer

In the 1980's the basic tenants of the integrated healthcare model were developed and subsequently evaluated as part of the Hawaii Medicaid Study (Cummings, Dorken, Pallak & Henke, 1993; Pallak, Cummings, Dorken & Henke, 1994). This prospective study of 36,000 Medicaid eligible patients and 90,000 Federal employees living on O'ahu demonstrated that providing quality behavioral care may drastically reduce medical utilization rates and total healthcare costs by as much as 8 million dollars per year (Cummings, 1997). The Hawaii Medicaid Study was the first step in exploring the possibilities of an integrated healthcare model.

In August 2001, The Hawaii Integrated Healthcare Demonstration Project began as a follow up to the Hawaii Medicaid Study. The overarching goal of the project was to provide patients with high quality, behavioral health services within the primary care setting and examine how these services impact a number of patient factors including clinical outcome, functional status, and satisfaction with healthcare services, medical cost, and medical service utilization. As with the original study, medical costs and utilization will also be examined.

In order to achieve this main goal, however, several others had to be set and accomplished along the way. These included: securing funds for the first year of operation, finding primary care sites to participate in the study, hiring personnel, training clinicians in the integrated healthcare model, developing outcome measures, and finding ways to integrate data collection with the delivery of clinical services. Another goal of the project was to create a transportable set of training materials so that researchers and healthcare organizations could duplicate the practices and procedures of the project with minimal effort. This preliminary report is a summary of progress made toward these goals. This is not a report of an efficacy trial but rather a report of a treatment development project. An important future goal is to develop appropriate and feasible control groups so that clearer inferences can be made regarding treatment effects.

Funding

Three organizations contributed money for the first year of the project. The Hawaii Medical Services Association Foundation provided $45,000. The Bureau of Primary Health Care provided $100,000, while the University of Nevada, Reno Research Initiative contributed another $100,000. In total, these funds were adequate to support the project for 1 year.

Participating Sites

Six primary care clinics on O'ahu were visited to assess their interest in participating in the project. In addition each clinic was assessed on a number of variables to determine if they were a good fit for the project. These variables included patient flow, types of problems seen at each clinic, office culture, etc. By the summer of 2001 three clinics agreed to participate in the project. These sites are described below.

Medical Arts Clinic

The Medical Arts Clinic is located in the rural city of Wahiawa. The clinic was founded in 1968 and serves approximately 30,000 patients a year. Of those patients, 20% meet poverty levels and are traditionally considered underserved. The clinic serves a patient population that is ethnically and racially diverse. In fact, for many patients, English is not their native language.

Haleiwa Family Health Center

Haleiwa Family Health Center is located on the rural North Shore of O'ahu. It was founded in 1967. Physicians there see approximately 20,000 patients a year. Of these, 9% are at less than 100% of the Federal Poverty Levels. Approximately 22.4% are on food stamps and are traditionally considered underserved. The patient population served by the clinic is also racially and ethnically diverse. For example, approximately 12.5% of the patients are Native Hawaiian.

Kokua-Kalihi Valley Comprehensive Family Services

Unlike the Medical Arts Clinic or Haleiwa Family Health Center, Kokua-Kalihi Valley Comprehensive Services (KKV) is located in Kalihi Vally, an urban setting just outside Honolulu. It was founded in 1972 and is located in a Health Personnel Shortage Area. Physicians at KKV see approximately 5,000 patients per year, 80% of which meet poverty levels and are traditionally considered underserved. Similar to the other sites, the patient population at KKV is racially and ethnically diverse. Over 90% of the patient population is Asian and/or Pacific Islanders.

On September 27, 2001, KKV withdrew from the project due to a misunderstanding regarding the nature of the project. The months of October, November, and December 2001 were used to secure the cooperation of another primary care site. On January 9, 2002, Waikiki Health Center joined the project.

Waikiki Health Center

Similar to KKV, Waikiki Health Center (WHC) is located in an urban setting. The clinic is situated in Waikiki, the famous beach resort area within Honolulu. Founded in 1967, WHC provides primary medical care and ancillary services for the residents of O'ahu. Physicians at WHC see approximately 6,000 patients a year. Of these, 60% are considered traditionally underserved and do not have health insurance.

Personnel

Four staff members were hired in O'ahu to execute the study. These included a full-time Project Coordinator and Clinical Director, and 2 half-time Behavioral Health Consultants. Position descriptions appear below.

Project Coordinator

The primary role of the Project Coordinator was overseeing the day-to-day operations of the study. In addition, the Project Coordinator helped develop clinical outcome measures, trained project staff on the proper use and timing of outcome measures, helped develop a research methodology that was seamless with the delivery of services, found solutions for problems as they arose at each of the three project sites, and ensured that all members at each site had the materials needed to ensure the smooth and efficient running of the project.

The Project Coordinator's secondary role was to collect, enter, manage, and analyze the outcome data from each of the three project sites. Results were used for clinical supervision, program development, and supporting grant applications. Finally, the Project Coordinator provided feedback to key stakeholders in the form of monthly and quarterly reports.

Clinical Director

The Clinical Director's primary role was to provide behavioral health consultation to the primary care providers (PCPs) at his assigned project site. This included providing brief, short-term psychological interventions for patients whose concerns and levels of functioning were appropriate for treatment within the integrated healthcare model. (Examples of appropriate patients included those suffering from severe distress, lifestyle problems, mood problems, relational problems, behavioral problems related to medical illness, and substance abuse.) The Clinical Director also provided other consultation services such as "curbside" consults, medicine recommendations, and when necessary, linked patients to specialty care. Finally, the Clinical Director also helped with project development by training and supervising other staff clinicians and developing treatment protocols.

Behavioral Health Consultants

Two half-time clinicians, or Behavioral health Consultants (BHCs) as they are called in this model, were hired to provide behavioral health consultations to the PCPs at their respective sites. Although these 20 hour/week positions were primarily clinical, BHCs were required to participate in other project development duties (e.g., write grants, helping with instrument development, attending meetings, etc.)

Training

As noted above, a necessary first step in conducting the project was to train clinicians on the delivery of integrated behavioral health services. The philosophy behind clinician training was simple. Clinicians would receive the highest quality training in the integrated healthcare model to ensure that they would deliver the best possible care to their patients. After training, the quality of services would be maintained through supervision with experts that could take the form of shadowing, conference calls, and review of clinicians' notes.

Provider training focused on these domains:

A. The Biodyne Model of Brief Focused Psychotherapy through the Lifespan. This is the famous form of therapy developed by Dr. Nicholas Cummings, Ph.D. and served as the core for provider training. It was developed in the 1980's in the Hawaii Medicaid Study and was the basis for American Biodyne's success (Cummings, Dorken, Pallak & Henke, 1993; Pallak, Cummings, Dorken & Henke, 1994). Each American Biodyne therapist was initially trained in this model and continually supervised for adherence and competence. It is based on an important therapeutic contract:

> "My job is never to abandon you as long as you need me, never to ask you to do anything until you can do it. Your job is to join me in a partnership to make me obsolete as soon as possible."

The techniques of this therapy are focused on correctly diagnosing patients' resistances, understanding the patient's implicit contract (the often unstated but real reason for entering therapy), making an operational diagnosis (understanding the answer to the question, "Why is the patient here now?"), and understanding the patient's position in a useful heuristic: the onion-garlic chart. The onion-garlic chart is a paradigm of a psychodynamic division that allows the formation of useful treatment plans. A key element of the Biodyne model of therapy is that the first session involves treatment and homework, rather than just assessment, as in more traditional psychotherapy.

B. Primary Care Model of Behavioral Health Service Delivery. This model was developed by Drs. Kirk Strosahl and Patricia Robinson. The core concept in this model is to translate evidence based therapies into the ecology of primary care medicine. Functional diagnosis utilizes efficient screens, testing, and interview techniques. Patients are then triaged into efficient, effective treatment such as cognitive behavioral groups for depression, stress management treatment, and disease management treatment. Trainees are taught a wide range of skills on how to work effectively as part of a team that is led by a medical professional. Core competencies include:

1. *Triage/Liaison*: Initial screening visits of 30 minutes (or less) designed to determine appropriate level of mental health care intervention.
2. *Behavioral Health Consultation*: Intake visit by a patient referred for a general evaluation. The focus is on diagnostic and functional evaluation, recommendations for treatment and forming limited behavior change goals. This service

involves assessing patients who are at risk due to a stressful life event. It may include identifying whether a patient could benefit from accessing existing community resources, educating the patient about these resources, or referring the patient to a social service agency.

3. *Behavioral Health Follow-up*: Secondary visits by a patient to support a behavior change plan or treatment started by the PCP on the basis of earlier consultation. This service is often conducted in tandem with planned PCP visits.

4. *Compliance Enhancement*: Visit designed to help the patient comply with an intervention initiated by the PCP. The focus is on education, addressing negative beliefs, or offering strategies to help cope with side effects of medical treatment.

5. *Relapse Prevention*: Visit designed to maintain stable functioning in a patient who has responded to previous treatment; often spaced at long intervals.

6. *Behavioral Medicine*: Visit designed to assist the patient in managing a chronic medical condition or to tolerate an invasive or uncomfortable medical procedure. The focus may be on lifestyle issues or health risk factors among patients at risk (e.g., smoking cessation or stress management) or may involve managing issues related to progressive illness (such as end stage COPD).

7. *Specialty Consultation*: Designed to provide consultation services over time to patients who require ongoing monitoring and follow up; applicable to patients with chronic stressors, marginal lifestyle adaptation, and so forth.

8. *Disability Prevention/Management*: Visit designed to assist patients who are on medical leave from job to return to work appropriately. The focus of this service is on coordinating care with the PCP, job site and patient. The emphasis is on avoiding "disability building" treatments and patient suffering.

9. *Psychoeducation Class*: Brief group treatment that either replaces or supplements individual consultation, designed to promote education and skill building. Often a psychoeducation group can and should serve as the primary psychological intervention as many behavioral health needs are best addressed in a group format.

10. *Conjoint Consultation*: Visits with the PCP and patient designed to address an issue of concern to both; this often involves addressing conflict between them.

11. *Telephone Consultation*: Scheduled intervention contacts or follow up visits with patients that are conducted by the behavioral health clinician via telephone, rather than in person. This consultation may also take place via email in some cases.

12. *On-Demand Behavioral Health Consultation*: Usually unscheduled PCP initiated contact with a patient, either via telephone or in person. This service is generally utilized during emergency situations requiring an immediate response.

13. *On-Demand Medication Consultation*: Usually unscheduled PCP initiated contact with a patient regarding medication issues such as compliance or possible behavioral side effects of treatment.

14. *Care Management*: Designed to contain extensive and coordinated delivery of medical and/or mental health services, usually to patients with chronic psychological and medical problems.
15. *Team building*: Conferencing with one or more members of the health care team to address peer relationships, job stress issues or process of care concerns.
16. *PCP consultation*: Face to face visits with the PCP to discuss patient care issues; often involves "curbside" consultation.

This model also involved PCP training. U/ABC's consultants Drs. Kirk Strosahl, Ph.D. and Patricia Robinson, Ph.D. have successfully trained physicians in a number of settings. This training is often done in an initial lunch and followed up by opportunities such as presentations at staffing and other informal contacts. Key core competencies include:

1. Accurately describing and selling behavioral health services when referring patients to a behavioral healthcare specialist.
2. Demonstrating an understanding of the relationship of medical and psychological systems to cultural contexts of individual patients.
3. Diverting patients with behavioral health issues to behavioral health consultants.
4. Using an intermittent care strategy such that the patient is receiving services from both the physician and the behavioral healthcare specialist by turn.
5. Referring patients appropriately to behavioral health classes in the primary care clinic.
6. Clearly stating the referral question in behavioral health referrals.
7. Interrupting the behavioral health provider as needed.
8. Conducting effective curbside consultations with the behavioral health provider.
9. Being willing to aggressively follow up with behavioral health providers when indicated.
10. Focusing on treatment plans that reduce physicians' visits and workloads.
11. Engaging in co-management of patient care with a behavioral health provider.
12. Documenting behavioral health referrals and treatment plans in chart notes.
13. Demonstrating knowledge of the behavioral healthcare provider role.
14. Being comfortable orienting the behavioral health provider to the primary care environment.
15. Paging the behavioral healthcare provider with urgent questions.

C. Medical Psychology. Generally the mental health professional is not well versed in basic medicine. This segment of training taught BHCs the relevant medical information needed to function in a primary care setting. Dr. Janet Cummings, Psy.D. led this training, in addition to lecturing on psychopharmacology.

D. Psychopharmacology. Generally PCPs look to the behavioral health consultant to provide advice and information about psychopharmacological approaches to treating mental health disorders. Behavioral health consultants need skills in discussing side effects, treatment adherence issues, and other feasibility issues with both the PCP and the patient. However, clearly it is the PCP or other medical professional's decision on whether and how to treat pharmacologically.

E. Quality Improvement. It is important that therapists understand the healthcare delivery system in which they operate, its goals, and its process of ongoing quality improvement (QI). Therapists were trained in the QI measures they were expected to use. Therapists were also trained in the supervision and continuing education procedures in which they were expected to participate. Drs. Ian Shaffer, M.D., M.M.M. and William O'Donohue, Ph.D. were key trainers.

This training was successfully conducted in the Hawaii project in September of 2001.

Supervision

As noted above, the goal of supervision was to help clinicians maintain the quality of their services. A multi-modal supervision model was employed in the project. For example, in the training phase of the project, BHCs observed Dr. Robinson working with patients. Later in the training phase, Dr. Robinson shadowed BHCs as they saw their first patients. Finally, Dr. Robinson also role-played various scenarios with BHCs to help them prepare for unique types of patients (e.g., resistant patient).

Since the initial training, BHCs have received individual supervision via conference calls and face-to-face sessions. For example, Drs. Robinson and Cummings regularly supervised individual BHCs via conference call. Meanwhile, the Clinical Director provided individual face-to-face supervision with the post-doctoral intern on staff.

Finally, Dr. Robinson conducted two separate site visits during the year to ensure that the BHCs were delivering high quality services. During these visits, she observed BHCs working with patients and reviewed patient chart notes. Suggestions ranging from improving service delivery to increasing patient referrals were discussed during these visits.

Administratively, there were several meetings that keep the project progressing towards its goals. First, there was a mandated bi-weekly staff meeting. These meetings served several functions including providing a regular forum to discuss issues related to data collection, methodology, and the day-to-day operation of the study. These meetings focused on improving efficiency in each of the aforementioned areas.

The Principal Investigator (PI), Project Coordinator and Clinical Director had weekly conference calls to discuss the needs of the project as they arise. Finally, the PI made quarterly visits to O'ahu to ensure that the project was running according to schedule.

Progress

The system of training and supervision has met with great success. As can be seen in the provider data presented below, primary care providers are quite satisfied with the quality of the services delivered.

Training Modules

Another major goal of the demonstration project related to training was to develop a transportable and economically efficient training regiment. To this end, each day of initial training was videotaped and archived, for use in training future project personnel.

In addition, project staff compiled a list of background reading materials with the following goals in mind: a) materials had to be blocked into coherent training units, b) these units had to be germane to the delivery of integrated healthcare, and c) materials had to be current. These materials were indexed and will serve to educate future personnel on the integrated healthcare model and other related topics (See Appendix A).

Dr. Cummings provided project staff with electronic copies of lecture materials, approximately 1,000 pages of readings, notes and references. These materials were condensed into "clinical fact sheets". Each sheet was designed to provide BHCs with background information related to various medical conditions. Project staff also compiled clinical fact sheets as well. An example of a clinical fact sheet for chronic pain appears in Appendix B, along with a comprehensive list of all available fact sheets.

Dr. Robinson also provided materials for use in the project. These included forms that could be used in the day-to-day practice of delivering services and several book chapters on the treatment of specific problems in primary care by various authors. A complete list of these forms and chapters appears in Appendix C.

Finally, staff compiled "resource lists" for use at the local level. These lists contain numerous names and numbers of organizations that deal with specific problems such as bereavement, homelessness, and general mental health. List(s) may be given to patients during the course of therapy to help them utilize community resources. An example of one of these resources lists appears in Appendix D, along with a complete inventory of available lists.

Progress. Headway is being made in the development of a transportable and economically efficient training regiment. Staff has been reviewing and indexing the training tapes, a first step toward editing the tapes into video training modules.

Another major long-term goal will be the development of an Integrated Healthcare Training Manual, which will be modeled after the United States Air Force's Primary Behavioral Health Care Services Practice Manual. This manual will be used to guide other sites in the development of an integrated healthcare system. It will cover a variety of topics from training to the day-to-day operation of an integrated setting. A chapter on data management will be included to cover such areas as creating data files, entering data, and analyzing data. Work has already begun compiling this manual.

Outcome Measures

Instruments that measure 1) patient satisfaction, 2) provider satisfaction, 3) substance abuse, 4) functional status, and 5) symptom complaints were constructed early in the opening weeks of the project. Instrument development was particularly challenging because the questionnaires had to fulfill the tenants of the integrated healthcare model. That is, they had to be brief, easily interpreted, and produce clinically useful information. Also, the resulting data must add to the quality of service delivery.

In early January 2001, after pilot testing, all instruments were revised to address a number of issues. The first had to do with the average number of days elapsed between visits. The average number of days between patient visits was quite short in the sample. Given this brief period between test and retest, the time scale for many of the instruments (e.g., in the past 30 days) was not well suited for our application.

To address this issue, several changes were made to the clinical outcome measures. For example, instruments incorporated separate instructions for baseline measures and follow-up measures. The baseline measure is uniform at two weeks prior to the patient's first visit with the BHC. Follow-up questions are phrased "since your last visit," giving a uniform frame of reference regardless of the number of days that have elapsed since the patient's last visit. This also eliminates any overlap in measures; thus, allowing us to accurately assess the impact of each session of therapy and determine dose-response curves and points of diminishing returns.

Also, Subjective Units of Distress Scales (SUDS) were adopted and developed for measuring patients' level of distress on several high frequency problems (anxiety, behavioral problems, depression, pain, and relationship problems). This allows for uniformity in administration across instruments, a move made to cut down response errors.

Finally, the patients' responses are based on a 10-point scale regardless of the specific problem being addressed. Again, this uniformity in administration and scoring was made to help reduce on response errors. An example of the Depression SUDS appears in Appendix E, along with a complete list of SUDS and other outcome measures that are available for clinician use.

Progress

The changes made to the instruments solved the intended problems. First, they measure distinct time frames within the patient's course of treatment. Also, since administration and scoring between instruments is uniform, recording errors have been reduced. Finally, since the uniform instruments are easier to administer, clinician usage increased.

A major future goal regarding product development is to continue refining the clinical outcome and quality improvement questionnaires until they are viable as *the* standardized measures in the field. Steps toward this goal would include establishing the construct validity and reliability of the instruments. Also, the consumer acceptability (clinicians, patients, and management) of the instruments would have to be examined. However, once these steps are accomplished, the end result would be a set of quality improvement and clinical outcome measures with known and acceptable psychometric properties. This would be a first attempt at constructing such instruments for use specifically in healthcare settings that employ the integrated healthcare model.

In the more distant future, once agencies begin adopting these instruments, databases will be compiled using information from participating organizations. Thus, organizations will be able to benchmark the quality of the services they are delivering against similarly sized entities, or against national standards. Currently we are working toward partnering with the United States Air Force to further develop our instruments, although addition funds would be needed to support instrument development. Additional grants will be written in year two to address this specific initiative.

The project is also interested in examining the efficacy of the integrated healthcare model in reducing patient medical costs and utilization. Steps are being taken to determine the most efficient and ethical manner in which to gather this information.

Methods

The research methods employed in the study were fairly straightforward. Primary care providers at each of the sites referred patients to their respective BHC. Depending on the issues facing the patient, the BHC may have seen the patient just once, several times within the next 30 days, or for a few sessions spaced over a longer duration. Patients who were seen for one treatment episode (e.g., weight loss) were not precluded from seeing the BHC for other treatment issues (e.g., anxiety) in the future.

Patients were asked to fill out a consent form during the initial session. This gave project personnel permission to review the patient's medical records at a later date to determine if the behavioral health services reduced their medical cost and/or utilization. Also, it gives the BHC permission to administer the clinical outcome and functional status surveys throughout the course of their treatment.

If a patient was seen just once, s/he was asked to complete a patient satisfaction survey after their session. All patients were asked to complete a patient satisfaction survey after their second visit. Patients that are seen over a longer period of time were asked to complete a patient satisfaction survey at the end of the treatment episode.

Data Collection and Impact

Data collection was integrated into the delivery of services in such a manner that it was not obtrusive or seen as something "extra" the clinician had to do. Instruments were intentionally brief and yielded information that was useful to the BHC and PCP. Also, of course, the instruments were designed to provide a demographic picture of our sample and determine whether or not the services were helpful. The results of the project's last 8 months of effort are presented below. As of April 30, 2002, 370 patients have been enrolled in the project, totaling 645 patient visits. The mean age of the sample is 42.79, while the median is 43.

Demographics

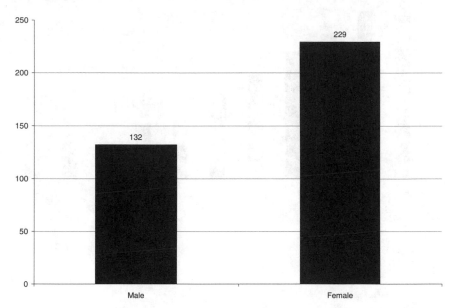

Figure 6.1. Patient Sample by Sex.

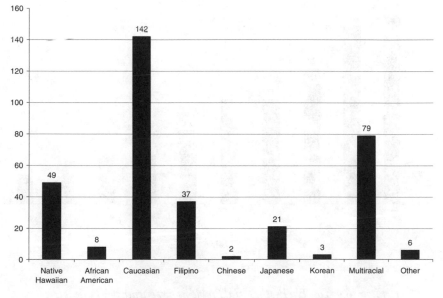

Figure 6.2. Patient Sample by Racial Category.

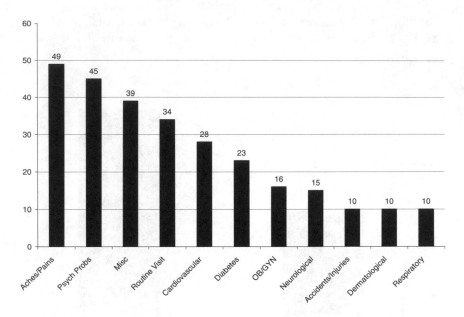

Figure 6.3. Top Ten Patient Medical Complaints.

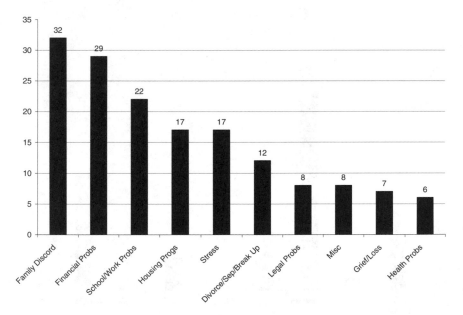

Figure 6.4. Top Ten Psychosocial Problems Experienced by Patients.

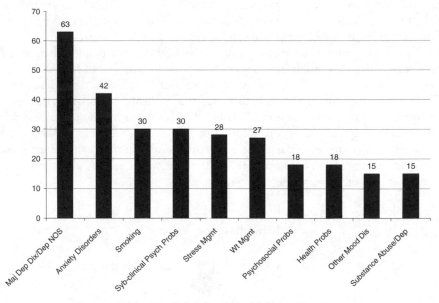

Figure 6.5. Top Ten Behavioral Health Treatment Categories.

Summary. Our sample consists mostly of middle-aged adults, with the majority being female. Although Caucasians comprise the largest single racial category, other racial backgrounds are well represented within the total sample. Interestingly, within the sample, there are a great many individuals who were seeing their PCP because of specific psychological problems such as anxiety or depression. This category was second only to "general aches and pains" in medical complaint categories (Figure 6.3). As can be seen in Figure 6.5, these two problems are also the two problems BHCs treated the most. Finally, in addition to psychological problems, patients experienced many psychosocial problems such as family discord, financial problems such as unemployment, problems at school and work, and homelessness.

Progress. Patient enrollment has been excellent. Our goal at the onset of the project was to complete 1,000 patient visits by the end of the first year. If patient recruitment continues at this same rate, that objective will be met.

Clinical Outcomes

Beck Depression Inventory-Primary Care Version

A main goal of the project was to demonstrate positive patient outcomes for those that were treated in the integrated healthcare model. One of the instruments used to examine patient outcome was the Beck Depression Inventory, Primary Care Version (BDI-PC) (Beck, Guth, Steer & Ball, 1997).

The BDI-PC is a very brief inventory used to measure depression. It contains seven items with raw scores ranging from 0 to 21. Raw scores in the 0-3 range indicate minimal symptoms of depression. Scores in the 4-6 range indicate mild symptoms of depression. Scores in the 7-9 range indicate moderate symptoms of depression, while scores in the 10-21 range indicate severe symptoms of depression.

Thirty-four patients were administered the BDI-PC as a pretest, then tested again several days later to determine how they were progressing in treatment. The average number of days between test administrations was 30.20 days. The mean BDI-PC score for the group at pretest was 9.2, indicating moderate to severe symptoms of depression. The mean BDI-PC score for the group at posttest was 5.5, indicating mild symptoms of depression. A paired-samples t-test was performed on the group's scores to see if there was a statistically significant change during the course of treatment. Results indicated that there was a statistically significant decrease in reported symptoms ($t_{(33)}$=5.7, p=.000).

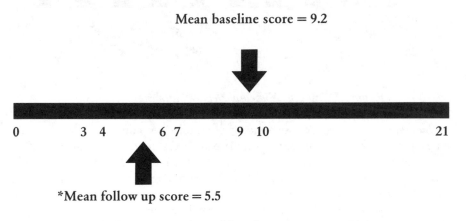

Figure 6.6. Group mean scores at baseline and follow up on the BDI-PC.

*Depression subject units of distress scale.*Fourteen patients were administered the Depression SUDS as a pretest, then tested again several days later to determine how they were progressing in treatment. The average number of days between test administrations was 9.5. The mean Depression SUDS score for the group at pretest was 6.5, indicating moderate to severe symptoms of depression. The mean Depression SUDS score for the group at posttest was 4.6, indicating mild to moderate symptoms of depression. A paired-samples t-test was performed on the group's scores to see if there was a statistically significant change during the course of treatment. Results indicated that there was a statistically significant decrease in reported symptoms ($t_{(13)}$=2.6, p=.02). Although these results are based on a small sample, they are quite promising.

On average, when you felt depressed, how you you rate your level of depression?

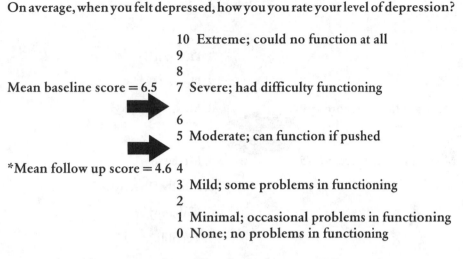

10 Extreme; could no function at all
9
8
Mean baseline score = 6.5   7 Severe; had difficulty functioning

6
5 Moderate; can function if pushed
*Mean follow up score = 4.6 4
3 Mild; some problems in functioning
2
1 Minimal; occasional problems in functioning
0 None; no problems in functioning

*Average number of days between tests = 9.5

Figure 6.7. Group mean scores at baseline and follow up on the Depression SUDS.

Quality of life. Twenty patients were asked a single question from Lehman's Quality of Life Inventory as a global measure of life satisfaction (Lehman, 1983). The question reads, "How do you feel about your life in general?" Responses to the question are measured on a seven-point scale: 1 or "Delighted" to 7 or "Terrible". These subjects were asked the question again several days later to determine how they were progressing in treatment. The average number of days between test administrations was 26.8. The mean response for the group at pretest was 3.75, while the mean response for the group at posttest was 3.25. Both responses were between "mostly satisfied" and "mixed". A paired-samples t-test was performed on the group's scores to see if there was a statistically significant change during the course of treatment. Results indicated that there was a statistically significant increase in the patients' self reported life satisfaction ($t_{(19)}$=2.24, p=.04). Although these results are based on a small sample, they are again quite promising.

How do you feel about your life in general?

	1. Delighted
	2. Pleased
*Mean follow up score = 3.25	3. Mostly Satisfied
Mean baseline score = 3.75	4. Mixed
	5. Mostly Dissatisfied
	6. Unhappy
	7. Terrible

*Average number of days between tests = 26.8

Figure 6.8. Group mean scores on the quality of life question at baseline and follow-up.

Progress. Preliminary data indicate that patients being treated for depression within the integrated healthcare model do improve with regard to reported symptomatology. However, the efficacy of treatment for other problems such as anxiety, chronic pain, and other behavioral problems need to be conducted. Also, patients report somewhat more satisfaction with life following a treatment within the integrated healthcare model. In future years, the project will introduce a control group to insure that the improvement rates are better than those that could be expected due to spontaneous remission. Meanwhile, more patients will continue to be tested and retested on all available instruments.

Consumer Satisfaction

In the integrated healthcare model, PCPs are the BHC's main consumer. It is the BHC's role to provide the PCP with consultation services. However, patients are seen as consumers of behavioral health services as well. In order to ensure that both sets of consumer were satisfied with the behavioral health services, each were asked to complete customer satisfaction surveys. Patients complete satisfaction surveys in the manner described in the methods section, while PCPs complete satisfaction surveys every quarter.

Patient Satisfaction

Patient satisfaction surveys consisted of three questions. In addition, patients were allowed to submit written comments on the surveys. Results from the survey appear below. The mean response to each question appears beside the respective question. The sample size for these results is 54.

Patient Satisfaction			
Item	N	Rating Scale	$\bar{x}$
How satisfied were you with the overall quality of the behavioral health consultation you received?	54	1=Low; 5=High	4.6
How do you feel about your health now that you've seen a behavioral health consultant?	54	1=High; 5=Low	1.7
Would you recommend similar behavioral health services to a friend or family member who had a similar problem?	54	1=Low; 5=High	3.7

Table 6.1. Patient Satisfaction mean response is indicated in the x column.

Patient Comments

- "Dr. Hall is so very much an encourager and supportive of my health improvement. Thank you for her."
- "Thank you for taking the initiative to treat the whole person, not just symptoms of what would be other problems."
- "This is a great way to reach people who would never think to talk to a professional about lifestyle changes. I'm one of them."
- "I like pragmatic-defined steps to improve behavior."
- "Suggestions provided by doctor served as a strong basis for my improved condition. This one on one interaction certainly gave me confidence that made me realize that my problem wasn't as bad as I thought."

Progress. In general the average response to each of the patient satisfaction survey questions is in the positive direction, indicating a high degree of satisfaction with the behavioral health services delivered. In addition, patient comments are quite positive. However, only 15% of the current sample completed satisfaction surveys. Greater effort needs to be taken to increase the number of completed patient satisfaction surveys in order to eliminate possible sampling bias.

Provider Satisfaction

Provider satisfaction surveys consist of three questions that were quite similar to those used in the patient satisfaction survey. In addition, providers were also allowed to submit written comments on the surveys. Survey results appear below. The mean response to each question appears beside the respective question. The sample size for these results is 16.

Provider Satisfaction			
Item	N	Rating Scale	$\bar{x}$
How satisfied were you with the overall quality of the behavioral health consultation over the past 90 days?	16	1=Low; 5=High	4.9
Overall how helpful were the behavioral health consultations you received in the past 90 days?	16	1=High; 4=Low	1.0
To what extent did the behavioral health services result in improved recognition and treatment of the behavioral components of health problems?	16	1=Low; 5=High	4.2
Would you recommend similar behavioral health consultation services to a provider dealing with similar patients?	16	1=Low; 4=High	3.9

Table 6.2. Provider Satisfaction mean response is indicated in the x column.

Provider Comments

"Susan has been very helpful and an excellent supplement for patient care. It is nice to have her easily accessible especially when a problem is identified and intervention can be done immediately after the visit with the MD."

"I think that there is a higher compliance rate with visits due to proximity (in office) behavioral health consultation services."

"Dr. Hall is a wonderful resource. I have had many patients who I've referred to her. She uncovers much more history and information which helps in managing the patients."

Progress. Results are generally positive across all survey items indicating that providers are satisfied with the behavioral health services their patient population is receiving. Providers' comments also suggest that they are pleased with the behavioral health services provided.

Summary

Training

The system of training and supervision employed by the project has met with great success. Providers perceive the BHCs' services to be useful and of high quality. In addition, the clinical outcome data support the notion that the services provided are meaningful to the patients. Overall, changes in patients' reported symptoms of depression are significant, and in the desirable direction.

Work still needs to be done in this area, however. First, the task of indexing and editing the tapes from the initial training need to be completed. Also, the major task of completing a training manual also needs to be completed.

Outcome measures. Staff has used the current versions of the clinical outcome measures and consumer satisfactions surveys satisfactorily since January 2002. The changes made at the beginning of the year have increased survey response and accuracy.

In the future, staff will conduct sub-studies to examine the psychometric properties of the instruments being used. Again, our goal is to refine these instruments until they have acceptable reliability and validity, then market them to other agencies that provide integrated healthcare services. Finally, later this year, staff will begin to examine the medical cost and utilization for the first cohort of patients.

Data Collection and Clinical Outcomes

Patient participation continues at an outstanding rate. Project staff needs to focus on conducting pre- and post-testing on patients who present with not only depression, but the myriad of other presenting problems. This would allow us to examine the efficacy of behavioral health services on other problems such as anxiety and pain. Furthermore, by increasing our sample size we can have greater confidence that our results are generalizable to other patient populations. With adequate funding we could begin collecting data on a control sample.

In summary, the first year of the project has been fruitful. In these first 9 months, clinicians have touched the lives of 370 individuals in what can be described by all accounts, as a positive manner. In the following years, patient contacts are expected to be even greater since all start up issues have been resolved, along with any problems with methods or instruments.

In addition to continuing to provide free behavioral health consultation services, the project is also working to increase its community involvement. First, the PI was officially voted on the faculty at the University of Hawaii, Manoa, which will allow him to work more closely with faculty and students there. Also, a stakeholders' steering committee was formed to help guide project goals. Members of this committee will be comprised of local consumers and primary care providers. The University of Hawaii, Manoa has approved the project as an official internship, which will allow doctoral students another local internship site, of which there are precious few, especially in Hawaii. One intern is already hoping to join project staff in the fall. Finally, future grant awards will bring money into the local economy.

Clearly there is more work to be done, however, most of these future goals simply involve refining aspects of what has already been a successful program. Given the past successes of the project, the future looks to be quite fruitful.

References

Beck, A. T., Guth, D., Steer, R. A., & Ball, R. (1997). Screening for major depression disorders in medical inpatients with the Beck Depression Inventory for Primary Care. *Behavior Research and Therapy, 35,* 785-791.

Cummings, N.A. (1997). Behavioral health in primary care: Dollars and sense. In N.A. Cummings, J.L. Cummings, & J.N. Johnson (Eds.) *Behavioral health in primary care: A guide for clinical integration.* Madison, CT: Psychosocial Press.

Cummings, N. A., Dorken, H., Pallak, M. S., & Henke, C. J. (1993). The impact of psychological intervention on health care cost and utilization: The Hawaii Medicaid Project. In *Medicaid, Managed Behavioral Health and Implications for Public Policy (Vol. 2). Healthcare and utilization cost series* (pp. 3-23). South San Francisco, CA: Foundation for Behavioral Health.

Lehman, A.F. (1983). The well-being of chronic mental patients: Assessing their quality of life. *Archives of General Psychiatry, 40,* 369-373.

Pallack, M., Cummings, N., Dorken, H., & Henke, C. (1994). Medical Costs, Medicaid, and Managed Mental Health Treatment: the Hawaii Study. *Managed Care Quarterly, 2(2).*

Appendix A

Index of Materials

1. Anxiety Disorders
    a. Phobia
        i. Mostly Phobia questionnaires, from Biodyne Materials
    b. Panic Disorder
        i. Panic Disorder Protocol, being developed by A. Kaplan
        ii. Panic Disorder and Agoraphobia, chapter by Craske & Barlow
        iii. Integrated Panic Disorder Treatment for Primary Care, by Regev et al., students at UNR.
        iv. Practice Guidelines for the Treatment of Patients with Panic Disorder, American Psychiatric Association Pracitice Guidelines,

v. Panic Disorder Practice Guidelines, from Practice Guidelines Coalition off the internet
c. Agoraphobia
    i. From Biodyne materials
d. Social Anxiety
    i. Social Phobia and Social Anxiety, chapter by Hope & Heimberg
e. OCD
    i. Obsessive Compulsive Disorder, chapter by Riggs & Foa
2. Other Specific Disorders
  a. Depression
    i. Depression Protocol, being developed by A. Kaplan
  b. ADHD
    i. Behavioral Treatment for ADHD: An Overview, by David Rabiner, athealth.com
    ii. ADHD Protocol, being developed by A. Kaplan
  c. Eating Disorders
    i. Cognitive-Behavioral Therapy for Binge Eating and Bulimia Nervosa: A comprehensive Treatment Manual, by Fairburn et al,
    ii. Cognitive-Behavioral Therapy for Bulimia, by Fairburn
  d. Borderline PD
    i. The Borderline Group Therapy Protocol, Cummings and Sayama, from Focused Psychotherapy
  e. Sexual Nuisances
    i. Chapter from Biodyne materials
3. Substance Abuse
  a. Adult Children of Alcoholics
    i. Group Protocol on Adult Children of Alcoholics, chapter from Biodyne materials
  b. Abstinence Training
    i. Group Protocol on Abstinence Training, developed by Foos and Ottens
  c. Chemical Dependency Psychoeducation
    i. Psycheducational Group of Chemical Dependency, from Biodyne materials
  d. Facts on Specific Substances
    i. Cocaine, fact sheet adapted from Janet's materials
4. Treatment Modalities
  a. Couples Therapy
    i. Chapter from Biodyne model
  b. Group Therapy
    i. The Immediate Group, Chapter from Biodyne model
    ii. Group Therapy, Chapter from Biodyne model
  c. Family Therapy
    i. Chapter from Biodyne model

    d. Biofeedback
        i. Chapter from Biodyne model
    e. Telephone Outreach
        i. Chapter from Biodyne model
    f. Psychoeducation
        i. Elements of Psychoeducational Protocols, by Cummings & Cummings
5. Life Style
    a. Weight Management
        i. Group Protocol on Weight Management, chapter from Biodyne materials
    b. Stress Management
        i. Group Protocol on Stress Management, chapter from Biodyne materials
        ii. Stress Inoculation Training, manual by Donald Meichenbaum
    c. Chronic Pain
        i. Chronic Pain Protocol, being developed by A. Kaplan
        ii. Group Protocol on Chronic Pain, chapter from Biodyne materials
    d. Smoking Cessation
        i. Nicotine Fact Sheet, adapted from Janet's materials
        ii. Group Protocol on Smoking Cessation, chapter from Biodyne materials
6. Medical Psych
    a. Cardiovascular Disease
        i. Fact sheet adapted from Janet's materials; includes facts about cardiovas
           cular disease, cardiovascular disorders, recovering from heart disease,
    b. Digestive Disorders
        i. Fact sheet adapted from Janet's materials; includes facts about gas
           trointestinal tract, digestive disorders, stress/psychological factors and
           GI tract,
    c. Disorders of immune system
        i. Fact sheet adapted from Janet's materials; includes facts about infection,
           infectious disorders, immune disorders, psychoneuroimmunology,
           stress/psychological factors and immunology
    d. Endocrine System Disorders
        i. Fact sheet adapted from Janet's materials; includes facts about endocrine
           system, endocrine disorders
    e. Cancer
        i. Fact sheet adapted from Janet's materials; includes facts about
           different cancers, psychological factors and cancer, and coping
    f. Blood disorders
        i. Fact sheet adapted from Janet's materials; includes facts about blood,
           blood disorders,
    g. Asthma
        i. Protocol for the Integrated Treatment of Adult Asthma by Byrd et al.,
           students at UNR,

        ii. A controlled Trial of Two Forms of Self-Management for Adults with Asthma (Wilson et al, 1993), Journal article of clinical study

    h. Hypertension

        i. Hypertension: an Evidence Based Approach, by Niccols, student at UNR

    i. HIV/AIDS

        i. Evaluating a HAART Adherence Enhancement Intervention for HIV/ AIDS Positive Patients, A Research Proposal, by Avina et al, students at UNR

    j. Urinary Tract Infections

        i. Treatment of Urinary Incontinence in Older Adults: A step-care model, by Buchanan and Hadden, students at UNR

    k. Musculoskeletal disorders

        i. Fact sheet adapted from Janet's materials

7. Other Training Materials

    a. US Air Force Primary Behavioral Health Care Services Practice Manual Version 2.0

    b. Focused Psychotherapy: A Casebook of Brief, Intermittent Psychotherapy Throughout the Lifecycle, Book by Cummings & Sayama.

    c. Brief Intermittent Therapy Throuought the Lifecycle, chapter from Biodyne Materials

    d. Psychotropic Medications, information from Biodyne Materials

    e. Biodyne Bootcamp outline

    f. Behavioral Medicine, Clinical Health Psychology, and Cost Offset, journal article by Friedman et al (1995)

    g. The Catalytic Function in Psychotherapy, Journal Article by Bennett (1989)

    h. The Anatomy of Psychotherapy Under National Health Insurance, Journal Article by N. Cummings (1977).

    i. The General Practice of Psychology, Journal Article by N. Cummings (1979).

    j. Prolonged (ideal) versus short-term (realistic) psychotherapy, Journal Article by N. Cummings (1977).

    k. Brief Psychotherapy and Medical Utilization, Journal Article by N. Cummings & Follette.

    l. Impact of Alcohol, Drug Abuse, and Mental Health Treatment on Medical Care Utilization, Journal Article by Jones & Vischi (1979).

    m. Turning Bread into Stones, Journal Article by N. Cummings (1979).

8. Assessment Scales and Measures

    a. SUDS Scales for: Anxiety, Behavioral problems, Chronic Pain, relational problems, depression, general SUDS scale

    b. Others instruments: Functional Status, Somatic Complaints List, substance Abuse Scale, Beck Depression Inventory-Primary Care version, provider Satisfaction, Patient Satisfaction, patient Contact Sheet

Appendix B
Chronic Pain FAQ Sheet for Clinicians

Assessment

1. Assess for type of pain, which may include:

- dull, aching pain in muscles and joints
- sharp, knife-like pain in tender areas
- widespread pain over multiple parts of the body
- headaches, migraines

2. Assess for Symptoms associated with chronic pain, including:

- tiredness, exhaustion
- problems concentrating and working
- decrease in the quality of life, relationships, and play
- anxiety, depression
- sleep difficulties
- feelings of anger, hopelessness, frustration

3. Assess onset and duration: (for Pain Disorder diagnosis, symptoms should persist for at least three months).

4. Assess previous attempts to manage pain (surgeries, medications, other treatments). There is often no medical or physical evidence to explain the intensity or persistence of the pain.

5. Identify a pain pattern:
   A. What time of day is the pain better or worse?
   B. During what activities does the pain improve or worsen?

6. Coping Strategies: What does the patient do to cope with pain (behaviors and thoughts)?

Patient Education

1. Why am I in pain?
- Pain is our body's natural way of telling us there is something wrong.

- Everybody experiences some pain, but when there isn't any solution to the pain the pain is not useful. Chronic pain is ongoing pain that is not fully cured by medical intervention.
- Pain can be exacerbated by several factors (e.g., stress, sleep problems, anxiety, interpersonal conflict, medical complications). There is a vicious cycle in that these factors can both contribute to pain and also be a result of pain.

- Explain to patient cognitive factors that exacerbate pain:
    1. focusing on the pain
    2. psychological state (e.g., helplessness, depression)
    3. attitude toward pain (e.g., rejection versus acceptance)
- Explain to patient behavioral factors that exacerbate pain:
    1. lack of physical activity
    2. sleep problems and poor eating habits
    3. obesity
    4. smoking, drugs, alcohol
    5. overexertion or over doing activities instead of pacing and recuperating in-between.
- Explain to patient environmental factors that exacerbate pain:
    1. cold, loud noises, unsupportive furniture
    2. lack of support (e.g., back braces, shoes)

2. How do we treat Chronic Pain?
- Lifestyle changes: learning techniques to cope with pain are safe and effective in treating Chronic Pain. Even if Chronic Pain does not completely resolve, behavioral changes can help the patient learn to live a rich and fulfilling life.
- Taking an active role: Patients need to work with their treatment team and take an active role in managing their pain.
- Medical interventions: Chronic Pain may be treated through medical interventions when appropriate, such as medications, surgery, trigger point injections, etc. However, caution should be used since medications for pain are often addictive and surgery is evasive and possibly dangerous.

Cognitive Intervention

1. Negative Stereotypes
    A. Have patient identify stereotypes s/he associates with Chronic Pain (lazy, useless, unproductive).
    B. Have the patient define the meaning of the stereotypes s/he identifies (e.g., A lazy person is one who lays around and doesn't do anything).
    C. Have the patient explore how true the definition is to him/her (e.g., I push

myself to do things but sometimes have to rest because I'm in pain).
D. Have the patient challenge the stereotype and come up with alternative beliefs (e.g., I try my best to do things even though I'm in pain. A lazy person wouldn't make any effort at all).

2. Feelings of Helplessness: Patients often believe that if the pain is limiting their ability to do activities, they might as well not bother at all (All-Or-Nothing Thinking)
   A. Make sure patient understands that it is possible to live a full life even with Chronic Pain. She just needs to learn to do things differently. Discuss All-Or-Nothing Thinking.
   B. Have patient identify activities that she thinks she cannot do (e.g., I can't hang out with friends because I'm in too much pain to do enjoyable activities with them).
   C. Even if these activities are difficult, there may be different ways of approaching the activity to make it possible (e.g., I can still hang out with friends and have fun. I may not be able to play basketball with them, but I can cheer them on and have a picnic afterwards. They will welcome my company).

3. Anger at self and others: Many patients understand that their pain is not their fault or anybody else's and to not take out their anger or frustration on themselves or others.

4. Coping Thoughts: Explore the patient's own thoughts that they use to relieve pain.

Behavioral Intervention

1. Making tasks more manageable: Have patient list "Things that are difficult to do". Address the "Things that are difficult to do" list and help the patient come up with practical solutions breaking down difficult tasks into manageable pieces and avoid overexertion and frustration. Also have patient identify things in their environment that are problematic and help patient find solutions (Ex. Patient cannot lift heavy groceries like they used so now they will have to make more trips to bring all the groceries inside.)
2. Goal setting: Have patient set short and long-term goals to keep them motivated
3. Make plans according to pain pattern: Use the patient's pattern of pain (identified in the assessment section) to help guide daily routine.
4. Plan enjoyable activities: Identify "Things that I can do" and plan to do them.
5. Relaxation techniques: plan ways to relax (baths, massages, meditation, heating pads, etc.)

6. Seek social support: Have patient identify their social network that they can rely on for support. Suggest local services (e.g., chronic pain support group)
7. Physical activity: Help patient establish a reasonable exercise routine to maintain flexibility and strength.
    1. Pleasant images (e.g., conjuring peaceful scene)
    2. Dramatized images (e.g., using pain, like a "wounded spy")
    3. Neutral images (e.g., planning weekend, doing budget)
    4. Focus on environment (counting ceiling tiles, trees)
    5. Rhythmic activity (e.g., counting or singing)

Medical/Adjunct Interventions

1. Medications:
- Analgesics, such as Vicodin, or the benzodiazpine drugs, may be used to decrease pain, but they are addictive and may negatively impact cognitive functioning.
- Neurontin may be moderately effective, helps inhibit the brain from receiving pain signals
- Antidepressents: may be helpful in relieving depression and anxiety related to pain. The tricylic antidepresents are known to have some pain relieving action.

2. TENS Units (transcutaneous electrical nerve stimulation): may provide temporary relief from pain. TENS works by sending small electrical signals that disrupt pain messages on their way to the brain. TENS Units are portable, safe, and have few side effects.

3. Nerve Blocks: a procedure in which a physician provides a local anesthetic which is injected into the areas of pain for temporary relief.
4. Biofeedback: A process that helps the patient learn to control physiological functioning, and may help him feel he has some control over pain.

Other Factors

1. Validate pain: It is important to validate the patient's pain. Patients are often frustrated and feel helpless because medical doctors cannot help them.
2. Primary gains: Patient's may receive primary gains (e.g., disability) for pain.
3 Secondary gains: Patients may not be motivated to help themselves because of secondary gains such as attention they receive for the pain. The therapist may work to help the patient receive the secondary gains in a manner that does not involve pain (e.g., get attention for creative activities). It is often helpful to work with individuals in the patient's support system.

Other Available Clinical Fact Sheets

- Blood Disorders
- Cancer
- Cardiovascular Disease
- Cocaine
- Digestive Disorders
- Endocrine Disorders
- Muscoskeletal Disorders
- Nicotine
- Pain
- Depression
- Chronic Pain

Appendix C

List of Materials Provided by Mountainview Consulting, Inc.

- Chronic pain information
- List of core behavioral health skills for depression
- Medication assessment questionnaire
- Information about medications and chronic pain

Appendix D

Resource Phone Numbers

Elderly Services

Catholic Charities Elderly Services   595-0077
· Transportation Services Program providing specialized island-wide transportation to and from group dining sites, shopping, medical appointments, entitlement agencies, excursions
· Housing Assistance Program to help in housing crisis, needing services such as counseling on housing options; assistance with information, referrals, application to permanently affordable housing units; advocacy; social and financial services; group homes/shared housing
· Money Management Assistance provides budget preparation and

maintenance services for the elderly who can no longer manage their finance or need assistance; bill sorting and advocacy

Quality Living Choices (part of Catholic Charities)–   595-0077
· provides foster family or residential care for persons on O'ahu and the Big Island who would otherwise be placed in a nursing facility; clients need to be Medicaid eligible and ICF/SNF level of care; case management is provided to the client to monitor social and physical needs

Lanakila Multi-Purpose Senior Center–   847-1322
· provides a focal point for elders living in the area from Ward Avenue to Fort Shafter to participate in educational sessions, recreational and leisure activities, volunteer opportunities, and ethnic club meetings and activities

Child & Family Service   543-8405
· Senior Case Management, a Kupuna care service, includes assessment of care needs by nurses and social workers, arranges for immediate and long-term assistance from community services to help preserve independence, works together with families to help them take charge of their own situations, and offers services seven days a week
· Health Support Group for Frail Older Adults–many locations on O'ahu, two weekly meetings per group, learn about topics important to seniors, share and socialize, safe exercises for seniors to improve fitness, case management as needed:

Gerontology – Honolulu   543-8468
    Gerontology – Ewa   681-1401

Senior Hotline   523-4545

Adult Intake Unit, Dept. of Human Services–   832-5115
· for dependent or frail elderly adults who are being abused or neglected

Temporary Financial Aid:
· Catholic Charities Elderly Services   595-0077
· Catholic Charities Community and Immigrant Services   528-5233
· CSI, Inc.   538-0353
· Domestic Violence Clearinghouse   531-3771
· Hawaii Centers for Independent Living   522-5400
· Jewish Community Services   258-7121
· Salvation Army, O'ahu   988-2136
· St. Sofia Ukranian Greek Church/
Waianae Community Outreach   696-4095

Utility Assistance:
- Verizon Hawaii Lifeline Service   643-3456
- HCAP (Honolulu Community Action Program)–
subsidies for gas and electric bills)   521-4531

Food Banks:
- Hawaii Foodbank   275-2000
- HCAP (Honolulu Community Action Program)–
federal surplus food distribution   521-4531

Meals: Group dining sites and home-delivered meals
- Alu Like Ke Ola Pono Project–
meal sites for Native Hawaiian elders   535-6728
- Hawaii Meals on Wheels–home-delivered meals, Honolulu
and Kaneohe   988-6747
- Lanakila Meals on Wheels–group dining sites and
home-delivered meals, island-wide   531-0555

Housing: Foster and care home placement agencies that place and monitor Medicaid eligible individuals in authorized foster or care homes. Agencies may also accept private pay clients.
- Abel Case Management, Inc.   486-7914
- Aloha Health Care Providers, Inc.   676-7505
- Case Management, Inc.   676-1192
- Case Management Professionals, Inc.   689-1937
- Catholic Charities Quality Living Choices Program   535-0138
- Quality Case Management, Inc.   423-2468
- Queen's Community Based Programs   547-4410
- Residential Choices, Inc.   676-3948

Housing Search and Information:
- Bob Tanaka, Inc.   949-4111
- CBM Group, Inc., Hale Mohalu Senior Apartments   456-0368
- Chaney, Books & Company   544-1600
- City & County Rental Assistance–Section 8 subsidies   523-4266
- Hawaii Affordable Properties, Inc.   589-1845
- Homeless Solutions, Inc.–transitional housing for the homeless 973-0600
- Housing Assistance Program, Catholic Charities Elderly
Services– help with housing needs for seniors   595-0077
- HUD (Dept. of Housing and Urban Development)   522-8175
- Kulaokahua–transitional housing for the elderly   780-6544
- Loyalty Enterprises   543-0511
- Mark Development, Inc.   735-9099

· Prudential Locations   738-3100
· Retirement Housing Foundation
    Weinberg – Philip St. Elderly   949-2555
    Pauahi Elderly   524-5844
· State Housing & Community Development Corporation of HI
    Applications (Housing)   832-5960
Rent Subsidy (including Section 8)   832-5960
Housing Hotline   587-0524
· Urban Management   524-2731

Household Goods:
· The Community Clearinghouse, a program of Helping Hands Hawaii
(apply through social agencies, welfare, churches)   845-1669
· Kaumakapili Church Free Store (Fridays, 8:30 a.m.-10:30 a.m.) 845-0908

Escort:
· Angels on Wheels, American Cancer Society—cancer patients to
doctor's appointment only
    Honolulu Unit   595-7544
    Central/Leeward Unit   486-8420
    Windward Unit   262-5124
· Catholic Charities Elderly Services   595-0077
· Moiliili Senior Center   955-1555
· Project Dana   945-3736
· Senior Solutions   454-0541

Inventory of Resource Lists

- Domestic Violence
- The Elderly
- Bereavement
- General Mental Health Services
- Anger Management
- Weight Loss
- Substance Abuse Treatment
- Remedial Reading Resources
- Job Training and Vocational Rehabilitation
- Depression
- Chronic Pain
- Suicide

Appendix E

Patient's Name: _____

Date: ____/____/____

Depression Scale

Administrator Instructions: For each item, please read the appropriate question based on whether this is a baseline administration or follow-up. Please record patient's responses in the area provided.

Baseline Questions: In the past two weeks how many days did you feel depressed? _____

On average, when you felt depressed, how would you rate your level of depression? _____

Follow-up Questions: Since you last visit approximately (prompt) days ago, how many days did you feel depressed? _____

On average, when you were depressed, how would you rate your level of depression? _____

10 **Extreme** depression; could not function at all
9
8
7 **Severe** depression; had serious difficulty functioning
6
5 **Moderate** pain; depression present but manageable; moderate difficulty functioning, but I could function if I pushed myself
4
3 **Mild** pain; mild depression; some problems in functioning
2
1 **Minimal** depression; only mild and occasional problems in functioning, but barely noticeable
0 **No** depression; no problems functioning at all

Complete List of SUDS

• Depression
• Anxiety

- Pain
- Behavioral Problems
- Relationship Problems

Other Outcome Measures

- Functional Status
- Cigarette Use
- Drug Use
- Alcohol Consumption
- Somatic Complaints

The authors would like to thank Charles Van Anden, Linda Brinkley, Andrew Aoki, Mike Sayama, Rick Chung, and Kay Wong, Patti Robinson and Kirk Strosahl for their assistance on this project.

Integrating Consultative Behavioral Healthcare into the Air Force Medical System

Christine N. Runyan, Vincent P. Fonseca, & Christopher Hunter

While other chapters of this book have focused on the logic, science, and overarching issues pertaining to integrated care, this chapter will explore how one system has used many of the principles previously described to integrate behavioral health providers into primary care using a consultative approach. After providing some background about the Air Force Medical Service (AFMS), this chapter will describe the planning, development, and implementation of an integrative care initiative using the *"Seven Habits of Highly Successful Integrated Care Programs"* framework previously introduced by Kirk Strosahl, Ph.D. A description of the training process that has been developed as well as preliminary outcomes from this project will be discussed.

Introduction

Mental health disorders are one of the most burdensome public health problems affecting society today, accounting for roughly 15% of the overall burden of disease in the United States (Murray & Lopez, 1996). Several health promotion and disease prevention agencies have offered recommendations for improving screening and treatment of individuals with mental health disorders. In 1999, the U.S. Surgeon General released a landmark report on mental health, calling for the recognition of mental health as a necessary component of overall good health and well being. One of the leading health indicators in Healthy People 2010[1] is to increase the proportion of adults with recognized depression who receive treatment. Additionally, the U.S. Preventive Services Task Force recently recommended universal depression screening of adults in clinical practices that have systems in place to assure accurate diagnosis, effective treatment, and follow-up (U.S. Preventive Services Task Force, 2002). Considering that approximately one in five Americans will suffer from a major mental illness each year, and that fewer than half receive any professional medical or mental health intervention (Kessler, Burns & Shapiro, 1993; Kessler et al., 1994; Reiger et al., 1993), it is not surprising that these agencies have coalescing goals targeting timely and accurate recognition, assessment, and management of mental illness.

Unfortunately, there are both economic and social barriers to achieving these goals. One of the biggest obstacles is the lack of health insurance. Roughly 39 million people are without healthcare coverage in the United States (Mills, Robert J: U.S. Census Bureau, 2001). Even among those with health coverage, few health plans offer parity in their coverage for mental health, as compared with physical health conditions. These barriers are compounded by a stigma that continues to surround mental illness in our society. Myths and misconceptions about mental illness and its treatment ultimately leave many individuals suffering unnecessarily with unrecognized, unassessed, and untreated mental health conditions.

Beyond individual suffering and disability, there is also an impact on healthcare organizations when behavioral issues and mental health conditions are not adequately addressed. For example, there is up to a two-fold increase in medical utilization among psychosocially distressed individuals as compared with their non-distressed counterparts (Simon, 1992; Greenberg, Stiglin, Finkelstein, & Berndt, 1993). Several studies have demonstrated a relationship between factors of psychosocial distress and poor general health status, morbidity, and mortality – all of which drive up medical care costs (Roy-Byrne and Katon, 1997). Whether psychosocial distress is caused by or a contributor to medical disease processes, the end result is likely to be a more complicated course of treatment, increased medical costs to the system and the individual patient as well as increased healthcare utilization (Strosahl, 2001).

In fact, it is estimated that as many as 70% of primary care visits are related to behavioral health needs (Fries, Koop, & Beadle, 1993). Waiting rooms of most primary medical care clinics are filled with patients whose psychosocial problems or behaviors contribute their health situation. Even among those with chronic or acute medical conditions, potential behavioral and lifestyle interventions are often overlooked or minimally addressed even though their impact on the patient's overall health and functioning could be profound. The rapid work pace, inadequate training to intervene with behavioral and emotional conditions, or fear of opening "Pandora's Box" create an atmosphere in many primary care clinics whereby there is a mismatch between the services that are being provided and the patient's needs. As long as this mismatch exists, it is difficult to deliver optimal and cost-effective care because the physical symptoms or pathology being treated is not what is most impacting the patient's health status. Even when a behavioral health condition is appropriately identified in primary care, treatment is most often delivered solely by a primary care provider (PCP), who may have limited behavioral health expertise (Kessler et al., 1994; Reiger et al., 1993). Time constraints and sub-optimal training and skills among primary care providers (PCPs) make improvements in recognition and management a daunting challenge.

Even if these barriers could be removed, another change that must occur is a shift among PC and behavioral health providers, medical systems, and even patients in how mental health and mental illness are conceptualized. That is, mental health and mental illness are commonly misunderstood as dichotomous entities, when in reality they are opposing points along the same behavioral health continuum (Figure 7.1). Historically, mental and behavioral health interventions have been reserved for those meeting DSM diagnostic criteria. Sir Geoffrey Rose, in his writing on the strategies of prevention (1992; 1993), stated that "case definitions are necessary...but they should be recognized for what they are, which is an operational convenience and not a description of nature. Recognition of the continuous distribution which unites the population, sick and healthy, is a first and necessary step…" Rose's comments reflect the evidence which suggests the progression from healthy to "caseness" is a gradual one, often marked by many missed opportunities to intervene, as well as individual suffering. Psychosocial stressors can manifest as somatic complaints or symptoms and adversely impact quality of life long before the traditional definition of "caseness" is met.

Behavioral Health Continuum in a Large Population

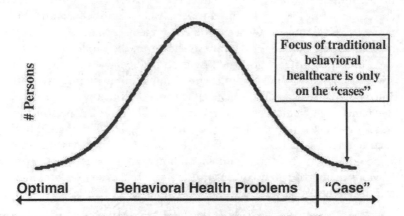

Figure 7.1. Behavioral Health Continuum.

Currently, recognition and intervention of even the most severe behavioral health cases is sub-optimal (Simon & VonKorff, 1995). This is partly because medical providers, who are typically trained from a Cartesian framework of mind-body dualism, are trying to assess, diagnose, and treat multiple complaints during the typical 15-minute visit. When behavioral health needs are detected, it is often because the symptoms are so pronounced that the patient, family, or caregiver can no longer ignore them. Behavioral health interventions, through a referral to a specialty care provider, may be offered at this point; however, only about one in four patients will actually seek mental health services (Strosahl, 2001).

In contrast, behavioral health intervention delivered by trained behavioral health providers on the "front lines" of primary care is emerging as a potential means of reducing the impact of mental and behavioral health conditions. Integrated primary care allows for a shift toward a population based approach of behavioral healthcare in which brief behavioral health services can be provided to patients at an earlier point in their progression along the health continuum, in a setting that minimizes resistance to care, and provides different types of services that may more closely match patient's needs. It is also likely to reduce the duration and intensity of treatment required to move individuals back towards the healthier end of the continuum as compared with the intensity of services required once an individual moves further down the health continuum towards illness.

The Air Force Medical Service

The vision is simple in the Air Force Medical Service (AFMS) – high-quality healthcare, at a reasonable cost, with easy access to health care providers. The AFMS comprises 78 discrete medical facilities and is responsible for the healthcare of roughly 1.2 million enrolled persons. The Air Force (AF) facilities are geographically distributed, spanning the entire United States as well as Europe, Asia and the Pacific. Similar to the U.S. Surgeon General, the AF Surgeon General's office sets global policy, regulations, and areas of emphasis; however, the implementation of such policy is almost exclusively governed by each facility. Each facility functionally operates as a unique hospital or clinic with a similar infrastructure as a staff-model Health Maintenance Organization. The facility is responsible for the care of their enrolled panel. If the facility cannot meet the needs of an enrolled person, the patient is then sent to a network provider in the community. In 2000, mental health care provided to AFMS beneficiaries outside AF facilities was one of the leading costs to the medical system, totaling about 8.3 million dollars. Thus, one key priority of the AFMS is to appropriately "recapture" the care that is sent to providers in the community because it costs significantly more than care provided in the direct care system.

Over the past five years, the AFMS has begun to re-engineer its entire healthcare delivery system. This effort is guided by a population health improvement strategy that is based on routine and comprehensive health assessment, preventive and primary care, and disease management. Most importantly, the focus has been on shifting from delivering more costly and less effective tertiary healthcare service towards prevention of injuries and illness. Identifying a variety of activities that would help optimize resource use, improve the health of beneficiaries, expand access to care, and increase customer and staff satisfaction led to a massive re-engineering of primary care clinics in the AF – Primary Care Optimization (PCO). Concomitant with PCO, the AFMS was evaluating the outcomes from a "proof of concept" project undertaken in 1998 at one AF base to demonstrate that behavioral health providers could work effectively and efficiently in primary care (PC) environments. By 1999, optimizing behavioral healthcare through the delivery of integrated primary care became part of the PCO initiative.

Setting the Stage for the Behavioral Health Optimization Project (BHOP)

Improving access to and delivery of behavioral health services in the direct care system was the primary objective of BHOP. To achieve this objective, PC clinics needed to change their processes of care to better recognize and appropriately treat individuals with behavioral health conditions. One of the essential lessons learned from the initial pilot effort in 1998 was that merely co-locating behavioral health providers was an insufficient solution. In the absence of changed processes, co-located behavioral health providers are likely to revert to delivering specialty services to only the small proportion of the population that PCPs clinically suspect need behavioral healthcare. Making an impact on the population, however, requires behavioral health providers to support improved detection through either targeted or universal screening, assessment, intervention and follow-up for behavioral health conditions. Ideally, these processes should also minimize the time-burden on the PCPs. Fortunately, many of the recommended services do not require a physician. Other members of the healthcare team, including the behavioral health provider, have the expertise to provide these services.

Our goals to optimize Behavioral Healthcare were to:

1. Increase access to BH care within the AF facilities to minimize patients being sent to network providers;
2. Provide healthcare options to patients and encourage shared-decision making;
3. Focus on prevention by identifying BH conditions early;
4. Work with the medical providers to break down common communication barriers;
5. Offer services along the entire continuum of health;
6. Offer services that were acceptable – and effective.

Dr. Kirk Strosahl's *"Seven Habits of Highly Successful Integrated Care Programs"* will now be used to describe how the AFMS is implementing this vision of integrated behavioral healthcare. The seven habits are: (1) Addressing political and organizational issues; (2) Creating financing strategies that manage risk and ensure long term stability; (3) Define core program parameters; (4) Define program mission, scope, and tactics; (5) Create administrative infrastructure; (6) Identify and address training needs; and (7) Define and measure performance indicators.

I. Develop Political and Organizational Support

Because the AFMS is both geographically distributed and decision-making occurs locally, gaining interest and support from local decision-makers was imperative. This occurred through a variety of informal communications; however, the single most effective process was bringing all of the key decision-makers into one room. In this two-day meeting, following substantial discussion, disagreement, weighing of the evidence, and addressing local concerns, a systematic plan for implementation was ultimately developed. Developing the plan and vision within the group took more time and compromises than were originally envisioned, but the end result was complete buy-in and commitment from these individuals as well as a sense of ownership for the process and outcomes. Although the AFMS supported this concept and initiative from the outset with written memos of endorsement, all involvement from local facilities was on a voluntary basis only – there was no requirement for any site to participate. Aligning the BHOP initiative with PCO, which also had political and organizational support at the highest levels, however, may have facilitated participation. This system-wide step was essential in developing a firm foundation on which to build the integrated care initiative.

II. Financing Strategy and Ensure Long Term Stability

Financing strategies. Because the AFMS essentially functions as 78 distinct staff-model HMOs, there was no need to negotiate a financial arrangement for BH services delivered in PC clinics. In the AFMS, the medical treatment facility is allocated an operating budget to provide healthcare for their entire enrolled beneficiary population, whether it be mental or physical healthcare. Provider staffing is based on the size of the enrolled population. Although providers account for all services they provide to patients, they are not under pressure to "earn" their salary from the number and types of appointments or procedures performed and coded each day.

At the BHOP project level, financial support for this initiative was provided internally from the Air Force Surgeon General's office. Much of this funding was allocated to the training of behavioral health providers because, rather than purchasing or carving out services, we shifted behavioral health provider's time from specialty mental health clinics to primary care clinics. That is, integrated care was implemented with no increased staffing and the AFMS will likely continue to rely on existing providers to provide integrated care. Since AFMS providers also frequently re-locate or leave the Air Force, and new providers join, a "train-the-trainers" model was adopted so that training can be sustained using only AF trainers.

Ensure long term stability. The AFMS hired an external consultant and subject matter expert to provide both initial didactic and clinical training to a selected cohort of AF providers. Seven BH providers, all of whom worked at one of the three Air Force psychology internship sites, were selected to serve as the original training cohort. The consultant was hired to both train these providers in the behavioral health consultation (BHC) model of care and to train them to train other providers in this model. Developing BHC trainers at the psychology internship sites allows a minimum of 20 interns a year to receive this specialized training. All of the original seven BHCs continue to practice this model, provide training, and have since made "trainers" out of several other BH providers. Over time, we are gradually increasing the pool of both BHC providers as well as BHC trainers, thereby reducing our reliance on an external consultant and trainer.

III. Define Core Program Parameters

The AFMS explored several possible models of delivering behavioral healthcare within the PC clinics and ultimately chose a consultative model of care that was rooted in a population health framework and consistent with the stated goals of this initiative. The model of care differs substantially from traditional specialty mental healthcare. The focus of this model is on brief, functionally based assessment with recommendations and delivery of interventions designed to improve the patient's functioning and quality of life. Along with the patient, the primary care provider is viewed as one of the key customers. Viewing the PCP as a primary customer enables the BHCs to remain focused on increasing the PCP's ability to address BH problems as part of PC treatment, without increasing the time or care burden directly on the PCP. Another aspect of this model is that it expands the behavioral healthcare options that are currently available to AFMS beneficiaries and does so at an earlier point along the health continuum. Table 1 details the core characteristics of the BHC Model.

IV. Define Program Mission, Scope, and Tactics

The AF's BHC Practice Manual is a comprehensive services manual with details of the BHC Service, including the mission, scope, and tactics (detailed in Table 2 below). Not only does the manual describe the suggested strategies for BHCs to successfully integrate into the clinic, it specifically details the minimum core competencies that all BHCs must meet before initiating their BHC Service. A substantial portion of the manual is dedicated to the academic and clinical training program used for BHCs (to be described later in this chapter) and is organized around the core BHC competencies. Thus, this manual is used both as a guide for new practitioners when core competencies are being developed and as an ongoing resource for BHC practitioners.

The BHC Practice Manual evolved over the course of this initiative as we learned more about the practice of this model in the AFMS. The manual, which began as a 70-page document, is now over 150 pages of text, appendices, and templates. In addition, the BHOP website now offers the BHC Service Manual as well as other resources for BHCs to share, such as patient handouts, marketing tools, etc. with others.

V. Create Administrative Infrastructure

We provided infrastructure support with detailed recommendations, tools, and training for critical administrative functions.

Tools. In the AFMS, patient visits are captured using work center codes. A new distinct work center code was created for BHC visits; this code is also linked to the diagnostic and CPT® codes for each patient visit. This method allows BHC visits to be analyzed by the distinct clinic in which BHC care was provided (e.g., family practice or internal medicine), as well as all BHC visits in aggregate.

Other tools included a BHC coding flowsheet and a BHC "superbill" to help BHCs more accurately document diagnostic and CPT® codes. Specific scheduling parameters were also recommended; BHCs were trained to allow maximum scheduled referrals while still maintaining open time for same-day referrals. For example, it was explicitly recommended that BHCs schedule in 15 – 30 minute blocks and to schedule 75% of their clinic time with new and follow-up patients,

Dimension	Characteristics
BHC's Role	- BHC seen as part of primary care healthcare team - BHC referred to as a behavioral specialist, not "psychotherapist" or mental health provider - BHC shares knowledge, provides options and collaborates with patients on healthcare decisions - PCP retains primary responsibility for care
Referral Structure	- Patient referred by PCP for suspected behavioral need or condition
Session Structure	- 15- to 30-minute visits - Limited to one to four visits in typical cases
Assessment Structure	- Brief assessment focused on presenting problem - Emphasis on functional status
Intervention Structure	- Lower intensity, longer interval between sessions - Visits conveniently timed around PCP visits - Long-term follow-up care reserved for high-risk cases
Intervention Methods	- Simple, specific behavioral or cognitive interventions - Interventions can be supported by PC clinic in ongoing care - Patient education and self-management used frequently - Emphasis on home-based practive to promote change - May involve PCP in visits with patient; always work with PCP to reinforce BHC's interventions and vice versa - Refer to specialty care if indicated
Documentation and Feedback to PCP	- Brief notes documented in primary medical record only - Same-day feedback (typically verbal) to primary care provider

Table 7.1: Core Characteristics of the AFMS Behavioral Health Consultation Model.

Dimension	Chapter Heading	Contents	Appendices
Mission	Background and Rationale	- Literature Review - Application to AF Medical System - Population Health Concepts	- Legal Memorandum of Support - Letter of Support for AF Surgeon General's Office
Mission	Primary Behavioral Healthcare	- Treatment Philosophy and Key Principles - Program Goals - Patient Goals	
Scope	BHC Service and Consultant Roles	- Parameters of BHC Service - Typical BHC Services - Role of Consultants - Role of Psychiatry Liaison to BHC - Excluded Services	- BHC Job Description
Tatics	Service Procedures	- How to Access BHC (Types of Referrals) - Patient In Crisis - Indications for Referral to Specialty Care - Assessment Protocol - Initial Consultation Response - Follow-up Consultations - Documentation - Feedback to PCM - Termination of Consultation	- Recommended Screening Measures for BH Problems in PC - Sample BHC Documentation Notes - Resources for Managing Depression in Primary Care
Tactics	Administrative Procedures	- Diagnostic and CPT Codes for BHC Visits - Scheduling Templates - Scheduling Standards - Informed Consent and Use of BHC Information Sheet - Technician Support - Staffing Guidelines - Program Evaluation - Clinical Evaluations	- Coding Glossary, Guide, and Flow Sheets - BHC Information Sheet - Peer Review of Records Form - BHC Program Self-Audit Form - Patient Satisfaction Questionnaire - Provider Satisfaction Questionnaire

Tactics	Recommendations for Clinical Practice	- The Gestalt of Primary Care
		- Step by Step Guide to BHC
		- The Training Program:
		  - Academic Detailing
		  - Skill-Based Training
		  - Continued Mentoring
			- BHC Poster
			- BHC Service Brochure
			- BHC Referral Forms
			- BHC Trainer Job Description
			- Core Competency Tools

Table 7.2: The BHC Practice Manual.

leaving 25% of their time open for "curbside" consultation with PCPs and same-day referrals. Specifically, BHCs were instructed that one way to do this could be to have one 30-minute appointment each hour; this allows approximately 40 scheduled appointments a week and easy access for patients to be seen as same day walk-ins during the second part of each hour. In addition, marketing materials for the BHC service, such as brochures for patients and posters for the PCP exam rooms were developed and distributed to the implementation sites. These are just several examples of how the administrative infrastructure was created. However, the opportunities to improve how administrative tasks are accomplished will continue to arise. Effectively responding to these opportunities will not only enhance the overall clinical effectiveness of BHC Services, but failing to do so could greatly impair an otherwise flourishing service.

Training. Ensuring consistency in BHC Services across AF facilities has been one of the biggest administrative challenges yet. Both patients and providers in the AFMS are a highly mobile population. As such, we are setting up a new expectation among patients for expanded access to behavioral healthcare as integrated care is implemented throughout the 78 facilities in the system. We are also establishing a new expectation among our PCPs for the types of BHC Services in PC. If the BHC Service is different at every clinic in which a PCP works, PCPs may become discouraged and rely less on the BHC over time. It is our goal to develop consistent processes, procedures, structure, and content of BHC Services across AF facilities. The primary means by which we have been able to work toward this goal is through education and training of all new BHCs.

Legal review. Since no case law has yet been established related to integrated primary care, we anticipated resistance from the BH community regarding ethical concerns and legal ramifications. Therefore, the proposed model of care was presented to the medical-legal consultants to the AF Surgeon General. The medical-legal representatives raised several concerns about the model. Specifically, there was concern that patients may not be able to distinguish primary BH care from specialty mental healthcare. They also voiced concerns that specific exclusionary criteria for PC work be established (e.g., imminently suicidal patients are not to be treated by BHCs in PC). However, they also strongly supported the model from the perspective of providing increased access to BH care and provided a written endorsement supporting this initiative. Anecdotally, the medical-legal endorsement alleviated anxiety about providing BH care without traditional informed consent, separate documentation records, and other specialty mental health care constraints.

VI. Identify and Address Training Needs

Overall approach. A "Train the Trainer" model was adopted from the outset of this effort, mainly to ensure sustainability and consistency in the model of integrated behavioral healthcare. Because the practice of consultative behavioral healthcare is considerably different from traditional mental healthcare, knowledge acquisition and clinical training are considered paramount to successful integration. As previously stated, seven BH providers were selected from three different Air Force facilities to serve as the original BHC cohort in the AFMS. The three facilities that were selected to participate each have a psychology internship training program and therefore serve as the entry point for 98% of all AF psychologists. Training was structured similarly at each location. The overall objectives of training were to have each of the original BHCs:

1. implement the model of integrated behavioral healthcare;
2. learn how to train others;
3. establish a training program for interns within their clinic; and finally,
4. establish an externship training program that allowed us to send behavioral health providers practicing at other AF locations to their clinic for on-site clinical training.

In order to accomplish these objectives, an external consultant was hired. This allowed him or her to become familiar with the AFMS model of integrated care, as we had tailored a model to fit our system. This also allowed the consultant to help develop recommendations that were provided to each site on how to select an effective "BHC champion." This effort was, and continues to be, entirely voluntary for every site so it was necessary to choose providers who were interested and willing to learn and practice in a new model of care. The consultant then trained each of the initial seven BHC providers, as described below. These BHCs have, in turn, trained several more providers in their externship training programs and have also trained roughly 20 psychology interns per year in this model of care. Providers trained in the externship model are all volunteers who are interested and committed to integrating into primary care at their local site. At this stage, the BHOP initiative in the AFMS is widely known and even though no policy or regulation exists directing the integration of a behavioral health provider into primary care, over half of the PC clinics in the AFMS are either integrated or are actively moving toward integration with a trained BHC. Using the train-the-trainer's model, this has been possible in less than two years since the project's inception.

Preparing the PC clinics. As the PCPs are one of the primary customers of this model and are responsible for the care for the other customers – the patients – all providers needed to understand the role of the BHC. Therefore, before any on-site training or implementation occurred, the initial groundwork was laid in the PC clinic and with the PC leadership and staff. The BHC met with the PC director to discuss the AFMS model of integrated behavioral healthcare. Once the PC director was supportive, the BHC introduced the model to the PCPs during a routinely scheduled meeting. After these introductory meetings, medical providers are quite eager to have a BHC as part of their healthcare team and often ask why this approach has not been taken sooner.

Initial BHC training. Initially, each BH provider received the AF BHC Practice Manual and was asked to start seeing patients in the PC clinic based on several phone consultations with the external consultant and using the information in the Practice Manual. After each BHC had been in the PC clinic for approximately one month, the external consultant visited the site for one week. During this training week, the consultant delivered a one-day workshop on the consultative model of behavioral healthcare in PC clinics, using a combination of didactic presentation and video clips of BHC practice in a similar model. The consultant also worked one-on-one with each BHC for the remainder of the week. He observed patient visits, giving tailored and highly specific feedback to help the BHC develop the core clinical and practice management competencies. Based on this feedback the BHC altered their practice accordingly and then continued to have ongoing training with the consultant via email and phone calls as needed, as well as monthly one-hour phone consultations. BHCs also videotaped BHC consultation appointments and sent them to the consultant for supplemental feedback. After approximately 9 months, the external consultant returned to each facility for another week to evaluate the BHC's progress on core competency skills and taught them how to successfully train others.

Training BHCs on setting up the service and what to expect. In training BHCs to set up their service for success, the general rule of thumb is that whatever resources, and support provided to PCPs in the clinic should be similarly provided to the BHC. In order for the BHC to function as a member of the PC healthcare team, it is imperative that they establish and negotiate with the PC director both what the BHC can offer to the clinic as well as what resources and support they need to do so. For example, BHCs were trained on the importance of and how to negotiate for office space appropriate for seeing patients within the PC clinic. While a permanent location where providers know they can find the BHC is ideal, this is often not possible nor is it essential. In addition, BHCs were trained on becoming familiar with the administrative processes and protocols that are followed in their PC clinic. For example, if PCP appointments are scheduled at the front desk of the PC clinic, BHCs appointments should also be scheduled here. The idea is that the BHC service looks and feels to patients and PCPs as similar to PC care as possible.

During initial training, BHCs are instructed about the importance of integrating into the overarching PC culture, since it substantially differs from the specialty mental health clinic culture. As there is no substitute for "being there," the BHC was encouraged to attend staff meetings, lectures, and social events with the medical providers when possible. Personal contact with the medical providers, nurses, and technicians is paramount to a good integrated service.

Another aspect of preparatory training for BHCs was to expect a low referral rate from PCPs when first starting an integrated service. Although the PCPs are generally glad to have the BHC service, it often takes time for them to integrate BHC services into their daily practice. BHCs are encouraged to use several different strategies to increase referral rates. First, BHCs were instructed to continuously remind providers what services are available – this can be done informally through conversations or more formally through information sheets or brief presentations at staff meetings. Often, some type of short handout that contains the BHC's name, pager number and the types of problems they can help the PCP manage is most useful. A second strategy was how to increase referrals by spending one minute at the beginning of the day to talk with each of the medical providers. The BHC should tell the provider the times they are in the clinic, when their schedule is open, that walk-ins are welcome, and also ask if they have any patients on their appointment list that the BHC might be able to help them manage. A third strategy was using a weekly handout describing a specific, clinical topic that the BHC could help the PCPs manage. This handout listed the symptom or problem area and how the BHC could help. These topics included sleep difficulties, obesity, tobacco, medication adherence, exercise, high blood pressure, diabetes, and gastrointestinal problems. The final strategy BHCs were taught was to spend time with the PCPs while they are seeing patients. BHCs were encouraged to observe the provider for a couple of hours to get an idea of their practice style and the types of patients they are seeing. This allows the BHC to get to know each provider's style as well as acculturate to the pace and practice of a typical clinic day for PCPs. The secondary benefit of this observation period is that BHCs are likely to encounter *teachable moments* with both PCPs and patients and, with the BHC in the room, the PCP is likely to be more aware of the behavioral health problems their patients may be having.

Training for AF psychology interns. Over the past one and a half years, each AF psychology internship-training site has been training interns in this model of integrated care. All three training sites use a core competency checklist and train BHCs to those specific knowledge and skill sets. However, the training program varies slightly at each site depending on the unique circumstances of the clinic and the overall internship. Although many different schedules can be used for training, it is important to ensure the schedule exposes the trainee to the model with sufficient depth and breadth in terms of the types of patients seen (new patients and follow-up patients), types of problems seen, and types of interactions with PCPs. The next section describes one of these training programs in detail.

All interns are required to read and study the AF BHC Practice Manual prior to any clinical training. Training then begins with a 1-day workshop detailing the specifics and supporting empirical evidence of the model. This phase also includes videotapes of an expert behavioral health consultant conducting a first appointment interview which demonstrates many of the core competencies required to effectively work in primary care. Each intern has a 4-day/week rotation in the primary care clinic for one month. During the first week of clinical training the trainer reviews each aspect of the manual with the intern in order to ensure a good working knowledge of the standards of practice. Training is provided on brief behavioral treatment of psychological and medical disorders most commonly seen in the primary care setting. Interns are also given reading assignments on the use of psychotropic medications with a special emphasis on how BHCs can support PCPs by educating patients on side effects and augmenting the pharmacotherapy of depression, anxiety, and post-traumatic stress disorder.

Also during the first week, clinical training starts with the intern observing the BHC trainer. They observe roughly 25-30 patients, most of whom are new consults. This allows for most aspects unique to the practice of integrated care to be observed and discussed before the trainee begins seeing patients. After each visit, the BHC trainer and the intern discuss what occurred during the appointment. The goal is to teach the intern about rapid functional assessment, designing behavioral change plans for new patients, and evaluating the success of plans for returning patients. The intern also learns how to document BHC visits in the medical record and provide feedback to PCPs.

During the second week of training the intern sees patients, under the observation of the BHC trainer. The BHC trainer observes and provides specific, actionable feedback to the intern on core clinical competencies. Each of the clinical and practice management competencies is reviewed, and the intern is provided feedback on what they did well, what they didn't do well and how they can improve. The BHC trainer also reviews all of the intern's documentation and observes them providing feedback to the PCP. Core competencies on documentation and feedback to the physicians are reviewed with the intern using the same format as with clinical and practice management skills.

During the third week of training the intern sees patients by themselves, with the BHC trainer available for questions and consultation. The intern also does all the documentation and provides feedback to PCPs on their own. This allows the intern to get a sense of what it is like to work independently as a BHC. During the final week of training, the BHC trainer again observes the intern on all aspects of their practice in order to give additional feedback on any areas needing further development. The BHC trainer also serves as an ongoing mentor for the intern if he/she will be practicing as a BHC after internship.

Externship training for other providers. In order to the increase the overall pool of trained BHCs, fully credentialed psychologists and social workers are also brought to the internship sites specifically for BHC training. Although these providers are not able to spend a full month at the training site, the training elements are identical but compressed into a one-week intensive training schedule. The educational components of training occur before the trainee arrives on site; however, on the first day of training the BHC trainer reviews the Practice Manual for clarification and to address any questions the trainee has about practice standards. The trainee then typically spends one day observing the BHC trainer, one-day seeing patients with the BHC trainer, and two days seeing patients on their own with ongoing feedback from the BHC trainer. All feedback to the BHC trainee is based on observations and ratings using the core competencies checklist for clinical and practice management skills. The BHC trainer is then available as a mentor for further feedback or consultation as desired. In fact, approximately a six month period of continued consultation and mentorship through regularly scheduled telephone calls, video review, and e-mail communication is recommended.

Final notes on training. While several lessons have been learned through the development of these training programs, the primary lesson is that there is no substitute for live observation, practice, and feedback. While the BHC Practice Manual is an invaluable resource to BHCs, it is insufficient in preparing BHCs on the nuances and clinical competencies inherent to integrated care. Particularly in a large system that is geographically dispersed, *clinical* training is a necessary component to ensure consistency and fidelity in the model of care. Recently, the AF has also created a series of "Best Practice" videotapes. These tapes detail the core elements of BHC practice along with real provider-patient video clips to demonstrate each of the competencies; these tapes are intended to be used to augment, not replace, clinical training.

VII. Define Measures / Performance Indicators

The initial evaluation focused on whether this model of care satisfied our primary care providers and their patients, whether access to care was improved by placing a behavioral health provider in the PC clinic, and whether BHCs were practicing within the standards of the model. Initial data collection only included the first six months from the originally trained BHCs. An expanded data collection and analysis that includes all AF BHCs who have been practicing for at least six months is currently underway.

Satisfaction surveys. All patients seen by the BHCs practicing in the pilot clinics for one month were anonymously surveyed (n=76). In addition, thirty-four primary care providers working within four of the initial PC pilot clinics were surveyed. All surveys were mailed directly to project staff and were not handled by the BHCs. Twenty-three PCPs responded (68% response rate).

Patient satisfaction. Of note, 97% of patients reported that they were either "satisfied" or "very satisfied" with BHC care and 69% said that they would "definitely" recommend BHC services to others. Almost all (95%) of the patients responded that behavioral healthcare options were at least "sufficiently" discussed. Also, 95% said that they were at least "sufficiently" involved in making decisions about their specific healthcare plan (Table 7.3). Of note, 76% responded they were "very much" or "completely" involved.

Provider satisfaction. All (100%) of PCPs stated they would "definitely" recommend other PCPs and clinics implement BHC Services and 91% felt the BHC Service helped them improve ("quite a bit" or "a lot") their recognition and treatment of BH problems. Also, 100% expressed overall satisfaction with BHC services (Table 7.4). Comments offered on this survey by the PCPs suggested that they were no longer reticent to ask patients about psychosocial concerns because they felt they would not have to manage that aspect alone. Providers also felt that the BHCs provided behavioral healthcare that was both accessible and acceptable to patients.

Level of Overall Quality of BHC Care	Poor	Fair	Good	Very Good	Excellent
	2%	2%	10%	33%	54%
Satisfaction with BHC service	Very Dissatisfied	Dissatisfied	Neutral	Satisfied	Very Satisfied
	2%	2%	0%	14%	83%
Would Recommend BHC Services	Definitely Not	Probably Not	Probably Yes	Definitely Yes	
	2%	2%	27%	69%	
Options Discussed	Not at All	Minimally	Sufficiently	Very Much	Completely
	1%	4%	24%	38%	33%
Shared Decision Making	Not at All	Minimally	Sufficiently	Very Much	Completely
	1%	4%	18%	33%	43%

Table 7.3. Patient Satisfaction Survey Results (n=76).

Access to Behavioral Healthcare

Among the 858 patients seen by the BHCs in PC clinics during six months of data collection, over half (58%) were not active duty military; they were family members of active duty military or retirees. Within these same facilities, fewer than 25% of the patients seen by the specialty mental health clinic were family members or retirees. This is due to the limited appointment availability specialty mental health clinics have for non-active duty individuals. Thus, without the BHC service, many of the patients seen in PC would have either gone without behavioral healthcare or used a network provider, increasing costs to both the patient and the AFMS.

BHC Service Description

Most of the patients interacting with BHCs are seen briefly (15-30 minutes) and their entire care is of short duration – typically one follow-up session is required (mean number of visits = 1.6). BHCs do not build-up a caseload of patients, which allows them to maintain relatively open access for new patients and same-day consultations as needed. If a patient's needs go beyond the consultative care typically offered in primary care, they are referred to more appropriate specialty services. However, among these 858 BHC encounters, fewer than 10% were referred

	Poor	Fair	Good	Very Good	Excellent
Level of Helpfulness	0%	0%	0%	9%	91%
Overall Quality	0%	0%	0%	13%	87%
Level of Overall Satisfaction	Dissatisfied	Somewhat Dissatisfied	Neutral	Somewhat Satisfied	Satisfied
	0%	0%	0%	0%	100%
Would Recommend BHC Services	Definitely Not	Probably Not	Probably Yes	Definitely Yes	
	0%	0%	0%	100%	
Improved Recognition of Behavioral Health Problems	Not at All	A Little Bit	Somewhat	Quite a Bit	A Lot
	0%	0%	9%	23%	68%

Table 7.4: Primary Care Provider Satisfaction Survey Results (n=23).

for specialty mental health services suggesting the majority of presenting complaints are managed quickly and exclusively by the BHCs.

In a descriptive analysis of BHC patients seen over a six-month period, 71% were in six diagnostic categories as depicted in Figure 2. Situational reactions are the most frequent diagnostic category overall; however, among females, depressive disorders were the most frequent category. Although the types of patients seen by BHCs are similar to those often referred to specialty mental health care, BHCs are able to care for these patients in far fewer visits, with substantially less administrative overhead, and still provide services within the direct care system. Therefore, both direct and indirect costs are decreased.

Conclusions

In summary, the AFMS has been able to develop and implement a standard model of consultative behavioral healthcare at 30 AF primary care clinics, while achieving high satisfaction among both primary care providers and patients. We have demonstrated increased access to behavioral healthcare that is both acceptable to patients and reduces the number of referrals to network providers. We now have services that we can provide to patients at earlier points along the health continuum, thereby reducing pain and suffering as well as the intervention intensity required, rather than waiting for mental illness "caseness" to emerge. In the AFMS, integrated behavioral healthcare is now a new tool in our armamentarium as we strive to deliver cost-effective, quality healthcare to our beneficiaries. Moreover, it has moved us closer to the goal of increasing the recognition and appropriate treatment of individuals with behavioral health needs as set forth by the U.S. Preventive Service Task Force, the U.S. Surgeon General and Healthy People 2010.

References

Fries, J., Koop, C., & Beadle, C. (1993). Reducing health care costs by reducing the need and demand for medical services. *The New England Journal of Medicine*, *329*, 321-325.

Greenberg, P. E., Stiglin, L. E., Finkelstein, S. N., & Berndt, E. R. (1993). The economic burden of depression in 1990. *Journal of Clinical Psychiatry*, *54*, 405-418.

Kessler, L., Burns, B., & Shapiro, S. (1993). Psychiatric diagnoses of medical service users: Evidence for the epidemiological catchment area program. *American Journal of Public Health*, *77*, 18-24.

Kessler, R. C., McGonagle, K. A., Zhao, S., Nelson, C. B., Hughes, M., Eshleman, S., et al. (1994). Lifetime and 12-month prevalence of DSM-III-R psychiatric disorders in the United States. Results from the National Comorbidity Survey. *Archives of General Psychiatry*, *51*, 8–19.

Mills, Robert J; U.S. Census Bureau; "Health Insurance Coverage: 2000;" September 2001; Current Population Reports.

Murray, C. J. L., & Lopez, A. D. (Eds.). (1996). The global burden of disease: a comprehensive assessment of mortality and disability from diseases, injuries and risk factors in 1990 and projected to 2020. Cambridge, MA, Harvard School of Public Health on behalf of the World Health Organization and the World Bank (Global Burden of Disease and Injury Series, Vol. I).

Reiger, D., Narrow, W., Rae, D., Manderschied, R., Locke, B. & Goodwin, F. (1993). The de facto U.S. mental and addictive disorders service system: Epidemiological Catchment Area prospective 1-year prevalence rates of disorders and services. *Archives of General Psychiatry*, *50*, 85-94.

Rose, G. *The Strategy of Preventive Medicine*. Oxford University Press: Oxford. 1992.

Rose, G. (1993). Mental disorders and the strategies of prevention. *Psychological Medicine*, *23*, 553-555.

Roy-Byrne, P. P., & Cowley, D. S. (1998). Pharmacological treatment of panic, generalized anxiety, and phobic disorders. In P. E. Nathan, & J. M. Gorman (Eds.), *A Guide to Treatments that Work* (pp. 319-338). New York: Oxford University Press.

Simon, G. (1992). Psychiatric disorder and functional somatic symptoms as predictors of healthcare use. *Psychiatric Medicine*, *10*, 49 – 60.

Simon, G. E. & VonKorff, M. (1995). Recognition, management, and outcomes of depression in primary care. *Archives of Family Medicine, 4*, 99-105.

Strosahl, K. (2001). The integration of primary care and behavioral health: Type II change in the era of managed care. In *Integrated Behavioral Healthcare: Positioning Mental Health Practice with Medical/Surgical Practice.* Cummings, N. A., O'Donahue, W., Hayes, S. C., & Follette, V. (2001). Academic Press.

Yehuda, R., Marshall, R., & Giller, E. L. (1998). Psychopharmacological treatment of post-traumatic stress disorder. In P.E. Nathan, & J. M. Gorman (Eds.), *A Guide to Treatments that Work* (pp. 377-397). New York: Oxford University Press.

U.S. Department of Health and Human Services. *Mental Health: A Report of the Surgeon General–Executive Summary.* Rockville, MD: U.S. Department of Health and Human Services, Substance Abuse and Mental Health Services Administration, Center for Mental Health Services, National Institutes of Health, National Institute of Mental Health, 1999.

U.S. Department of Health and Human Services. *Healthy People 2010: Understanding and Improving Health.* 2nd ed. Washington, DC: U.S. Government Printing Office, November 2000.

U.S. Preventive Services Task Force. Screening for Depression: Recommendations and Rationale. *Ann Intern Med* 2002;136(10):760-764.

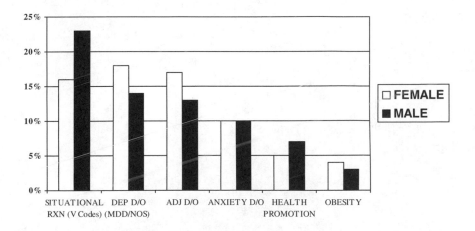

Figure 7.2. Most common presenting complaints to BHCs over six months (n=858 patients).

Footnotes

[1] The leading health indicators of Healthy People 2010 reflect the major health concerns in the United States at the beginning of the 21st century and will be used to measure the overall health of the Nation.

Quality Improvement in Behavioral Healthcare in Integrated Care Settings

Kyle E. Ferguson & William T. O'Donohue

While the U.S. is the wealthiest nation in the world and spends more on healthcare than other industrialized nations, it ranks 37th (out of 191 countries) in terms of overall quality according to the World Health Organization (Conyers, 2003). The quality of healthcare in this country is a serious and pervasive problem (Levesque et al., 2001). Scores of people suffer needlessly or worse, die prematurely, when their healthcare needs are improperly managed. A striking statistic is that as many as 98,000 people die each year as a result of medical errors (Simpson, 2001). Whereas certain errors are impossible to eliminate (e.g., on account of the complexity of disease processes), many are. Most notably, many healthcare providers are not delivering guideline-concordant care in keeping with the current scientific standards of practice. As a case in point, in a recent study involving 350,000 covered lives, 16 of 40 standard medical procedures were "improperly omitted more than a third of the time" (e.g., 80% of heart-failure patients did not receive a crucial beta-blocker as prescribed by acceptable standards of cardiac care; Consumer Reports on Health, 2002, p. 1).

Mental health in the U.S. is similarly beleaguered by poor quality (the reader should note that the terms "mental health" and "behavioral health", "patients" and "clients", and "customers" and "consumers" are used interchangeably throughout this chapter). During any given year, while approximately 22% of the population (50 million) suffers from a diagnosable mental disorder, serious enough to cause marked functional impairment (e.g., employment, school, daily life), only half of those individuals receive some form of treatment (American Psychiatric Association, 1994; Kessler et al., 2001). And should a mental illness be properly diagnosed and the patient undergo treatment from his or her family physician or mental health professional, most patients will receive a treatment that deviates from acceptable standards. For example, in a recent study conducted between 1997 and 1998 involving a national clinical sample (N=1,636), only 35% of those with a depressive or anxiety disorder were receiving treatment in accordance with intervention guidelines for psychosocial treatment and pharmacotherapy (Young et al., 2001, p. 55). Quality is reportedly worse in treating the seriously mentally ill (e.g., chronic schizophrenia or bipolar disorder), who arguably are in greater need of effective treatment given the extent of overall impairment. According to Wang, Demler, and Kessler (2002), who examined data from the National Comorbidity Survey, fewer than 1 in every 6 patients with serious mental illness received treatment that could be considered "minimally adequate" (p. 92).

The present chapter addresses quality improvement (QI) in behavioral healthcare. Problems with healthcare quality as shown in the above examples generally fit into one or more of three broad categories: underutilization, misuse, and overutilization. The first part of the chapter discusses these and in particular how utilization patterns affect healthcare expenditures. The second section defines what is meant by QI and the notion of quality as used in business more generally. Whereas many readers have worked within organizations that have made efforts at quality improvement, the benefits in doing so are rarely obvious; most likely due to the fact that these data rest in the hands of upper management and are largely cast in organizational concepts and terms, more akin to business and economics. Moreover, QI is almost always in the hands of administration and accreditation agencies, and the variables of interest are at best only remotely related to clinical outcomes. All too often, QI involves getting paperwork in on time and calling clients within X number of days for intakes and follow-ups. While such variables are necessary in improving the quality of an organization's services, they are not sufficient. More clinically relevant data enable organizations to adapt treatment protocols to better address the ever changing needs of patients. The third section of this chapter discusses the clinical and economic benefits of clinically oriented QI. A fundamental issue in quality improvement concerns service variability. As will be taken up later, one class of variability is tolerable, and in fact, unavoidable, while another class poses insurmountable barriers to QI when it is poorly managed or predominantly ignored. The fourth section discusses these two types of variability with respect to the delivery of behavioral healthcare technologies and how agencies ought to manage these using a data analytic tool called a Control Chart. The fifth section provides a general framework that details the most important aspects of developing and evaluating QI programs. This framework is born out of a philosophy and set of guiding principles known as Total Quality Management (TQM; Deming, 1982, 1986; Oakland & Followell, 1990; Rampersad, 2001). Specially, Demings's (1982) 14 points of quality management are at the core of TQM and are considered at some length in the last part of the chapter. The remainder of the chapter provides guidelines in setting up QI systems.

As it turns out, QI programs do not have to be elaborate or labor intensive to yield useful information. Quite the contrary, depending on the organization's goals, very little additional effort might all be that is required on the part of management, staff, and clients. QI programs should require only minimum effort; otherwise they run the risk of becoming yet another bureaucratic exercise. After all, QI is not efficacy or effectiveness research. Efficacy studies determine the extent to which a given intervention produces desired changes in some clinical variable of interest in a targeted population, broadly defined (e.g., patients with early stage dementia; Chambliss, 2000). Effectiveness research concerns the applicability and feasibility of interventions, broadly defined (e.g., community mental health clinics in the United States). Conversely, QI is concerned with the extent to which clinicians employ *known* efficacious and effective interventions to clinical settings, and how these interventions employed within particular settings affect clinical outcomes, regionally or locally, depending on the size of the catchment area of the company (Strosahl et al., 1997).

Patient Utilization Patterns and Quality

Underutilization

Problems with healthcare quality generally fall under three broad categories: underutilization, misuse, and overutilization (Chassin & Galvin, 1998). Underutilization is failing to provide services that would otherwise prove beneficial for clients. For example, roughly half of older adults with suspected mental health problems (especially depression) do not receive treatment (Lebowitz et al., 1997). And given the fact that our elderly population is ever burgeoning (it increased elevenfold between 1900 and 1994; cf. the nonelderly population increased only threefold; U.S. Census Bureau, 2001), more people each year will suffer needlessly unless some vital changes are made in the delivery of behavioral healthcare technologies. Interestingly, on the other end of the age continuum the results are similar. Namely, approximately 50% of children and adolescents who meet diagnostic criteria for emotional or behavioral problems do not receive treatment (Leaf et al., 1996; Zahner et al., 1992). Obviously, better early detection efforts in primary care and outreach would help alleviate this problem (e.g., Cummings, 1997, depression/bereavement outreach program for widowed older adults).

Many patients who are not receiving needed behavioral health services turn up in primary care. However, rather than present to primary care with mental health issues, such individuals in need of assistance present with a host of somatic complaints. In an internal medicine clinic, for example, Kroenke and Mangelsdorff (1989) found in their sample (N=1,000) that less than 16% of somatic complaints (e.g., chest pain, fatigue, dizziness, headache, back pain, numbness, cough, constipation) had an identifiable organic cause. Similarly, at Kaiser Strosahl (1998) estimated that approximately 70% of all primary care visits (N=25,000) were driven by psychological factors (e.g., panic, Generalized Anxiety, Major Depression and somatization). The remaining 30% were corroborated by medical test findings. Most notably at follow-up, after 10 years, none of the somatic complaints of the 70% eventuated in positive medical test findings, thus ruling out that organic problems went initially undetected.

It is not to be overlooked that every psychological problem has accompanying physical symptomology. And those symptoms drive healthcare visits as shown in the above examples. Panic attacks and heart attacks, for example, have overlapping symptoms that are oftentimes indistinguishable and equally distressing (Barlow & Craske, 1994). Chest pain or pressure, tachycardia, shortness of breath, dizziness, and chills, are reported by those individuals who have experienced panic and heart attacks (Huffman, Pollack, & Stern, 2002). Physical medicine is by and large ill equipped to make the distinction between symptomology due to disease processes and underlying psychological disturbances. After all, their diagnostic instruments and procedures (e.g., blood work) are typically designed to detect organic etiology (e.g., liver failure) not mental health problems. Unfortunately, in traditional primary care settings (i.e., nonintegrated) psychological factors usually aren't considered until after an armamentarium of clinical laboratory tests have been exhausted.

Misuse

Unnecessary utilization of medical/surgical procedures (or behavioral care) is considered a misuse of healthcare. In the above examples, while individuals are underutilizing behavioral care, they are misusing general medical services (though in many cases, "unintentionally"). Other examples would include, though are not limited to:

- Providing counseling for a purported psychiatric disorder when in effect the client has a misdiagnosed medical condition (e.g., mistaking a thyroid problem for depression; Morrison, 1997).
- Utilizing emergency medicine when such cases could be better managed on an outpatient basis (e.g., treating parasuicidal behavior individually or in groups using Linehan's, 1993, empirically-supported treatment protocol, as opposed to waiting for clients to turn up in the emergency room with potentially life-threatening self-inflicted injuries).
- Using sand tray therapy for treating Panic Disorder when efficacious, cost-efficient treatments are readily available (e.g., Barlow, 2001; Barlow, & Craske, 1994; Clark, 1989; Hecker, & Thorpe, 1992; Salkovskis, & Clark, 1991). This is especially problematic when patients frequently turn up in the emergency room thinking they are having a heart attack, given the fact that psychoeducation plays such a major role in the above cognitive-behavioral therapies (CBT).

Overutilization

From the patient's perspective, overutilization is providing appropriate services though in excess, where the "potential for harm exceeds the possible benefit" (Chassin & Galvin, 1998, p. 1002). For example, while opioids are usually indicated for marked acute pain, they are contraindicated for prolonged or excess use on account of iatrogenic effects (e.g., drug tolerance, chemical dependency, and functional impairment; Aronoff & DuPuy, 1997). From a public health perspective, overutilization is considered an opportunity cost as overutilizers "bottleneck" the system. Thus, in a sense, overutilization harms the "greater good". Namely, as such individuals undergo expensive diagnostic tests and clinical procedures other patients who would otherwise benefit from such services are kept out of the system (this logic holds for misuse as well). For example, clients with medically unexplained physical symptoms called somatizers, utilize three times more outpatient services when compared to clients without the disorder (Swartz, Blazer, George, & Landerman, 1986). Unfortunately more services usually do not amount to beneficial outcomes and to make matters worse, more care often causes additional harm. Indeed, somatizers experience high rates of iatrogenic illness, resulting from complications from multiple ineffective surgeries, adverse reactions to a "pharmacopia" of medications, and the like (Fink, 1992; also see the chapter on high utilizers by Cuciarre and O'Donohue in the present volume).

Patient Utilization Patterns and Healthcare Expenditures

Underutilization, misuse, and overutilization of healthcare have placed a tremendous financial burden on the government and private agencies, as these have driven healthcare expenditures up. Notably, over the last several decades healthcare expenses have risen at multiples of the general rate of inflation, with current estimates of $1.3 trillion, annually, or 14% of the gross domestic product (GDP; O'Donohue, Ferguson, & Cummings, 2002; Phelps, 1997). By 2012, economists predict that it will reach 18% of the GDP, or $3.1 trillion (Spors, 2003). As spending continues to rise more individuals will be without health insurance. Over and above current estimates of 14% of uninsured citizens (approximately 40 million Americans; U.S. Census Bureau, 2001), increasing numbers of employers will not be able to afford such benefits for employees and individuals simply will not be able to pay out of pocket.

Utilization patterns of the uninsured contribute to this inflationary spiral. The uninsured typically underutilize preventive services and misuse or overutilize emergent care (O'Donohue et al., 2002). That is, the uninsured typically do not enter into the healthcare system until it is too late, once numerous complications arise. For example, asthma and diabetes that can otherwise be effectively managed on an outpatient basis are two of the top ten reasons for hospitalizations for the uninsured, accounting for 65,000 unnecessary hospital admissions each year (Agency for Healthcare Research and Quality, 2003). Thus a vicious cycle begins: uninsured individuals drive healthcare costs up on account of misuse and consequently, more beneficiaries lose their insurance. Whether this current trend will stand or fall will ultimately depend on QI efforts with the uninsured.

From Fee-for-Service to Capitation:

Market-driven Quality Improvement

Within the last several decades the provision of healthcare has become increasingly market-driven. In fact, some authors go so far as to call it a revolution, whereby the cottage industry, characterized by solo practice and fee-for-service financial arrangements, has been for the most part supplanted by large multibillion dollar conglomerates, called managed care (Cummings, 1986). This revolution, of course, was sparked by the aforementioned economic factors (i.e., increasing healthcare expenditures). Managed care stepped in as a means of dampening this inflationary spiral, by employing a capitated financial system in lieu of fee-for-service, that will be taken up shortly (Cummings, 2000). From an economic perspective the reason for this shift is obvious.

Fee-for-service arrangements often lead to inefficient practices. This is to be expected given that the more work one makes for oneself the more money the individual or organization receives. It pays to employ an inordinate amount of tests, to garner as many clients as possible in spite of diminishing quality of services (perhaps with iatrogenic effects), and to delay the course of treatment well beyond reasonable limits. Fee-for-service systems simply create financial incentives for providing more services than necessary. Under such arrangements there is very little push for QI.

By contrast, in capitated systems where healthcare is provided at a fixed cost, there are financial incentives for delivering the most efficient, effective treatments (Chambliss, 2000). Because providers assume financial risk, there is an emphasis on prevention versus crisis management in an effort to forestall the need for expensive procedures and hospitalization. Treating asthma-related Panic Disorder, for example, can markedly reduce the rates of rehospitalization in groups of asthmatics that manifest certain patterns of illness-specific panic fear (Carr et al., 1994; Feldman, Giardino, & Lehrer, 2000). Of course, providers might also deny services or set up a "firewall" of sorts, whereby patients get so bogged down in an overly elaborate application process that they eventually give up; both of which temporarily cut costs. However, in a market-driven healthcare environment, those organizations that "cut corners" by denying services or otherwise prevent ready access to necessary care, eventually go out of business on account of more mishaps (e.g., clinical crises), paying out damages resulting from malpractice suits, and losing customers to competitors. And indeed, this has been the case in the U.S., as what started out as dozens of managed behavioral healthcare organizations has been winnowed down to just several. Incidentally, the largest, Magellan Behavioral Health with over 70 million covered lives (or 1 in 3 insured Americans), has recently declared bankruptcy.

With over half of the country now belonging to one of the managed behavioral health organizations, healthcare has undergone industrialization, comparable to other industries (e.g., computer industry; Cummings, 1986; Oss et al., 1997, as cited in Sturm, 1999). This so-called industrialization of healthcare has placed a premium on accountability and cost-effectiveness, as third-party payers are now in a position of making greater demands on providers (e.g., demanding detailed justification of services and economies of scale; Cummings, 1986; O'Donohue, Graczyk, & Yeater, 1998). This increase in accountability behooves healthcare administration and clinicians to deliver quality services all the while containing costs within fixed boundaries. It goes without saying that under such financial arrangements, there is a tremendous push for clinically-relevant QI – companies eventually go under without it.

The Concept of Quality and Quality Improvement

What is Quality?

The term "quality" as used in business is a multidimensional construct, the emphasis of which depends on the industry and the kinds of outcomes a company values (Cameron & Barnett, 2000, p. 272). To provide a few popular examples, some individuals define quality as "achieving or reaching the highest standard possible" (Tuchman, 1980, p. 38), while others define it as conformance to specifications (Shewhart, 1931), rate of errors or defects during the production process (Crosby, 1979), and the "the extent to which a product or service meets and/or exceeds a customer's expectations" (Reeves & Bednar, 1994, p. 420). Of the four definitions, the fourth one has gained wide acceptance in the service industry and seems most relevant to the current market-driven healthcare environment.

QI from this perspective is an iterative process, designed to continuously "upgrade" products and services in keeping with consumers' ever changing needs and expectations (Rampersad, 2001). By continuously upgrading products and services everyone involved, the organization, clinicians, clients, as well as key stakeholders (e.g., insurance companies) can potentially benefit from these efforts.

The Benefits of Quality Improvement

There are at least five major benefits of quality improvement. QI programs: 1) improve productivity, 2) utilize all interesting technologies, 3) improve value, 4) are sensitive to unintended negative effects, and 5) are focused on the long-term.

1) QI improves productivity. QI is designed to continuously improve the efficiency of a specified process. Efficiency, of course, is related to productivity. All other things being equal, a more efficient process produces more output units relative to a less efficient process in the same timeframe. Take psychotherapy for depression, for example. The gold standard of treatment is Beck et al.'s (1979) depression protocol. While this is a highly efficacious empirically supported treatment, it requires about 14 to 16 sessions for moderately-severe clinical cases, and possibility more for treatment non-responders. Although it is the treatment of choice when conditions are optimal, in many clinical settings conditions are far from optimal.

Thus, Beck et al.'s protocol is not always the most efficient mode of treatment delivery because patients often do not last long enough in therapy to realize its full benefits or possibly, as we are about to see, any benefits. Indeed, the modal number of psychotherapy sessions is only one; specifically, about half of the patients who present to clinic do not return after their first visit (Phillips, 1985). Accordingly, an otherwise superb treatment is effectively useless half the time (as patients would have only been briefly exposed to assessment, not treatment). Given that many patients only attend one session, perhaps a QI program might pare down Beck et al.'s 14-16-session treatment so that its core principles (e.g., cognitive restructuring) fit into the first session. Should patients elect to continue with psychotherapy then those core principles would be extended or built upon over the course of subsequent sessions.

Now consider two competing agencies, one that uses Beck et al.'s protocol as prescribed and the other that uses the same protocol though also employs the adapted first-session protocol. With the latter agency, because more patients would be exposed to the "active therapeutic agents" (e.g., challenging dysfunctional beliefs), we might expect better clinical outcomes and correspondingly, fewer healthcare visits with those depressed patients who attend only the first session (e.g., Katon et al., 1990, found that "high utilizers" of medical-surgical interventions, the highest 10% of patient visits, had prevalence rates of 25% for current depression and 68% for lifetime depression). Said differently, in addition to Beck et al.'s standard protocol, the second agency provides a more efficient mode of depression treatment for at least half of the patient load.

2) QI utilizes all interesting technologies. In market-driven, capitated systems, QI provides an incentive for research and development (R & D) of new technologies. Effective use of state-of-the-art technologies like telecommunications and data processing (e.g., software) or clinically, innovative treatments and more streamlined systems of care, help agencies gain a competitive advantage over other agencies vying for the same market share. Indeed, the old adage rings true: Time is money. New technologies are first and foremost designed to save people time, in which case companies are afforded more opportunities to earn more capital as employees can increase their catchment area. Video-conferencing, for example, provides similar access to specialty care in rural communalities as face-to-face contact with a therapist. Thus, companies employing this technology can carve out a greater market share because their specialists are not wasting time traveling to rural sites (and possibly, rural patients are not tying up urban clinics).

Before proceeding to the next item it is important to note that computer information systems enable organizations to link clinical settings across a network, culling and integrating clinical, financial, and operational data (Hermann et al., 2000, p. 252). Every major QI project requires this technology. The upshot of utilizing this technology is that it facilitates communication among professionals from disparate areas, that otherwise would work independently even though they might very well be working towards similar goals. Information systems also cuts down on redundancy – the duplication of services.

3) QI improves value. Value as used in healthcare economics is inexplicably tied to a company's resources and the cost of providing these in the care of patients (Phelps, 1997). According to Hargreaves et al. (1998):

> *Resources* include time inputs by clinicians and others required to provide treatment and services, medication, supplies, and space. *Value* is the worth (i.e., inputs in relation to outcomes) of one unit of a specific resource (p. 46, emphasis added).

Colloquially, "more bang for the buck", signifies greater value. For example, if newly developed Treatment Y is more efficient (i.e., requiring fewer resources) or produces better outcomes than the existing Treatment X (utilizing the same resources), all other things being equal, one unit of Treatment Y (e.g., number of hours) is of greater value compared to one unit of Treatment X.

4) QI increases sensitivity to unintended negative consequences. Behavioral healthcare is not the same as the widget-producing industry or even its related cousin, medicine. No one would argue that restructuring a depressed individual's thought patterns or dealing with parasuicidal behavior is as straightforward as mending a broken wrist or making the nth fast food customer happy by changing the grease in the deep fryer every other week. Thus, it would seem unrealistic for psychology to be held to the exact standards as other industries because it has more *unintended consequences* (Popper, 1972). Setting and splinting a broken wrist or changing the grease in the deep fryer has highly predictable outcomes: bones usually fuse and fresh grease makes customers happier than 3- or 4-week-old grease. Cognitive restructuring, while *intended* to produce healthier thinking patterns, might very well produce the negative *unintended consequence* of causing a person to ruminate more over his or her problems, thus causing increased distress and possibly increased utilization. Targeting parasuicidal behavior for intervention, while *intended* to reduce harmful self-mutilation might actually promote such behavior as the *unintended consequence* of attention from the therapist differentially reinforces further escalation. While treatment guidelines might issue general warnings about *unintended negative consequences* (usually in the form of proscriptions), they cannot tell therapists what clients, with what presenting problems, under what set of circumstances are we more likely to expect these. By continuously measuring process variables (e.g., patient satisfaction), QI is in a better position to flag *unintended negative consequences*. And once *unintended negative consequences* are flagged (e.g., X number of patients with certain types of presenting problems are highly dissatisfied after being taught cognitive restructuring), an organization can then try to figure out what went wrong and ultimately, make efforts at reducing or preventing these. In a sense, therefore, QI gets at addressing Gordon Paul's (1969) ultimate clinical question: "What treatment is most effective for which type of individual, and under which set of circumstances?" (p. 44). Or more pointedly, our QI question is thus: "What treatment for which type of individual, and under which set of circumstances should we expect *negative unintended consequences?*"

5) QI is focused on the long-term. As we shall see later on in the chapter, clinical and administrative processes are fluid and as such, there is always room for improvement. QI, therefore, is always oriented to the future and committed to long-term goals (e.g., reducing *unintended negative consequences* as protocols, by degrees, are adjusted to better suit patient needs). QI never asks: How can this product or service be perfected, as if there were an end in sight. Rather, QI asks: How can I make improvements to this product or service in accordance with the ever changing needs and expectations of my patients; realizing full well that expectations and needs are likely to change over time? Chronic Fatigue Syndrome, for example, only emerged as a "clinical problem" fairly recently. While still controversial in many professional circles, informed patients who believe that they have the disorder expect some form of treatment and would be highly dissatisfied if these services were not available.

Quality and Variability in Service Delivery:

Normal versus Abnormal Variation

In every healthcare environment there is variability in the way behavioral technologies are employed. Fluctuations in the provision of these services are due to two sources of variation, normal and abnormal (Mainstone & Levi, 1987). Normal variation reflects natural unsystematic factors. These are chance factors that may be reduced though never eliminated. When staff are ill, for example, one would expect a change in the quality of services. In most cases, clinicians are more likely to make errors when they are running a fever, feeling nauseous, and the like. These fluctuations in service quality, of course, cannot be eliminated as all staff fall ill at some point in time. Likewise, using Barlow and Craske's (1994) manual for Panic Disorder, during early stages of treatment we expect therapists to talk about the nature of panic and anxiety (e.g., fear being seen as a natural response, part of the body's "fight or flight" mechanism). Through careful training in the use of this protocol, along with assessing therapists' adherence at regular intervals, we assume some variance from therapist to therapist, though by and large variability should not exceed that which is normal (e.g., the therapist won't be talking about the client's inner child).

Abnormal variation, by contrast, reflects the presence of unusual non-random factors affecting a system (Mainstone & Levi, 1987). Take treatment for Obsessive-Compulsive Disorder, as a case in point. When clients are frequently sensitized to aversive stimuli in the therapist's office, when they should be desensitized in accordance with exposure and response prevention (ERP) guidelines (e.g., Foa, 1996), we would consider this abnormal variation that mitigates against the quality of our services. Possibly, therapists aren't adequately preparing patients for what to expect (e.g., telling their patients that ERP trials cause marked distress in some individuals). Perhaps the exposure trials are cut short, not allowing for the cessation of autonomic arousal.

Abnormal variations in performance are to be identified and thus remedied in order to bring a process back under "control" (e.g., therapists are doing what they were initially trained to do; Oakland & Followell, 1990). But before normal or abnormal variations can be identified, processes must first be measured.

Quality Improvement and Measurement

The popular mantra in quality improvement is "you can't improve a process or outcome without measuring it" and its corollary, "don't waste time and effort measuring it if you aren't going to try and improvement it" (Meyer, 2001, p. 171). Accordingly, by measuring variables targeted for change in a systematic, consistent manner, we gain a better understanding of how certain processes work. A "process" as used here is the transformation of a company's inputs (e.g., materials and labor) into desired outcomes (e.g., products and services; Oakland & Followell, 1990). Clinically, as far as inputs are concerned, this would include triage, assessment, employing various modes of therapy, maintenance, and follow-up. Regarding outcomes, this would include clients' clinical and functional status, quality of life, cost, and consumer satisfaction (Hermann et al., 2000).

By understanding the workings of a process we can then bring it under our influence or control (Rampersad, 2001). That is to say, using this feedback we can then identify performance deficits on the part of staff and make efforts at improving these (though we hasten to add that staff are not to blame – it is the organizational system that is called into question). To this end the primary tool, designed to identify normal and abnormal variation, is described in what follows. However, as we shall see later on, agencies do not necessarily have to employ this method to flag abnormal variation. Simpler methods, that will be taken up shortly, usually suffice.

Control Charts[1]: An Overview. The primary tool for flagging normal and abnormal variability is the Control Chart. Control Charts are the primary means of identifying whether the process in question is or is not in control, or more technically precise, statistical control (O'Donohue et al., 1998). A Control Chart is essentially a run chart[2] with statistically derived upper and lower limits superimposed over the process average (Walton, 1986, p. 114; see Figure 8.1). Specifically, these upper and lower confidence limits are 3 SDs above and below the grand mean (i.e., the average of the sample means for those variables taken during baseline) of all the services garnered during the baseline phase (this accounts for 99.7% of the variance in a normal distribution) (O'Donohue et al., 1998, p. 183). In light of the fact that due to chance factors alone only approximately 3 out of 1000 outcomes fall outside of these control limits, any sample falling outside such limits are deemed as abnormal variation and as such the process is said to be out statistical control (Mainstone & Levi, 1987).

W. Edwards Deming and Total Quality Improvement

The impetus for the American quality movement began in the late 1970s, as manufacturers became increasingly aware of the competitive threat posed by Japanese industry (e.g., automobiles, office machinery, electronics). American consumers began turning to Japanese products because they were simply of superior quality (e.g. more durable, fewer defects, and greater technological sophistication). Moreover, due to greater efficiency in producing their goods and services, Japanese industries were also producing their products at lower cost.

Interestingly, it was an American by the name of W. Edwards Deming, who was responsible for taking a struggling Japanese industry post-World War II, and turning Japan into an economic superpower (Sanders & Sanders, 1994). Deming also had a profound impact on American industry facing similar crises, such as Ford Motor Company and Xerox, among countless others (Gabor, 1990).

Deming relied heavily on the statistical process control (SPC) methods developed by Walter Shewhart (1939; the aforementioned Control Chart is one such method). However, to Deming statistical inspective methods were more than

---

[1] *Because the literature is replete with examples in how to construct control charts, only critical points will be highlighted here. For those readers interested, please consult the following for an in-depth discussion of how to implement such tools: Mainstone & Levi, 1987; Oakland & Followell, 1990; Shewhart, 1939; Wheeler & Chambers, 1992).*

[2] *Running records preserve the time-order sequence in which the values occur (Wheeler & Chambers, 1992).*

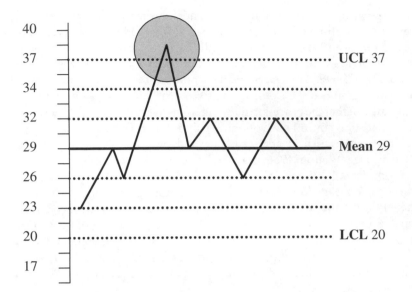

Figure 8.1. Control Chart. The data point highlighted by the translucent disc falls outside of statistical control, thus suggesting non-random, abnormal variability. **UCL** = Upper Control Limits; **LCL** = Lower Control Limits. *Standard Deviation = (approx.) 3.0*; Modeled after Swanson, 1995, p. 156).

mere tools. Deming went so far as erect an entire management philosophy around these statistical techniques (Redmon, 1992). From his position statistical methods allow a better understanding of processes (Walton, 1986). Only by way of understanding how a process works can we then bring it under our influence or statistical control. And finally, once a process is under statistical control, we can readily flag harmful abnormal variability should it arise.

Quality for Deming is defined in terms of critical dimensions (e.g., performance, endurance, expenses, accessibility, and ease of implementation) as they pertain to consumer satisfaction (Babcock, Fleming, & Oliver, 1998; Oakland & Followell, 1990). According to Deming (1986), a company's vitality hinges on a continual process of improving the quality of its products or services, Deming's so-called "chain reaction" equation. This equation indicates that quality and cost share an inverse relation. Namely, as quality goes up, costs go down from fewer mishaps, lower waste and so on, and as a corollary, production is driven up.

Deming's approach contrasts with what he called "retroactive management," whereby a company's focal point is on end products, work standards, and annually appraising workers. From his standpoint a product or service is continually reworked in accordance with consumer satisfaction and as such there is never an end product per se, but only a "fluid" product that has yet to be improved. This notion of quality control runs parallel to Karl Popper's (1963) philosophy of science (O'Donohue,

Graczyk, & Yeater, 1998). According to Popper, the highest status that a scientific theory can attain is not yet disconfirmed (Hergenhahn, 1997). Likewise, the highest status that a product or service can achieve from a quality control perspective, is not yet refined to suit the customer's current needs. Products and services are only provisionally held until something better comes along (i.e., something more attuned to customers' current needs and expectations).

Let us turn next to Demings's (1986) 14 points of quality management, as these core principles underlie QI.

The Deming Management Method

Point 1. Create constancy of purpose toward improvement of product and service with the aim to become competitive and to stay in business, and to provide jobs (p. 24 ff.).

Comment: Management should make QI routine practice. For example, in the Hawaii Integrated Care Project II (see Laygo et al. in the present volume), therapists devote a certain percentage of their work week to QI. Eventually, QI becomes a "habit".

Point 2. Adopt the new philosophy. We are in a new economic age. Western management must awaken to the challenge, must learn their responsibilities, and take on leadership of change (p. 26 ff.).

Comment: Management cannot ignore this point when one considers the fact that healthcare has undergone industrialization and is now largely capitated versus fee-for-service (Cummings, 1986). As mentioned, capitated financial arrangements place a premium on accountability and cost-effectiveness. Moreover, industrialization brings added consumerism as third-party payers are in a better position to "shop around".

Point 3. Cease dependence on mass inspection to improve quality. Eliminate the need for inspection on a mass basis by building quality into the product in the first place (p. 28 ff.).

Comment: Quality should be built into a product or service at the outset. For example, Cummings (1990), in what came to be known as "Biodyne boot camp", trained his therapists in the Biodyne model of brief intermittent therapy throughout the lifecycle during the first couple of weeks of employment. Training therapists in this model cut down on abnormal variation attributable to different therapeutic orientations.

Point 4. End the practice of awarding business on the basis of price tag alone. Instead, minimize total cost (p. 31 ff.).

Comment: In capitated financial systems, the most successful companies provide comparable services at lesser cost.

Point 5. Improve constantly and forever the system of production and service, to improve quality and productivity, and thus constantly decrease costs (p. 49 ff.).

Comment: In his Biodyne model, for example, Cummings (1990) made physical arrangements to clinical settings such that supervisors had ready access to therapists' sessions, by way of a one-way mirror and microphone. With increased access, supervisors could provide clinical supervision in real-time (as therapists wore a small earphone) for particularly intractable cases. Moreover, protocol adherence could be assessed at any given time (e.g., a supervisor might "tune" into a session at random times).

Point 6. Institute training on the job (p. 52 ff.).

Comment: In the Biodyne model, should a therapist's practices depart greatly from protocol guidelines, then supervisors would provide immediate corrective feedback (e.g., while a therapist is in session or immediately thereafter; Cummings, 1990). One principle of behavior that the learning laboratory has taught us is that the sooner feedback[3] is delivered the more likely behavior will change accordingly (Ferster & Skinner, 1957; Miltenberger, 2001). Conversely, all other things being equal, staff are less responsive to delayed feedback. Behavior is thus sensitive to the interval between observing the problematic behavior and the point at which feedback is delivered. Ideally, staff should be informed immediately whenever there is a problem.

Point 7. Institute leadership. The aim of supervision should be to help people and machines and gadgets to do a better job. Supervision of management is in need of overhaul, as well as supervision of production workers (p. 54 ff.).

Comment: Of course, part of QI is identifying better ways in which supervision might be optimized. Insofar as supervisors provide feedback to staff so too should staff provide feedback to supervisors. A certain amount of QI is set aside for this purpose. Quality circles, where clinicians meet with supervisors to discuss clinical process issues, would be an appropriate venue to discuss supervisor issues (Milakovich, 1995).

---

[3] *Or technically, a reinforcer or punisher.*

Point 8. Drive out fear, so that everyone may work effectively for the company (p. 59 ff.).

Comment: Punishing nonconformance or speaking up should be avoided. As Deming (1982) aptly noted, "No one can put in his best performance unless he feels secure" (p. 59).

Point 9. Break down barriers between departments. People in research, design, sales, and production must work as a team, to foresee problems of production and use that may be encountered with the product or service (p. 62 ff.).

Comment: The underlying philosophy of integrated care is to break down barriers between health and mental health fields, as clinicians from either profession work together on managing cases. QI involves everyone in an organization, from front-line staff who answer the phone to upper management.

Point 10. Eliminate slogans, exhortations, and targets for the workforce asking for zero defects and new levels of productivity. Such exhortations only create adversarial relationships, as the bulk of the causes of low quality and low productivity belong to the system and thus lie beyond the power of the workforce (p. 65 ff.).

Comment: Obviously, given the high prevalence of unintended negative consequences in behavioral care it is impossible to employ any service with "zero defects". Rather, staff are encouraged to do the best they can in meeting the needs and expectations of their patients.

Point 11. Eliminate management by numbers, numeric goals. Substitute leadership (p. 70 ff.).

Comment: Clinicians and supervisors should be oriented to continuous quality improvement every day, during the entire day. Numeric goals suggest that an endpoint is in sight, which is not the case.

Point 12. a. Remove barriers that rob the hourly worker of his [or her] right to pride of workmanship. The responsibility of supervisors must be changed from sheer numbers to quality
b. Remove barriers that rob people in management and in engineering of their right to pride of workmanship. This means, inter alia, abolishment of the annual or merit rating and of management by objective (p. 77 ff.).

Comment: Annual evaluations as a means of control and discipline foster mediocrity and instill fear in clinicians (Milakovich, 1995, p. 53). Regarding the first point, because no one really knows how performance ought to be measured meaningfully, the factors that are considered in merit reviews are generally unrelated to variables of clinical interest (e.g., getting to work on time).

Point 13. Institute a vigorous program of education and self-improvement (p. 86).

Comment: In integrated settings, for example, behavioral health clinicians might participate in grand rounds or continuing medical education to better understand how disease processes might affect behavior, improving medication adherence, and the like (Strosahl et al., 1997).

Point 14. Put everybody in the company to work to accomplish the transformation. The *transformation is everybody's job* (p. 86 ff.).

Comment: Again, the participation of all parties involved is key in implementing effective QI programs. Clinicians share in this responsibility with middle and upper management.

Let us next discuss the most important aspects of developing and evaluating QI programs. Of course, an extensive overview is beyond the scope of the present chapter. Rather, our purpose here is to provide general guidelines.

General Guidelines

As in the Hawaii Integrated Care project (see Laygo et al., present volume), all clinically relevant QI programs are based on at least three meta-principles:

1. All data are collected in a *minimally burdensome* and *minimally intrusive* way (otherwise management will be unable to rally support from staff).
2. All data are *clinically relevant*. In the Hawaii Integrated Care project the measures had to pass a "smell" test. That is to say, only those measures of interest to front line clinicians were used.
3. All data are *relevant to management decision-making*. The "smell" test here is, "shouldn't the manager need to know this information in order to really understand what he or she is managing". *We also recommend that supervisors (when appropriate) set aside some of their work week to see patients. This way they will be more in tune with the workings of the clinic, as regards client issues.*

Based on the above principles, brief measures are then developed to assess the following domains:

1. *Patient satisfaction*: Every patient must be given a patient satisfaction form and allowed to complete this anonymously. The form should only be

comprised of several items, perhaps using a Likert scale. In some cases, consider implementing focus groups, especially when designing new programs. Focus groups are used to obtain knowledge about patient needs and expectations at the outset as well as provide a forum for constructive feedback, delivered by representative patients (e.g., use a focus group comprised of family caregivers when designing a group for family caregivers; Swanson, 1995). Focus groups should not exceed 12 participants otherwise they become too unwieldy.

2. *PCP satisfaction (of the behavioral health services)*: PCP satisfaction is measured quarterly so as not to become burdensome. Again, as is the case with patient satisfaction, the form should only be comprised of several items.

3. *Clinical change on target variables*: Every patient must have some baseline and terminal measure on their presenting problem(s) (e.g., depression measured with a Beck Depression Inventory; Beck et al., 1979). As in the Hawaii Integrated Care project, clinicians are allowed to choose their measures, though are not given the option to opt out of measuring clinical variables.

4. *Functional status change*: Functional status change will pertain to one or more of the following: employment, school, familial or interpersonal effectiveness, and psychological and/or behavioral health. Functional status with respect to employment might involve fewer days absent from work or increased productivity. Regarding school, this might entail grades or, as it pertains to children, how a student gets along with classmates. A change in familial functional status as regards parenting might involve supplanting more appropriate disciplinary strategies (e.g., time-out) for corporeal punishment. Regarding interpersonal effectiveness, this might entail being more assertive with one's spouse. A change in functional status psychologically or behaviorally might involve a reduction in overall distress or increasing one's menu of pleasant activities (so called quality-of-life issues). In any case, functional status should be assessed during baseline, immediately following treatment, and optimally, several months after receiving services. And once again, it should be measured using a form comprised of only a few items (e.g., "How many days of work have you missed within the last 6 months?").

5. *Medical utilization*: Medical utilization might entail the following: number of primary care or outpatient visits; itemized laboratory tests and the cost of these; number of emergency visits; days in the hospital; medication/surgical costs; and behavioral health costs, to name only a few. These data are largely garnered from patient charts.

Control Charts: Step-by-step implementation. Data gathered from the above measures are culled and analyzed. These data might be represented by summary statistics (see Laygo et al., present volume), involving measures of central tendency (e.g., mean, median, mode, and standard deviation). This, of course, is the easiest method of analyzing process data. Or, should an organization wish to do so, it might employ the use of a Control Chart. In what follows we briefly outline the chronological steps in using a Control Chart.

1. The first step is to identify a datum or data for analysis (patient satisfaction, PCP satisfaction, clinical change across targeted variables, changes in functional status, and medical utilization). A datum can be anything of relevance to the successful workings of a system, though it must be quantifiable.
2. Once identified, we need to measure this datum under natural conditions (i.e., prior to reworking the system). A behaviorally-based term for this phase is called baseline (Sidman, 1960).
3. Once we have derived an adequate sample of data from the baseline phase, we then calculate a mean or grand average should our analysis involve more than one datum.
4. With the mean situated in the middle, we then superimpose the upper and lower confidence limits (i.e., 3 SDs) (see Walton, 1986, pp. 114-115; see Figure 8.1 earlier in this chapter).

What to do when a process is out of statistical control: troubleshooting. Whenever systemic problems are identified on Control Charts or otherwise, management should track down the sources that are believed to contribute to abnormal variability. This is no easy task, though more often than not, such sources will most likely be found either in the contingencies in the work place or perhaps abnormal variability is due to inadequate staff training or drift. Questions to ask are as follows (Mager & Pipe, 1984):

• Are staff not doing what is expected because they are lacking the necessary skill set, or does the problem lie in the environment per se? *At no point in time do we blame staff for deficient performance. Rather, the problem is systemic in origin. We cannot stress this enough.*
• Regarding skills deficits, do employees require booster training, more opportunities for practice, or is additional environmental support in order to perform their duties (e.g., prompts such as checklists)?
• Regarding environmental factors, performance deficits might also be attributable to contingencies residing in the setting in which behavior is expected to occur.
• The first question to ask in the series of questions related to contingencies concerns whether performance is punishing. *Should performance be punishing then a suitable target for intervention would be to make efforts at lowering response cost or response effort in carrying out work-related activities. Perhaps more frequent staff rotations or redistributing staff resources at critical moments is what is called for.*

• On the opposite end of the continuum, the following question needs to be asked: Is non-performance reinforcing? *If this is indeed the case, then one needs to further tease apart why this is so by identifying the contingencies of which incompatible work-related behavior is a function. To take an obvious example, are staff using work time for other purposes (e.g., studying or talking on the phone with friends)?*

Benchmarking. Recall that abnormal variation reflects the presence of unusual non-random factors affecting a system (Mainstone & Levi, 1987). It is important to note that in this definition there is no mention that abnormal variation is necessarily bad. For example, data falling outside 2 or 3 SDs above or below the mean might mean that a clinician or clinicians is/are doing something particularly well. They might have happened upon a clinical technique that is especially effective with certain patients. Once flagged on a Control Chart or identified using another analytic method, other clinicians might try to emulate these practices. In the TQM

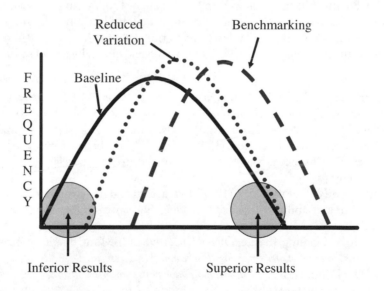

Figure 8.2. A schematic of the QI process. On a Control Chart, inferior results would fall outside of statistical control as one moves further down the one end of the distribution (LCL). QI attempts to eliminate this abnormal variation and as a result, we see a reduction in overall variation (the new distribution indicated with a dotted line). Of course, superior results also fall outside of statistical control (UCL), in which case the organization can learn from these exemplars and teach these skill sets to others. When other staff effectively learn these skills, the above distribution will ultimately shift to the right (the new distribution indicated with a dashed line; Modeled after Mortimer, 1991, p. 32).

literature this process is called *benchmarking* (Reider, 2000). Specifically, "benchmarking is the systematic and continuous process of determining the best performance and underlying skills (and once identified, teaching these skill sets to others that might benefit from this training)" (Rampersad, 2001, p. 22, parenthesis ours). Benchmarking is therefore a critical component in the development of a clinically relevant QI system.

Ultimately, by reducing abnormal variability due to deficiencies in performance, overall variability is thus reduced. Benchmarking simply shifts the distribution to the right, as shown in Figure 8.2.

Conclusion

Health and mental health have been slow at adopting a clinically focused QI approach. This is likely due to the fact that QI usually rests in the hands of upper management and accreditation agencies that may or may not be knowledgeable in clinical issues. More often than not, QI concerns getting paperwork in on time or whether form X or Y has been correctly filed. While such variables are necessary in QI, they are insufficient as far as improving patient functioning is concerned. QI programs must address patient satisfaction as well as clinically relevant variables such as changes on target variables and functional status. Moreover, QI does not have to be overly elaborate or labor intensive to yield clinically useful information.

References

Agency for Healthcare Research and Quality. (2003). *Nationwide Inpatient Sample(NIS): Healthcare Cost and Utilization in Project (HCUP)*. Rockville, MD: Author. Retrieved March 29, 2003, from http://www.ahrq.gov/data/hcup/hcupnis.htm

American Psychiatric Association. (1994). *Mental Illness (An Overview)*. Washington, DC: Author. Retrieved March 29, 2003, from http://www.psych.org/public_info/overview.cfm

Aronoff, G. M., & DuPuy, D. N. (1997). Evaluation and management of back pain: Preventing disability. *Journal of Back and Musculoskeletal Rehabilitation, 9*, 109-124.

Babcock, R. A., Fleming, R. K., & Oliver, J. R. (1998). OBM and quality improvement systems. *Journal of Organizational Behavior Management, 18*, 33-59.

Barlow, D. H. (Ed.). (2001). *Clinical handbook of psychological disorders: A step-by-step treatment manual* (3rd ed.). New York: Guilford Press.

Barlow, D., & Craske, M. (1994). *Mastery of your anxiety and panic - II*. San Antonio, TX: The Psychological Corporation.

Beck, A. T., Rush, A. J., Shaw, B. F., & Emery, G. (1979). *Cognitive therapy of depression*. New York: Guilford.

Cameron, K. S., & Barnett, C. K. (2000). Organizational quality as a cultural variable: An empirical investigation of quality culture, processes, and outcomes. In R. E. Cole & W. R. Scott (Eds.), *The quality movement organization theory* (pp. 271-294). Thousand Oaks, CA: Sage Publications.

Carr, R. E., Lehrer, P. M., Rausch, L. L., & Hochron, S. M. (1994). Anxiety sensitivity and panic attacks in an asthmatic population. *Behavior Research and Therapy, 32*, 411-418.

Chambliss, C. H. (2000). *Psychotherapy and managed care: Reconciling research and reality.* Boston: Allyn and Bacon.

Chassin, M. R. & Galvin, R. W. (1998). The urgent need to improve health care quality: Institute of Medicine National Roundtable on Health Care Quality. *Journal of the American Medical Association, 16*, 1000-1005.

Clark, D. M. (1989). Anxiety states: Panic and generalized anxiety. In K. Hawton, P.,Salkovskis, J. Kirk, & D. M. Clark (Eds.) *Cognitive behavior therapy for psychiatric problems.* Oxford: Oxford University Press.

Consumer Reports on Health. (2002). When doctors don't know best. *Consumer Reports on Health, 14*, 1-5.

Conyers, J. (2003). A fresh approach to health care in the United States: Improved and expanded Medicare for all. *American Journal of Public Health, 93*, p. 193.

Crosby, P. (1979). *Quality is free.* New York: New American Library.

Cummings, J. L. (2002). Psychopharmacology and medical cost offset. In N. A. Cummings, W. T. O'Donohue, & K. E. Ferguson (Eds.), *The impact of medical cost offset on practice and research: Making it work for you* (pp. 25-143). Reno, NV: Context Press.

Cummings, N. A. (2000). The first decade of managed behavior care: What went right and what went wrong? In R. D. Weitz (Ed.), *Managed care in mental health in the new millennium* (pp. 19-37). New York: The Haworth Press.

Cummings, N. A. (1997). Behavioral health in primary care: Dollars and sense. In N. A. Cummings, J. L. Cummings, J. N. Johnson (Eds.), *Behavioral health in primary care: A guide for clinical integration* (pp. 3-21). Madison, WI: Psychosocial Press.

Cummings, N. A. (1990). The Biodyne model of brief intermittent therapy throughout the life cycle. In N. A. Cummings, H. Dorken, M. S. Pallack, & C. J. Henke (Eds.), *The impact of psychological intervention on healthcare utilization and costs* (Tech. Rep. No. 11-C-9834419, Appendix II, pp. 152-177). San Francisco: Foundation for Behavioral Health.

Cummings, N. A. (1986). The dismantling of our health system: Strategies for the survival of psychological practice. *American Psychologist, 41*, 426-431.

Deming, W. E. (1986). *Out of crisis.* Cambridge, MA: MIT Press.

Deming, W. E. (1982). *Quality, production, and competition.* Cambridge, MA: Center for Advanced Engineering Study, MIT.

Feldman, J. M., Giardino, N. D., Hehrer, P. M. (2000). Asthma and Panic Disorder. In D. I. Mostofsky & D. H. Barlow (Eds.), *The management of stress and anxiety in medical disorders* (pp. 220-239). Boston: Allyn and Bacon.

Ferster, C. B., & Skinner, B. F. (1957). *Schedules of reinforcement.* New York: Appleton-Century-Crofts.

Fink, P. (1992). Surgery and medical treatment in persistent somatizing patients. *Journal of Psychosomatic Research*, 36, 439-447.

Foa, E. B. (1996). The efficacy of behavioral therapy with obsessive-compulsives. The Clinical Psychologist, 49, 2, 19-22.

Gabor, A. (1990). *The man who discovered quality: How W. Edwards Deming brought the quality revolution to America: The stories of Ford, Xerox, and GM*. New York: Time Books.

Hargreaves, W. A., Shumway, M., Hu, T., & Cuffel, B. (1998). *Cost-outcome methods for mental health*. New York: Academic Press.

Hecker, J.E., & Thorpe, G.L. (1992). *Agoraphobia and panic: A guide to psychological treatment*. Boston: Allyn & Bacon.

Hergenhahn, B. R. (1997). *An introduction to the history of psychology* (3rd ed.). New York: Brooks/Cole Publishing Company.

Hermann, R. C., Regner, J. L., Erickson, P., & Yang, D. (2000). Developing a quality management systems for behavioral health care: The Cambridge Health Alliance experience. *Harvard Review of Psychiatry, 8*, 251-260.

Huffman, J. C., Pollack, M. H., & Stern, T. A. (2002). Panic Disorder and chest pain: Mechanisms, morbidity, and management. *Journal of Clinical Psychiatry, 4*, 54-62.

Katon, W., Von Korff, M., Lin, E., Lipscomb, P., Russo, J., Wagner, E., et al. (1990). Distressed high utilizers of medical care: DSM-III-R diagnoses and treatment needs. *General Hospital Psychiatry, 12*, 355-362.

Kessler, D. A., Berglund, P. A., Bruce, M. L., Koch, J. R., Laska, E. M., Leaf, P. J., et al. (2001). The prevalence and correlates of untreated serious mental illness. *Health Services Research*, 36(6), 987-1007.

Kroenke, K., & Mangelsdorff, D. (1989). Common symptoms in ambulatory care: Incidence, evaluation, therapy, and outcome. *The American Journal of Medicine, 86*, 262-266.

Leaf, P. J., Cohen, P., Horwitz, S., Narrow, W. E., Regier, D.A., Alegria, M., et al. (1996). Mental health services use in the community and schools: Results from the Four Community MECA Study. *Journal of the American Academy of Child and Adolescent Psychiatry, 35*, 889-897.

Lebowitz, B. D., Pearson, J. L., Schneider, L. S., Reynolds, C. F., Alexopoulos, G. S., Bruce, M. L., et al. (1997). Diagnosis and treatment of depression in late life. Consensus statement update. *Journal of the American Medical Association, 278, 1186-1190*.

Levesque, D. A., Prochaska, J. M., Prochaska, J. O., Dewart, S. R., Hamby, L. S., & Weeks, W. B. (2001). Organizational stages and processes of change for continuous quality improvement in health care. *Consulting Psychology Journal: Practice and Research, 53*, 139-153.

Linehan, M. M. (1993). *Cognitive-behavioral treatment of Borderline Personality Disorder*. New York: The Guilford Press.

Mager, R. F., & Pipe, P. (1984). *Analyzing performance problems or you really oughta wanna* (2nd ed.). Belmont, CA: Pitman.

Mainstone, L. E., & Levi, A. S. (1987). Fundamentals of statistical process control. *Journal of Organizational Behavior Management, 9(1)*, 5-21.

Meyer, G. S. (2001). Balancing the quality cycle: Tackling the measurement-improvement gap in health care – Part I. *Nutrition, 17*, 171-174.

Milakovich, M. E. (1995). *Improving service quality: achieving high performance in the public and private sectors*. Delray Beach, FL: St. Lucie Press.

Miltenberger, R. G. (2001). *Behavior modification: Principles and procedures* (2nd ed.). Belmont, CA: Wadsworth.

Morrison, J. (1997). *When psychological problems mask medical disorders: A guide for psychotherapists*. New York: Guilford Press.

Oakland, J. S., & Followell, R. F. (1990). *Statistical process control: A practical guide* (2nd ed.). Oxford: Heinemann Newnes.

O'Donohue, W., Graczyk, P. A., & Yeater, E. A. (1998). Quality control and the practice of clinical psychology. *Applied and Preventative Psychology, 7*, 181-187.

O'Donohue, W. T., Ferguson, K. E., Cummings, N. A. (2002). Introduction: Reflections on the medical cost offset effect. In W. T. O'Donohue, K. E. Ferguson, & N. A. Cummings (Eds.), *The impact of medical cost offset on research and practice: Making it work for you* (pp. 11-25). Reno, NV: Context Press.

Paul, G.L. (1969). Behavior modification research: Design and tactics. In C. M. Franks (Ed.), *Behavior therapy: Appraisal and status*. New York: McGraw-Hill.

Phelps, C. E. (1997). *Health economics* (2nd ed.). Reading, Massachusetts: Addison-Wesley.

Phillips, E. (1985). *A guide for therapist and patients to short-term psychotherapy*. Springfield, IL. Thomas.

Popper, K. R. (1972). *Objective knowledge*. Oxford: Clarendon Press.

Rampersad, H. K. (2001). *Total quality management: An executive guide to continuous improvement*. New York: Springer.

Redmon, W. K. (1992). Opportunities for applied behavior analysis in the total quality movement. *Journal of Applied Behavior Analysis, 25*, 545-550.

Reeves, C. A, & Bednar, D. A. (1994). Defining quality: Alternatives and implications. *The Academy of Management Review, 19*, 419-445.

Reider, R. (2000). *Benchmarking strategies: A tool for profit improvement*. New York: John Wiley & Sons.

Salkovskis, P. M., & Clark, D. M. (1991). Cognitive treatment of panic disorder. *Journal of Cognitive Psychotherapy, 3*, 215-226.

Sanders, R. R., & Sanders, J. L. (1994). W. Edwards Deming, quality analysis, and total behavior management. *The Behavior Analyst, 17*, 115-125.

Scaturo, D. J. (2001). The evolution of psychotherapy and the concept of manualization. *Professional Psychology: Research and Practice, 32*, 522-530.

Shewhart, W. A. (1931). *Economic control of quality of manufactured product*. New York: Van Nostrand.

Sidman, M. (1960). *Tactics of scientific research: Evaluating experimental data in psychology*. Boston: Authors Cooperative, Inc., Publishers.

Simpson, L. (2001). Quality of care: Time to make the grade. *Pediatrics, 107*, p. 171.

Spors, K. K. (2003, Feb. 7). Health spending is likely to slow but still exceeds economic growth. *Wall Street Journal*, p. A1.

Strosahl, K. (1998). *A model for integrating behavioral health and primary care medicine.* Paper presented at the annual meeting of the American Psychological Association, San Francisco, USA.

Strosahl, K., Baker, N. J., Braddick, M., Stuart, M. E., & Handley, M. R. (1997). Integration of behavioral health and primary care services: The Group Health Cooperative model. In N.A. Cummings, J. L. Cummings, & J. N. Johnson (Eds.), *Behavioral health in primary care: A guide for clinical integration* (pp. 61-86). Madison, WI: Psychosocial Press.

Strum, R. (1999). Cost and quality trends under managed care: Is there a learning curve in behavioral carve-out plans? *Journal of Health Economics, 18*, 593-604.

Swanson, R. C. (1995). *The quality improvement handbook: Team guide to tools and techniques.* Delray Beach, FL: St. Lucie Press, c1995

Swartz, M., Blazer, D., George, L., Landerman, R. (1986). Somatization disorder in a Community population. *American Journal of Psychiatry, 143*, 1403-1408.

Tuchman, B. W. (1980, Nov. 2). The decline of quality. *New York Times Magazine*, 38-41, 104.

U.S. Census Bureau. (2001). Current Population Reports: Series P23-190. Washington, D.C.: Author. Retrieved March 29, 2003, from http://www.census.gov/prod/www/abs/popula.html

Young, A. S., Klap, R., Sherbourne, C. D., & Wells, K. B. (2001). The quality of care for depressive and anxiety disorders in the United States. *Archives of General Psychiatry, 58*, 55-61.

Walton, M. (1986). *The Deming management method.* New York: The Berkley Publishing Group.

Wang, P. S., Demler, O., Kessler, R. C. (2002). Adequacy of treatment for serious mental illness in the United States. *American Journal of Public Health, 92*, 92-99.

Wheeler, D. J., & Chambers, D. S. (1992). *Understanding statistical process control* (2nd ed.). Knoxville, Tennessee: SPC Press.

Zahner, G. E. P., Pawelkiewicz, W., DeFrancesco, J. J., Adnopoz, J. (1992). Children's mental health service needs and utilization patterns in an urban community: An epidemiological assessment. *Journal of the American Academy of Child and Adolescent Psychiatry 3*, 951-960.